Project Management Institute

ASPECTS OF COMPLEXITY: MANAGING PROJECTS IN A COMPLEX WORLD

Editor in Chief
Terry Cooke-Davies, PhD

Contributing Editors
Lynn Crawford, DBA, John R. Patton, PMP,
Chris Stevens, PhD, and Terry M. Williams, PhD

Library of Congress Cataloging-in-Publication Data

Aspects of complexity : managing projects in a complex world / editor in chief,
Terry Cooke-Davies ; contributing editors, Lynn Crawford ... [et al.].
    p. cm.
  ISBN 978-1-935589-30-3 (pbk. : alk. paper) 1. Project management.
I. Cooke-Davies, Terry, 1941- II. Crawford, Lynn.
  HD69.P75A77 2011
  658.4'04—dc23

2011024450

Published by: Project Management Institute, Inc.
                       14 Campus Boulevard
                       Newtown Square, Pennsylvania 19073-3299 USA
                       Phone: +610-356-4600
                       Fax: +610-356-4647
                       Email: customercare@pmi.org
                       Internet: www.PMI.org

To inquire about discounts for resale or educational purposes, please contact the PMI Book
Service Center.
                       PMI Book Service Center
                       P.O. Box 932683, Atlanta, GA 31193-2683 USA
                       Phone: 1-866-276-4764 (within the U.S. or Canada)
                       or +1-770-280-4129 (globally)
                       Fax: +1-770-280-4113
                       Email: info@bookorders.pmi.org

10 9 8 7 6 5 4 3 2 1

Table of Contents

Acknowledgments

This book owes a great deal to many people.

The presenters at each of the Research Open Working Sessions, who so generously provided their experience and insights, and the participants who made the conversations so lively. The contributors who have provided such stimulating chapters. The contributing editors, whose wise advice and ready support helped to give the book both shape and substance. And finally, of course Project Management Institute for funding this project and its many staff who have made this publication possible.

My grateful thanks to you all. It has been a privilege and a pleasure to work with you on this project.

Introduction

Managing Projects in a Complex World

Chris Stevens, John Patton, and Terry Cooke-Davies

And when it comes to solutions, simple is better. Elegant is better still.
Elegance is the simplicity found on the far side of complexity.

Matthew May, 2007, p. 3

This book has been written with three different audiences in mind: people who manage programs and projects (practitioners), line managers in organizations to which programs and projects make a substantial contribution (managers), and members of the academic research community who have an interest in how complexity shapes and influences the practice of program and project management (researchers).

Chapter 1 will be of interest to all three audiences, because it summarizes a series of dialogues between practitioners, managers, and researchers. These dialogues provided this book with its shape and led to the choice of topics in the remaining chapters of the book.

Increasingly in the world of business today, practitioners and managers find themselves potentially overwhelmed by the amount of complexity that they encounter. Successful project and program managers in these situations have had a natural or learned proactive perspective of what needs to be done. For many, obtaining this valuable skill of thinking and acting holistically can be accelerated, but not substituted, by exogenous learning. However, for most, such skills are obtained through years of experience. This experience is given another "C" designation, meaning Craftsmanship rather than Complexity. Chapters 2 to 7 (Part 1 of this book) will focus primarily on the experiential learning of experts, often labeled the "practical" application of the topics covered from a research point of view in Chapters 8 to 11 (Part 2). Finally, in the two concluding chapters, the first 11 chapters will be mined for "nuggets" of insight that are then used to outline the implications of the book as a whole for research (Chapter 12) and for management practice (Chapter 13).

Project managers in early documented achievements, such as the construction of monuments or biblical narratives, had to both think and practice their leadership systemically to be successful. Systems engineering has in the past 100 years evolved from a "hard" systems perspective to a professional discipline based on systems thinking and practice. Project management is an important relation based on similar ideas, even though success is generally based on the "soft" systems aspects of managing people. All projects at some level can be viewed as complex, but for most project managers it is not only their understanding of the "how it will be delivered" but "how they can manage it" that can be, and is often seen as "complex."

Of "complex" projects and "complexity" as a term, it is clear that for most people when confronted with something they don't understand, it will be considered as complicated. Where there are exponentially "complicated relationships" making up the whole, they may see it as complex.

Breaking programs or portfolios of work down into parts to be managed better has been a common and important practice for handling complicated situations. However, from a systemic perspective, this practice ignores all of the important relationships between those parts. As more parts such as subprojects are added, the relationships between them continue to expand exponentially, so perceived complexity rises.

During many large and long projects, change is ongoing and normal. Managers need to be more holistic in the way they view changes and current situations, as today's solutions have the potential to be tomorrow's problems. For many to understand a situation with a systemic and holistic discipline, as a means for both perceiving and understanding, it becomes possible to manage around the adverse aspects of change, and indeed leverage the positive.

Now, let's move from the consideration of the complicated to that of the truly complex. Part 1 brings together some of the practical perspectives of utilizing systems theory and practice in the context of complex projects and their management.

Progress during the history of the human race has always been fraught with challenges. For many, there was little or no precedent to build upon. For many centuries, humans have wondered about and studied from earth what the rest of the universe contains, and how it came about. Progress and understanding were not initially the results of pure study and contemplation. The real adventures in space started through the development of weapons of war. They then progressed to putting astronauts into low earth orbit, then reaching out to the moon and finally deep space.

These achievements may be seen as progressive advancement of knowledge and application. The unknown and new complexities of each stage were better understood because they were based on the experience gained from earlier projects. In addition, in the most successful cases, each stage was preceded by a strategic focus (for example, the mission to the moon spearheaded by President John F. Kennedy). Using previous experience, plans were established for the moon landing and they became operational, resulting in a final achievement of the goal (Apollo 11 landed on the moon on 16 July 1969).

As Doctor Jon Whitty explained during the March 2008 PMI Research Working Session in Sydney, Australia, the "C" word for describing the unknown and new challenges should not be seen in the context of complexity. Rather, to achieve an outcome in such situations, we should consider them in the context of challenges of craftsmanship.

Other presenters, at the same event, used complexity to refer to what appeared to be simple tasks, such as the refurbishment project of a local hotel, in contrast with building a large power station: (1) in another country on the other side of the world; (2) in the middle of an earthquake zone; and (3) using contractors from yet another distant country.

In another example, shoeing a horse was compared to building three advanced warships. In each case, one can learn some skills through an apprenticeship or experimentation. In the case of the larger projects, one can contract in those skills, and use one's experience in the leadership and dealing with large numbers of people, together with the experience gathered previously on similar projects.

Each one of the complex aspects of the simple projects was seen as such because they involved people, or, in the case of shoeing a horse, a large animal. The mutual conclusion was that it is the interaction with living sentient beings, rather than the technical issues of projects, which make a project complex. "It's all about people," said one of the leaders present.

Let us support this point by reflecting on NASA and their space projects. They suffered three very disastrous and public failures. It was determined that these failures were not just technical, even though the technology was admittedly complex. The failures were caused by failures in communications and interpersonal relationships.

Pellerin (2009, p. 11) stated that a Congressional investigation determined that between 80% and 95% of project failures are a result of either human or miscommunication (which is still human) issues. People can clearly be seen as a, or the, critical component in the difference between 'complicated' and 'complex' projects. Furthermore, history has shown that irrespective of how those projects have been labeled, their success or failure will be due to the behavior of the people in the teams, as well as how they are managed and led.

Good leadership is common across all successful organizations. The ability to communicate and negotiate, to have integrity and people skills, and to be a proactive and systemic problem solver are all considered to be essential tributes to manage projects.

Where Part 2 will provide the systemic foundation for consideration, Part 1 concentrates on the context and practice of dealing with project complexity. As with all endeavors, albeit a program or a project, one needs to understand where we are going or what we want to achieve. What is the goal?

In the terms of that quote from *Alice in Wonderland*, as long as Alice didn't care where she was going, but as long as she was going somewhere, then the Cheshire Cat's answer was appropriate in that she would get somewhere, if she was to walk long enough (Carroll, 1865).

A similarly focused approach is not acceptable for most organizations. In any discipline or sector, commercial/not-for-profit, or public/private or government, there clearly needs to be a focus and strategy. This strategy must cascade down through portfolios, programs, projects, and knowing what tools are appropriate to help those who manage them with a high degree of complexity.

Part 1 addresses the pragmatic aspects of these issues. Within the context of developing strategies, there are many considerations. These include risk and financial and resource allocations. However, one issue that needs the most focus is that of the "do-ability" of the goal. Can an outlined endeavor or strategy be achieved given the right management structure, adequate financial support, appropriate risk analysis (for *all* the stakeholders involved), along with the required skills and time?

This has to be considered in the context of the organization as it aligns with its overall ability to run a larger portfolio of short-, medium- and other longer-term projects and programs that need to be collectively managed. Their interactions and relationships, including time, finance, and risks (and shortages of appropriate levels and numbers of resources with the required skills to deliver) make up a portfolio of considered deliverables. Considered individually, the projects would be seen as simple or even routine. Yet, when the parts are brought together, and the relationships between them are considered as in a portfolio or large program of work, the situation often becomes complex.

For organizations to manage the potential conflicts within the portfolio(s), understanding the interaction among projects and programs can require both simple and sophisticated tools. Without making the management of complex work more difficult, one must not fall into the trap of assuming that expensive and large computerized management applications for project/programs/portfolios will help. They will only help if the fundamental and simple concepts of their foundations and needs are clearly understood. If they are not understood, sophisticated, expensive, and inappropriate tools will certainly overcomplicate the situation, accelerating the journey to project and program failure.

For Part 1, at some level, every project can be seen as complex, especially if it is not understood by those who either sponsor or deliver it. In the past, by splitting a project into small subprojects has been a way of simplifying or reducing project complexity. However, within the systemic view, it is clearly the interaction between the elements (subprojects, tracks, and deliverables) that is more important to manage than the larger projects. Such interaction invariably involves people; it was clearly agreed by academics and practitioners alike, during the PMI-ROWS sessions in that this point was a significant component in defining the difference between complicated and complexity.

In Part 2 of this book—Chapters 8 through 11—the topic of complexity will be explored from the point of view of researchers in different fields, each of whom has something to contribute to our understanding of complexity.

Much has been written in this introduction and in the first seven chapters of this book about the contribution that human behavior makes to complexity in projects. So Part 2 opens with Chapter 8 with a review of research into some prominent aspects of human behavior, judgment, and decision making, which are so important to the fields of project and program management, and which are explored from a variety of behavioral and cognitive aspects.

Reference has also been made to the multiple fields of study, arising from the systems movement in the natural and life sciences and that have been grouped together initially as "chaos theory," and later as "complexity theory." Chapter 9 explores how these theories apply to the management of projects, and acknowledge the conceptual challenges that they present to both researchers and practitioners.

The 1950s and 1960s saw, at least in the popular imagination, a confluence of the fields of science, technology, and management such that the U.K. Prime Minister-to-be Harold Wilson could campaign in 1963 with a slogan promising the "white heat of the technological revolution" (Pearce & Stewart, 2001). It seemed as if approaches such as systems engineering, management science, and the study of systems in the natural sciences were all broadly aligned with one another and that they were leading toward the achievement of common goals, with the control of both organizations and technological systems lying within reach. It was in this milieu that modern project management first flourished, and that the seeds were sown of what is now known as complexity science, or complexity thinking. In terms of understanding project management, complexity, and the relationship between them, it is necessary to understand the systems movement.

The systems movement as a whole is multifaceted, and through studies of both natural and artificial systems, has developed in a myriad of ways since the early days of project management. Chapter 10, presents an overview of this development, with special reference to soft systems methodology and to system dynamics, each of which provides a different research window through which we can catch glimpses of the causes of complexity in projects.

That part of the systems movement, out of which project management grew, included systems engineering, cybernetics, and management systems. It has been argued (Johnson, 2002) that it was this approach that distinguished the success of the U.S. space program culminating in the moon landing of 1969 from the failure of the European space program at the same time. This relationship between modern project management, management systems, and systems engineering remains an important one. Chapter 11 highlights recent perspectives on systems engineering and explores the respective contributions made by systems engineers and project managers to the challenges of complex projects that attempt to provide valuable solutions to "wicked" problems. In so doing, he makes the case both for new tools to be adopted by project managers, and for the kinds of behavioral skills and competencies that are necessary to bring about success in such environments.

These four perspectives (systems thinking, systems engineering, complexity science, and cognitive studies) may not, on their own, be sufficient to reach a comprehensive understanding of the nature of complexity on projects, but each one of them is most certainly necessary, and each of the chapters in Part 2 provides deeper insights into topics that were introduced in Chapter 1. Although they are written primarily with an eye on the research community, it is our intention that they will hold many insights that are of value to practitioners and managers.

Although Chapter 1 serves as an overview of the whole field, Part 1 has been written mainly with practitioners and managers in mind and Part 2 mainly for the research community, the final two chapters show very clearly how interwoven the interests of the three audiences really are. Chapter 12, written for the research community, contains many issues and topics drawn from Part 1, whilst Chapter 13 finds many insights for practitioners and managers in Part 2. Indeed, the careful reader who is pressed for time may well wish to start with one of these closing chapters, depending upon which audience they belong to, and then allow these summaries to direct their attention to the chapters that are most of interest to them.

References

Carroll, L. (1865). *Alice's adventures in wonderland.* London, England: Macmillan.

May, M. E. (2007). *The elegant solution: Toyota's formula for mastering innovation.* New York, NY: Free Press.

Johnson, S. B. (2002). *The secret of Apollo: Systems management in American and European space programs.* Baltimore, MD: The Johns Hopkins University Press.

Pearce, M., & Stewart, G. (2001). *British political history, 1867–2001: Democracy and decline.* London, England: Routledge.

Pellerin, C. J. (2009). *How NASA builds teams: Mission critical soft skills for scientists, engineers, and project teams.* Hoboken, NJ: John Wiley.

Chapter 1

Complexity in Project Management and the Management of Complex Projects

Terry Cooke-Davies

In some ways, complexity is rather like love: Everybody has experiences of it and knows what it is, but ask them to define precisely what they mean by it and you will end up with a broad range of definitions. In the realm of project management, the terms "complex" and "complexity" have been cropping up extensively during the past few years.

In order to shed some light on the topic, Project Management Institute hosted a series of four Academic-Business Roundtable Discussions and Workshops on the topic of "Complexity in Project Management and the Management of Complex Projects." These sessions were held in Atlanta, GA, Sydney, Australia, St. George's, Malta, and São Paulo, Brazil. Nearly 100 attendees at each location, heard from a panel of six invited presenters. The participants were then invited to take part in an open discussion and workshop session. The presenters were composed of business-people, project management practitioners, academics, and consultants.

These events, and the lively discussions that took place during them, were the inspiration for this book. Presenters and delegates offered insights that were as varied in their topics as they were well grounded in practice, in theory or in both. In the course of the dialogue, it emerged that managing projects in an increasingly complex world is both a growing challenge, and one for which no easy solutions exist. The field itself is multifaceted, continually evolving and in pressing need of expert practitioners, supportive organizational environments, and well-grounded research to support both.

This first chapter provides an understanding of complexity in project management as it emerged from the presentations and discussions at each of the four events. Made up, as it is, of the insights from 19 distinguished practitioners, managers, consultants, and academics, it inevitably has something of the "scatter gun" about it. It also does not include references and citations, since the points it is making all emerged during the events themselves from one of the participants. For ease of reading, a single "voice" has been adopted for the narrative, to present the breadth of ideas as coherently as possible. Subsequent chapters, which each elaborate on a particular theme introduced during the discussions, have the added depth and understanding of the expert authors and refer to the source of the information.

What Do People Mean When They Talk About Complexity?

As far as projects are concerned, there is a difference between "complex" and "complicated." It doesn't help to look up the dictionary definitions of the words, since each tends to be defined in terms of the other. If sense is to be made of the topic, then it is important to understand the concepts that people tend to have in mind when they use the terms, rather than educate them in one or the other particular dictionary definitions.

Similarly, although the term "complex" has a technical meaning (or, to be precise, several different ones) when it is applied to "complex systems" in the worlds of science and technology, these technical definitions (which will be explored in Chapter 4) should also be distinguished from the everyday sense in which people speak about complex projects. Furthermore, they should seek to assess the degree of "complexity" that any particular project or program can be said to possess.

You could describe a system or a project as "complicated" if it has a large number of interconnected and interdependent parts, whereas complex means something more. The Latin roots of the word imply "woven together," so that changes in one part have an impact on the others. If this "woven togetherness" is combined with changes that can occur within individual elements, then a project can be said to be complex if it consists of many interdependent parts, each of which can change in ways that are not totally predictable, and which can then have unpredictable impacts on other elements that are themselves capable of change.

You could say that a modern saloon car or a laptop is complicated, whereas a Formula 1 racing car or the human brain is complex. As one of the contributors said, "If you don't understand what will happen when you kick it—that's complex."

Aside from being a memorable way of describing complexity, this particular description also introduces a second important concept alongside the interaction of multiple parts—that of human "understanding." Many activities or fields of knowledge appear to be complex when they are first encountered, but as understanding and experience grow, they appear much less complex to the accomplished practitioner. To many beginner drivers or people with no knowledge of the workings of an internal combustion engine, a saloon car is daunting in its complexity, whereas it holds few mysteries for the drivers and engineers in a Formula 1 racing team. Thus, a single project might appear to be more or less complex to different people associated with it, such as the project sponsor or the project manager.

Complexity, then, is relative to an individual's understanding. But what about collective understanding? There are limits to the understanding of groups of people, organizations, professions, and even of humanity itself. This would suggest that complexity is a characteristic that is always encountered in endeavors or activities at the frontier of the knowledge or technology of the people who are undertaking the activity. Projects to build ancient wonders of the world such as the Pyramids or Stonehenge must have appeared complex in their time, but look very simple in contrast with NASA's programs leading to human flight to the moon, or some of the intricate and complex building and infrastructure projects that have been undertaken in the modern era.

On the other hand, the different components that make up the global economy are themselves complex elements that change unpredictably and then interact in unpredictable ways. As a result, in the postindustrial global world, apparently simple concepts such as a single integrated business appear to be increasingly complex, difficult to manage, and prone to failure.

The tools and techniques of modern project management were developed to help people and organizations reduce the amount of complexity in projects by breaking complex activities down into simpler ones wherever possible—thereby designing complexity out of the project as far as possible and leaving the resulting activity simply complicated. Removing complexity remains a laudable goal, and it should be the first resort for many project managers. However, a combination of the ambition that keeps humanity constantly pressing onward to new frontiers, coupled with increasing complexity in the global economy, ensures that there will always be projects that present their promoters and implementers with a high degree of complexity.

If projects with a substantial amount of complexity are also likely to have aspects that need to be managed in ways that extend the traditional tools and techniques of project management, then just what factors can be identified that cause a particular project to be "complex" in this common sense use of the term? And what challenges do these pose for project managers?

What Causes Complexity, and Why Is It a Problem?

Many organizations have developed their own means of assessing how complex a project is for varied reasons, such as assisting with the appointment of appropriate management or governance resources or positioning it within a portfolio of projects that are being considered for funding. Typically, such assessment schemes consider factors such as technology, size and scale, supply chain, geography, time pressure, stakeholders, and so on. The lists are long and varied.

Research into categorization systems has shown that organizations typically rate a project using, on average, 5 attributes, although the number of attributes can vary from as few as 2 to as many as 12. Factors assessed may include project scope, technical complexity, number of functions and skills involved, organizational involvement, level of ambiguity/uncertainty, number of sites locations or countries, organizational impact, clarity of goals and objectives, or source and location of risks.

Some organizations, recognizing that complexity depends on understanding, consider how familiar it is with the particular type, scale, or technology of the project.

It is worth looking into the different factors in this long and varied list and that can be said to cause complexity, and consequently, problems for project managers.

Unhelpful Behavior

There is widespread agreement among practitioners that one factor that makes projects complex is the interaction of human beings who are faced with making complex decisions. Complexity occurs when people with different interests, loyalties, cultures, and interactions with one another are put together to deliver a particular project or program. This can be seen as variants on "organizational politics," but it is actually more widespread than that.

All but the simplest projects involve teams of people coming together to accomplish goals, and when physical teams come together, unpredictable behavior emerges. The larger the team, and the larger the number of teams involved, the more complex the project. People are not always rational in their decision making, and tribal instincts are deeply rooted in humankind, which makes the behavior of individual teams liable to evolve and be difficult to predict. In addition, the interactions between different teams are themselves unpredictable, especially if there are differences in national, organizational, or professional culture.

These differences are often magnified by the different perspectives of the people involved: Those who are implementing the projects, those who will use the products or services that result from the project, those who stand to benefit from the success of the project, or those who establish the regulatory environment for the project.

Complexities like these in human behavior can reveal themselves in many different ways, for example: Clients of projects can cause changes to project scope, delay important decisions, interfere with the project implementation team, or complicate actions and decisions through a lack of trust; the workforce that is implementing the project can become disincentivized through poor morale or exhausted through excessive schedule pressure; and managers can react inappropriately to cost, schedule, scope, or quality pressures. Indeed, in projects with a high degree of complexity, communication can be a significant cause of failure. This is perhaps not surprising, since the need to communicate, relate, and interact is a basic human need. Such processes of relating are complex and responsive, because interaction among humans is always unpredictable to some extent.

Anyone who has ever been involved in large-scale organizational change will most likely have experienced for himself or herself what happens when the rumor begins to circulate that reorganization is imminent. The complex human system begins to evolve, to react in unpredictable ways, and to develop its own response in anticipation of the announcement. On the other hand, when a fleet of contractors' vehicles rolls up to start a major roadwork scheme with an inanimate system such as a road network, the roads don't react!

Project managers can expect to be faced with such behavioral complexity, but their own response can create additional complexity of its own. Responding to disruption by taking decisions that seek to recover the original planned schedule can lead to feedback loops, with unintended consequences and even, on occasions, catastrophic failure. This response is a particular manifestation of a phenomenon that is well understood in the systems view of the world, and one that is a major cause of complexity in projects: systemicity.

Failure to Appreciate Systemicity

When people talk about projects being complex, as we have seen, they are talking about not only the number of separate elements in the project but also about how these interact. In other words, about the behavior of the project as a "whole system"—what could be called the "systemicity" of the project.

When project managers look at projects, they are used to breaking them down into their constituent parts (e.g., using work breakdown structures). However, when feedback loops begin to develop, quite simple behaviors in each element can combine and cause complex behavior to emerge for the system as a whole. Perhaps the easiest of these effects to imagine is positive reinforcing loops, or "vicious circles." It is frequently encountered in amateur events making somewhat inexpert use of public address systems. The voice of the announcer is amplified through the loudspeakers, and this louder voice is picked up by the microphone and amplified further, and so on until the familiar ear-splitting "howl" results.

Similar effects can be experienced on complex projects, as unintended consequences from well-intended decisions result in the magnification and escalation of the original problems, until catastrophic failure results.

A pattern can be detected: project risks or perturbations create interactions that feed on themselves causing vicious circles; project managers respond to the disruption by making decisions that seek to retain planned delivery and planned quality, usually by accelerating certain actions; these actions are also disruptions that, in turn, must be contained within a shorter time scale, therefore, increasing the power of the vicious circles.

Models

Each of us interacts with the world as we understand it to be, based on our own mental "models" of what reality is and how it works. Most commonly, these models are more implicit than explicit, and they are likely to differ in important respects from other people's models. This diversity of models can be a major factor in causing complexity in projects.

Arising out of our models, we use symbols that are created, reproduced, and transformed by our interactions, and out of these symbols, we create and re-create meaning. That meaning in turn informs and directs what we do, so if our models are left intuitive and unexamined, they are likely to lead to unforeseen systemic effects at interfaces within the project.

Here, creating explicit shared models throughout the project team can help to improve understanding of the complexity inherent in the project. Conversely, having inadequate models that, for example, fail to recognize the extent of complexity in the project makes dealing with it that much harder.

Simplistic Project Management

One mental model that most project managers bring with them to the management of complex projects and programs is their understanding of the tools and techniques of project management. Where these are incomplete or inappropriate, they can add to project complexity. For example, a simplistic model of project risk management that fails to recognize systemic risks caused by the interactions between individual risks, or that fails to identify the significant risks, can contribute directly to a need for the kind of decision making and behavior that causes the kind of issues with systemicity that have already been described.

Complexity can also arise because of assumptions that are inherent in traditional models of project management and that are incompatible with actual systems and practices in the organizational environment of the specific project or program. For example, project managers may lack the authority necessary to manage the project effectively.

None of this, of course, is any excuse for failing to implement the "basics" of project management and use the tools and techniques in an appropriate manner to reduce avoidable complexity.

Over-Ambitious Strategic Management

A number of factors lead to increased complexity in projects in business and government. At least in the Western economies, the work force is aging while simultaneously the number and value of projects being undertaken are increasing.

Against this background, projects are managed and governed within a context created by the management and governance systems of the promoting and implementing organizations, and the resulting "system of systems" adds a further dimension to the systemicity that has already been discussed.

So too does the number of interactions (or "ripple effects") between projects undertaken within a project portfolio aimed to accomplish strategic business objectives, particularly when a number of projects independently are each intended to create business change that has to be managed and integrated at the point of delivery by the same business unit's operational staff.

Other Factors

The foregoing may be five of the most prominent factors that come to mind when seeking to understand the causes of complexity, but there are many others as well.

For example, project management training that reduces all the tasks of a project manager to a simple and straightforward rational, linear, and deterministic set of predefined processes and activities, tends to increase the challenges of systemicity by developing project personnel who are not on the lookout for the project's interconnectedness.

In the global marketplace today, supply chains frequently consist of people and organizations from very different geographical and ethnic cultures, which place great challenges on the social systems that need to be created within a complex project. In addition, the same forces that lead to such culturally diverse supply chains place great pressure on the expectations of superior project results, creating what often turns out to be unrealistic stakeholder expectations and can lead to time pressure and resultant systemic problems and/or stress on members of the project team with a consequential increase in unhelpful behavior.

In general terms, insights from the study of complexity in the life sciences suggests that there is a natural tendency for all organisms (including humankind and its "social" organisms such as project teams) to evolve complex responses to challenges that they encounter in their environment. Which, taken together with the causes we have just examined, provide a compelling argument for why there is a pressing need for a coherent research agenda to understand both the causes of complexity, and what can be done to prevent it resulting in problems, waste, and economic and social failure. That is why Chapter 12 of this book is so important.

In the meantime, however, it appears that many of the factors that contribute to complexity can cause consequential problems for practitioners of project management are also the factors that hold out the promise of both mining the benefits from it and minimizing its harmful consequences.

How Can Practitioners and Organizations Best Respond To Complexity in Projects?

Perhaps the most important observation about responding positively to complexity in projects is that the response should come from both the organization and from individual practitioners. To respond positively, there is a need for transformational leadership of the complex project or program, collective creativity to develop the system that is right for the particular project, shared knowledge among all those involved in the project, and processes that are adapted and adaptive to the project needs.

This kind of organizational and personal leadership is the measure by which one can engage, embrace, and drive to effect positive influences in delivering on strategy in the face of complexity. It is a leadership that recognizes that wherever possible, simplicity is the preferred option—possibly even elegance.

A great deal can be achieved by the rigorous and adaptive application of project management such that the fundamentals of a project manager who is skilled in leadership, a project controls system that is systemically sound, team members who know how they fit in and what they have to do, and well-conducted communication and people skills. But doing so in a way that doesn't create unwelcome complexity requires the first of the factors that are critical to success in managing complexity in projects, developing sufficient practitioners with the right competencies to deliver the whole portfolio of strategic projects.

Developing Practitioners

There is general agreement that good managers of complex projects are not born with skills they need, but rather that they learn them and perfect them over time. They develop a tacit sense of what needs to be done and become proactive in doing it. These skills are learned over time, much as a craft is learned, through the acquisition of experience with the help of mentorship. It is appropriate to talk about craftsmanship—the old system of mentoring or apprenticeship where the tacit knowledge of an elder can be passed on to the pupil. A craft skill is a memory embedded in your very being. It takes guidance and time to acquire the skill. Therefore, it is not a matter of training people how to do something; rather it is the repetitive and improving nature of honing practices to perfection.

As has been discussed, there is a shortage of people who are capable of leading large, complex projects and programs. With this in mind, Australian, U.K., and U.S. governments and senior representatives of the defense industry have supported an initiative to improve the international community's capability to deliver very complex projects across all industry sectors. It includes not only a competency standard for use as a framework for assessing and developing managers of complex projects but also an executive master's degree and continuing professional development in complex project management. This program allows people to think about what they do (as project managers) for an entire year. It provides employers with valuable experience and credentials, not one or the other; allows project managers an opportunity to develop a language for complex project management; and provides project managers with a credential that can develop a positive correlation with competent practice over time through the ongoing evaluation of the performance of credential holders.

The program acknowledges that too often industry expects engineers to go to college for their degree but they are not given a complex project to manage as soon as they qualify. However, all too often there comes a time when overnight they are given one to manage. That can be harmful for both the individual and the organization, whereas what is needed is awareness that people's experiences in this field should be developed only when they are ready to accept more difficult (complex) projects. After all, in the medical profession, a new doctor may have knowledge but is not going to be allowed to do surgery on someone until he or she has gone through a residency program for the specialty.

Not every organization will be in a position to support such a master's degree program, which, in any case, can reach only a finite number of candidates each year. There is a real need to recognize that developing a workforce capable of delivering a portfolio of complex projects requires more than acquiring a set of technical skills and competencies from a mentor over time. Many of the attributes required to manage complex projects successfully are directly connected to emotional intelligence and interpersonal abilities. For example, one factor that seems to be important is something called "ego resilience." Project managers need big egos if they are to believe that they can get the project done, yet need small egos to get out of the way and let people do what they need to do to get the project done. Therefore, the development program needs to contain elements such as this ego resilience. It is also a question of the project managers' comfort zone—they need to be comfortable managing up and around in the environment rather than just managing technical aspects of a project.

Other development needs include understanding cultural differences on a deep level to bring out the best from multicultural teams; focusing on how to organize teams, which people should be put together to deal with such cultural developments; and understanding all the commercial and risk management techniques that are necessary to deal with complex projects.

Finally, it is important to understand not only the skills that are needed, but also how they can be acquired. How do practitioners get better at learning skills? Learning from experience on projects presents a difficult challenge. The difficult part is mapping out what happened and what went wrong and learning the complex lessons, and yet unless this is done, any lessons learned are likely to be trivial or mistaken.

Appropriate Project Management

Perhaps not surprisingly, since modern project management had its birth in the ambitious and (then) complex projects of the post–World War II technology systems development, project management itself is seen as a powerful antidote to complexity. After all, the modular design of a project management system, together with the modular design of the system that was the project's output, was explicitly developed to reduce complexity to manageable proportions.

Not all projects are equal, of course, and allowances need to be made to acknowledge that different types of projects have different characteristics. For example, in R&D projects, initial estimates of cost are far more difficult to make than in (say) refurbishment projects.

There are also some organizational practices in the implementation of project management processes that can help to combat unwelcome complexity. Project management offices (PMOs), for example, can reduce unintentional complexity in project management implementation if they are responsible for implementing standards in portfolio management and program management as well as project management. Similarly, careful attention to the relative authority of line managers and project managers can help. The aim is to strike the right balance between those processes that need to be tightly controlled and rigorously followed, and those that are better applied flexibly.

How project scope is defined has a big impact on how complex the project ultimately is. Some organizations have reported taking the stance that anything that can affect a project should be considered as part of the project, so there is no "macro" environment. In other words, as many external influences as possible are brought within the scope of the project. However, since there is considerable evidence that smaller projects of shorter duration are significantly easier to control than larger projects of longer duration, than this suggests that program management, combining as it does a single integrated program with a succession of shorter more tightly defined projects, is an important weapon in the armory used to combat unwelcome complexity.

A second implication of this increased scope is that the design of processes for projects that affect a large public and use public funds will need to be established using highly visible independent bodies for such roles as conducting risk evaluation publicly and accountably.

Complexity in projects probably has its greatest impact in the sphere of risk management. What is called for is a shift toward "impact risk analysis." This involves asking questions such as, "What is the effect if it continues? What is the effect of multiplicities of this?" Risk mapping, looking at overall pictures, can help and may help to scale up for larger, more complex projects, for which traditional risk analysis is often useless. Risk has to be monitored and tiered in a complex project or program, balancing threats with opportunity management and creating wealth not only for the business but also on individual projects. It can often be beneficial for all potential stakeholders to be involved in the risk management process by identifying the risks that they are most conscious of and allowing proactive management to mitigate external problems.

Unfortunately, the current state of knowledge about projects that are late and overspend, does not distinguish clearly between projects that are well estimated and poorly managed, and those that have the opposite problems. It is clear, however, that getting the estimate right in the first place is important for success, and the more complex the project, the more challenging this task becomes.

Constructive Behavior

In examining the causes of complexity, people's behavior and the nature of human beings were well highlighted. The good news is that just as we collectively have the capacity to create unwelcome complexity, people are also capable of possessing competencies that provide the antidote to complexity.

Competencies that can mitigate complexity include:

- Passive empathy. The level of consciousness in anticipating and predicting situations and taking control of them before they become problems.
- Active empathy. The ability to quickly and accurately act on or communicate the situation. Ability to get to the core of problems through analysis and to develop and present solutions.
- Persuasiveness. Ability to influence others by listening, assimilating, and communicating information. Ability to negotiate and be flexible yet provide accurate information to key stakeholders.

Project managers accomplish their work only through other people—it is the members of the project team that actually deliver the end product. Therefore, it is particularly important to look for and develop those behaviors that encourage and build up the team. For example, it is important to give team members hope, so that they are motivated both to plan well and prepare for implementation and to carry out the actual implementation.

Especially on complex projects, it is a good idea to be prepared for things not to go according to plan, and if project managers find things getting over their heads, they need to be prepared to ask for help. It is crucial and important to ask for help in those situations. To that end, the project manager needs to manage and collaborate with all stakeholder groups.

It is perhaps a truism to say that managing complexity in projects is all about managing people, both upward (through upper management and influential external groups) as well as downward. What that implies, however, is that it would strongly benefit the project management profession if it had a stronger theoretical foundation for understanding why people behave the way they do where projects are concerned.

The effective manager of complex projects also needs to be able to "turn things around" when the project gets into difficulties, and this can often involve making some fundamental changes to the culture that has developed within the project team. They need the ability to step outside the culture . . . to start evolutionary change processes that are more adaptive; to look at change processes to enable the team to progress; to articulate visions, embody values and create the environment within each team member, where things can be accomplished; and last but not least, to get the team involved in the values of creating an environment where the project can succeed.

If it is appropriate, project managers today can call on many advanced communication technologies including not only information and communications technology (ICT) but also advanced tools such as social networking capabilities or products such as Second Life, which can transform the experience of working virtually. Used unwisely, such tools can add to the complexity of projects, and that is where the project manager needs to demonstrate not only sound judgment, but also leadership ability.

The task of managing a complex project combines project management with leadership. To that extent, it is at least as much about *who you are* as a project manager as it is about *what you do*. People that successfully manage complex projects have creativity, imagination, openness, and flexibility, and they go with the flow. On the one hand, it is a good thing to schedule, but when the project is complex, it is important to let the creative juices come forward. Speak with successful managers of complex projects and you will discover that they constantly have to have the big picture in mind, are willing to go into detail, and ask those burning, penetrating questions that cause people to see when they are off track.

It is only human to take setbacks personally when managing complex projects, and there are techniques for cooling down when you are emotionally upset. For example, trying to look beyond somebody who is antagonistic and responding neutrally to him or her. Teams can be extremely defensive because they got the project in trouble and if you get people really tired doing worthwhile work, it breaks down some of their defensiveness. This is not manipulative, but it helps people open their minds.

Like all effective leaders, the project manager needs to focus on the end goal of the project and manage all elements to that end, rather than managing the individual (technical) parts. It is in that context, that the effective manager of complex projects is able to understand the systemic implications of what is happening in different parts of the project.

Appropriate Response to Systemicity

Just as interactions between different elements of a project can have unintended consequences such as vicious circles, as we have seen, so understanding the systemicity of a complex project (the inter-relationships between the different elements of the project) is central to a project manager's ability to manage the project efficiently and effectively. It is this understanding of "the whole" rather than "the sum of the parts" that enables the effective integration of processes, knowledge, and leadership.

This is an area where a skilled project manager can add value to an organization by connecting all the dots to help the successful delivery of complex projects.

Reference has already been made to the consequences of not having appropriate shared models of complexity, but in a positive sense, mapping techniques and diagrams can aid in simplifying complex projects and demonstrating how the different parts combine. Feedback loops need to be understood, recognized, and evaluated for mitigating actions. Soft issues such as culture, language, leadership, and personal relationship management all contribute to a project's complexity, so visual means of expressing them help with understanding and management. Indeed, if a complex project is understood as a complex system, then the activity of managing the project through taking informed decisions and the like is inseparable from the activity of learning about the project.

Understanding this systemicity is important when making upfront decisions with what inevitably turns out to be inadequate information, and so is building up that understanding as the project progresses and more information becomes available. Sometimes actions or risks do not have the effect that was expected; in particular, as we have seen, feedback loops must be recognized, analyzed, and controlled. For this to happen, the systemicity needs to be understood and modeled.

Frequently, such systemic interactions bring the project's own systems and processes into direct contact with those of the promoting and implementing organizations, and this can bring many if not all of these different ways of mitigating complexity together in the form of the organizations' strategic management.

Focused Strategic Management

The ripple effects caused by interactions between multiple projects have already been mentioned earlier in this chapter, as has the "system of systems" created by the interface between the project's systems and those of its promoting and implementing organizations.

In a more positive light, however, the recognition by an organization of the strategic importance of managing its complex projects effectively and efficiently can lead to a significant mitigation of unwelcome complexity. A major defense contractor, for example, can have as many as 15,000 projects being undertaken at any given time, and it is far from certain whether all of their project managers understand their project's strategic intent and how it relates to the whole organization. This quantity of projects creates its own form of complexity, as has already been discussed, but it also creates the opportunity to create a "roadmap" of how the projects fit into the overall picture from a stakeholder perspective, showing how the outcomes from each projects contribute to the overall strategic success of the enterprise.

Similarly, the creation of an effective means of identifying the complexity of projects, and matching that to the competencies and skills of project managers is a significant help in the strategic leadership of an organization's most critical projects. Indeed, to deliver strategy effectively, an organization needs the following: leadership in the form of supportive and appropriate behaviors within policies and applications processes; information that has integrity and meshes systemically; knowledge in the forms of appropriate interventions and experiential opportunities for people as was seen in the discussion of "behavior"; and processes that are not restrictive but rather, policies that are adaptive processes.

With this in place, there is a systemic and dynamic link between mission, management of programs and projects, information, knowledge, learning, and understanding in a given context and under given conditions.

Other Considerations

These five groups of actions that can be taken by either individuals or organizations to exploit any opportunities presented by complexity, or to mitigate its unwelcome threats, will have the effect of linking more closely a complex project to the organizations that collectively provide its environment.

It is also good practice to have a C-level project manager to represent key projects to the executive level of the organization, to further the connection. It also has the effect of educating business leadership in issues around the delivery of strategy, while educating project management to the complexities and pressures of business leadership.

In the course of such dialogue, it is likely that there will be an increase in evidence-based measurement of outcomes, which is surely desirable.

Is Complexity in Projects a "Friend" or a "Foe"?

It is easy to form the opinion from reading much of the literature on complexity in project management that it is somehow undesirable—something to be resisted and overcome wherever possible.

That is, at best, a partial picture of reality. Some complexity is the inevitable consequence of changes in society, technology, and the global economy. As such, it is neither a friend nor a foe, but simply a feature of the environment within which the art and science of project management are practiced. Some complexity, as we have seen, is the result of humankind continually striving for goals that are more ambitious and as such, if the goals are well formed, they are surely to be embraced as a friend and welcomed for the benefits it can bring. What remains are those unwelcome aspects of complexity that are not properly understood, are not responded to sensitively and appropriately, or are the result of misguided management decisions in the first place.

The remainder of this book is a serious attempt both to pull together what is currently known and understood about the topic, to help practitioners and their managers improve future practice, and to guide researchers into answering those questions that will best help to improve our understanding of this multifaceted topic. If it is successful in these goals, it will support the profession of project management as it seeks to adapt to inevitable complexity, to turn desirable complexity into tangible benefits, and to minimize the harmful effects of unwelcome complexity.

Part 1

With Practitioners and Their Managers in Mind

Chapter 2

Managing Projects With High Complexity

Stephen Hayes and Daniel Bennett

Introduction

During 2009, the International Centre for Complex Project Management (ICCPM) hosted its first international roundtable series on complex project management in the United States and Australia. The roundtable series was titled "The Conspiracy of Optimism—Why Mega Projects Fail." The *conspiracy of optimism* is a term used in areas as diverse as economics, environmental change, and complex project management. It describes a situation where a number of stakeholders, each with their own priorities and unique worldviews, tacitly ignore the reality of a situation in order to gain approval to proceed with a venture no one would sanction if the true outcome was known. The roundtable series provided the opportunity for senior government and industry officials from Australia, the United Kingdom, the United States, and Canada to analyze the issue, reach consensus on some of the drivers, and propose a future course of action. A position paper and findings paper have subsequently been written and an international task force has been established to help improve the international community's knowledge and ability to better deliver complex projects.

This chapter examines the findings from the 2009 roundtable series and considers the implications for program managers when dealing with complex projects, both from a public and private sector perspective. How does the presence of a high degree of complexity influence the behavior and practice of a project manager? What does it feel like to be a program manager in a complex project? From an existing good practice perspective what has been found to work or not to work? What are the key elements that help or hinder a program manager? How does a project manager influence his or her environment to better manage the affects of complexity?

Complexity

In situating this chapter, it is also necessary to frame what makes a project complex while noting the contextualization of complexity ultimately depends on an individual or organizational "lens." In 2007, the ICCPM led an international meeting that described complex projects as those that:

- can be characterized by uncertainty, ambiguity, with emergent dynamic interfaces, influenced by significant political or external changes;

- run over a period which exceeds the product life cycles of the technologies involved or where significant integration issues exist;
- defined by effect (benefit and value) but not by solution (product) at inception.

Key Issues as Highlighted by ICCPM Roundtables

The following paragraphs highlight a range of issues that complex project management practitioners, from both the public and private sectors, believe have a significant impact on the success of complex projects.

Unaccommodated or misaligned stakeholder views of success. The view of success is driven by divergent stakeholder expectations of project success that is derived by assuming each other's interests to be aligned. As the number of stakeholders increase, there is an increase in risk associated with attributes such as outcome, control, ownership, and schedule.

Tension between product success and project success. The tension arises from, and encompasses the clash of paradigms associated with stakeholder interests—private versus public, product versus project outcome. The purchase of a new defense capability, such as an airborne early warning aircraft (product), without consideration for its role in a much larger network-centric environment (outcome) is a useful example.

Political and public relations pressure militating against doing the right thing. How often do we fail to see the timely cancellation of multibillion dollar projects due to the implications for political and corporate image? To resist pressures of this kind, and to improve timely/difficult decision making, requires clear situational awareness and a comprehensive understanding of the facts coupled with personal and organizational courage supported by effective senior leadership.

Lack of understanding or acknowledgment of nontechnical risk. Traditional or classical project management focuses on hard system theories such as systems engineering that fully account for technical aspects of project risks. However, complex projects need to be viewed as organic systems of systems and should include soft systems issues such as politics and more often than not a significant number of external stakeholders. Consider planning risks (and opportunities) associated with the global financial crisis. Few of these relate to technical risk and, as with the potential policy changes and implications following a change of government, result in the need for a paradigm shift for many programs in the approach to understanding and managing risk.

Use of competition as a weapon. Competition within an open environment promotes effective and efficient use of resources. However, within monopsonistic environments, the use of artificially created competition has the potential to drive a misperception of competition, resulting in relative ineffective and inefficient outcomes such as driving the contract price below an achievable level. This is analogous to perceived economic free markets that employ the use of tariffs to enable artificial competition. In a monopsonistic environment, both the customer and supplier have a responsibility to ensure they have a rational understanding of the real cost for capability through the implementation of systems to de-risk cost uncertainty.

Institutionalized procurement practices. Classical project management responds well to institutionalization of procurement practices and standardized methodologies. Within complex project environments, adhering to rigid procurement processes and procedures can limit the agility and ability of an organization to respond to complexity and therefore avoid the realization of unknown risk.

Few project managers are equipped to be project delivery leaders. It is becoming sufficiently evident that a project manager's skill base needs to be multidisciplinary, encompassing source knowledge from discrete disciplines such as law, economics, engineering, and human resources. In the future, managers of complex projects need to be developed and selected based on a range of leadership skills that enables them to operate in uncertain and ambiguous environments. With globalization and greater complexity, we are increasingly moving into an environment of globally interconnected organizations focused on strategic benefits realization. In this environment where outcomes are being managed using both operations and projects, project delivery leaders need to look and operate beyond the existing paradigms of project process and controls. Procedural compliance and engineering management are necessary but not sufficient for complex projects. In addition to the process and engineering of project management, our future complex project delivery leaders need to be developed and selected with consideration to the "art and strategy" of program leadership that incorporate aspects such as systems thinking.

Lack of opportunity for engagement between government and industry. ICCPM's 2009 roundtable series provided an opportunity for senior government and industry officials from around the world to have a safe and nonattributable discussion around the key issues causing complex project failure. Enabling this sort of activity through organizations such as ICCPM, Project Management Institute (PMI), and Aviation Week allows development of a shared understanding and agreed on definition of the issues we face in the project management community. More importantly, the engagement provides the starting point and a vehicle to begin to address these issues.

Future capability (projects) is predicated on attaining rational estimates. There is a need to improve project planning and estimation to be "realistic" and "affordable." Improvement in cost estimation tools as well as benchmarking cost of capability are important aspects of reining in the often overly optimistic view of cost of capability. Failure to do so will result in unaffordable long-term government capability or corporate investment plans.

Current tools and decision processes unsuitable for analyzing uncertainty. In an increasingly complex and ambiguous world, the inability of current tools, processes, and the human mind to analyze uncertainty poses a significant problem. Research investment is required to develop tools that focus on project relationships and interconnectedness of those parts of the "system" that cause uncertainty and thus complexity.

Complex Project Management in Practice

Perhaps the first question to consider in a discussion about complex project management is why would anyone ever contemplate a complex undertaking? Given historical issues with performance and risk of massive and intricate projects, reason might suggest that complexity should be avoided or reduced whenever possible. In most ordinary situations, that approach is entirely appropriate. Nonetheless, there is a powerful and compelling reason for accepting the challenge and risk of a complex project—the potential for greater benefits than would be possible by resorting to a more conventional and simplistic approach. Complexity in any situation must be characterized in terms of not only its principle context-specific attributes but also in terms of what it means from the standpoint of risks and rewards, and to whom both risks and rewards accrue.

So, how do organizations decide to take on the challenge of a complex project? And, once they decide to do so, how do they manage complexity to achieve benefits that make the endeavor worthwhile? Let's examine the nature of what organizations do and how they think about complexity in order to begin to answer these questions.

Stakeholder benefits and the measures of success and failure. One key attribute of nearly all complex projects is that they typically involve a large number of diverse stakeholder communities with a broad range of interests, issues, and levels of activism. In many cases, very powerful and influential stakeholders have no direct involvement in or, in some cases, no real awareness of what is happening within the project. Furthermore, and rather interestingly, we find that quite often the complex project manager has no direct responsibility to key high-level stakeholders, nor do they have any formal accountability (credit or blame) for achieving the desired stakeholder benefits.

For example, in the 1960s U.S. space program, the American public, as stakeholders, was advised by national leaders of the imperative for manned lunar exploration. However, the public had little need or desire for access to information about what was actually being done by NASA project management. Nonetheless, public support was vital to sustain the effort. Generally, however, although NASA leaders and managers had a keen sense of the national will and the high stakes involved, their direct accountabilities were for execution of the manned space project only. They had little or no responsibility for the stakeholder benefits that were to derive from successful project management.

It would be a mistake to discount those stakeholders or to ignore project benefits that should accrue to them. One lesson learned from experience in managing complex projects is to pay attention to the entire stakeholder set and their expected benefits. More stakeholders generally make the effort more difficult to manage, but the reason for giving them voice and consideration is tied to the value proposition of what it means to realize stakeholder benefits. In essence, the more a complex project manager can be accountable to deliver benefits to stakeholders at all levels, the more likely the project will be successful. In this sense, complex project managers draw within the project some of those accountabilities to stakeholders that would ordinarily be external to the project.

The organizational capacity for managing complexity. Ross Ashby, in his pioneering work on cybernetics and systems thinking, contributed what is called the Law of Requisite Variety, which essentially states that the controller of an activity must have the capacity to deal with at least as much variety as is presented within the activity being controlled. Though seemingly simple, this law has far-reaching implications for complex adaptive systems and the organizations that propose to manage them. One fundamental issue in this regard relates to the choices a management team makes in determining the project's internal scope, and thus the variety within the project system.

As noted in the previous section, for highly complex undertakings where success or failure may hinge upon risks and benefits as seen and experienced by external stakeholders, the organization must often adapt to bring direct or at least indirect responsibility for those requirements into the project domain. For example, the F-35 Joint Strike Fighter program, a U.S. Department of Defense mega-project of unprecedented proportions, affects and is dependent upon many factors that are normally a matter of national or international policies and diplomacy. Although program leaders do not engage directly in international politics, they have in some ways adapted the project organization and its capacity for internalizing and influencing things, such as economic and industrial policies in relation to F-35 worldwide industrial participation. Similarly, some effort has been expended to help ensure alignment of international financial institution expectations in relation to provision of financial support to industries participating in the program. In this latter case, financial institutions benefitted from a better understanding of the nuances of U.S. defense procurement and how limiting factors, such as annual contracts versus single longer-term contracts, affect the risk and profitability of participating international companies. The program has adapted to provide industry engagement that, to a degree, has influenced changes in long-standing practices that would have proven to be overly restrictive if left unaddressed.

The organization as a hierarchy, or a network, or both? Many complexity theorists and researchers are occupied with the study of how complex projects are organized, and how they conduct business in response to a constant demand from the environment for rapid self-directed reorganization. According to complexity leadership theory, complex projects require a balance between administrative, adaptive, and enabling leadership. In this model, administrative leadership implements and manages administrative or bureaucratic policies, procedures, and practices that are essential for any successful operation. Adaptive leadership produces effective and timely responses to the changing business environment and embodies the most innovative and Agile behaviors within the organization. The key contrast here is that administrative leadership generally follows hierarchical lines of authority and positional power structures, whereas adaptive leadership adheres to more of a neural network form of organization and operation that many traditionalists may have difficulty understanding.

A critical truth, however, is that most work in every organization is done without engaging the formal hierarchy. People within even strong hierarchical organizations learn the rules of engagement and then interact with each other with some degree of autonomy to get the job done. The difference in the most capable of complex project organizations is that they possess a strong enabling leadership function that moderates between administrative and adaptive leadership functions to purposefully enhance the adaptive neural network capacities for speed, agility, and innovation, even while maintaining essential discipline and control throughout the business.

Enabling leadership achieves these outcomes by fostering one-to-one and one-to-many employee engagement and other forms of networking and self-organizing behaviors, while using values- and principles-based leadership techniques to guide the network toward self-control. As one example, Google is well known not only for its innovation, but also for its internal self-control within an environment that is notably unrestrictive except for a simple mantra of "do no evil." It is interesting to note that individuals and work teams at Google usually determine for themselves what is good and what is evil; they do not need the organization to dictate that information to them.

People and discipline. Within the framework of what complexity leadership theory suggests, our real focus is on what people need and how they respond within the work environment to produce outcomes that, in turn, drive value in the form of stakeholder benefits. Although complex situations clearly present new challenges requiring seemingly radically different management approaches, the notion of administrative leadership correctly establishes the need for stability, order, and clarity in organization, processes, and procedures. In essence, a well-formulated organizational context establishes values, boundaries, and operating principles that serve as a stabilizing and guiding reference frame that helps people to accurately interpret meaning from their environment, to make sound judgments, and to maintain effective relationships with one another.

It is vitally important for individuals to maintain very high standards in the practice of their respective disciplines, as lapses in those disciplines, even under ordinary circumstances, can lead to catastrophic consequences. In complex projects, lapses in discipline initiate slow and steadily building erosion affecting the capacity of the organization to hold its ground, eventually leading to failure that is metaphorically akin to a landslide. Thus, although there are certainly some detrimental mindsets created by many traditional forms of education and training, it is vitally important for people to possess a compelling drive for rigor and discipline within their fields of practice.

At this point, it becomes clear that effective organizations give attention to two critical networks that must be developed and maintained. First, leaders support and direct their energy to the building of core disciplines and professional connections that might best be described as communities of practice, where individuals guide and strengthen one another—formally and informally—to drive standards and continuous improvement into their professional practice. Second, leaders also build each project team network by linking nodes in and between the communities of practice networks. That is, they select team members from the communities of practice to participate in the project, where a key *communicated* objective for each individual is to contribute value not only from their personal skills and efforts, but also by leveraging value from their professional network.

Systems thinking and paradoxical leadership. As noted previously, one of the key contradictions facing complex project managers is the tendency for formal training in any field to produce closed or narrow-minded perspectives. Almost every business enterprise or government organization is confronted with this problem, and its impact is more serious as complexity increases. Although the professional disciplines are critical, how those disciplines are taught and practiced is also very important.

Because complexity presents us with nonlinear and counterintuitive interactions and effects, we need holistic perspectives and systems views of projects and the problems they seek to resolve. For example, traditional teaching, beginning with elementary grade mathematics, science, and even language, gives us insight into the tremendously powerful concept of reductionism—the breaking down of problems into smaller, more manageable parts. This learned practice, though immensely valuable, produces an almost automatic and habitual response to virtually all problems. We become blind to the assumptions inherent in the approaches and tools we choose to apply, and we fail to appreciate how much error those assumptions have introduced. Is reductionism bad? No. It is very good and effective in a wide variety of circumstances, as long as we recognize the limitations of reductionist thinking and where super-position principles—that is, the recombination of the solved parts of a problem—are not valid.

Systems thinking raises our awareness of these limitations and contradictions. A good example of this kind of systems level, holistic thinking is to consider the treatment of physiological problems in the human body. We would find it ridiculous to physically take the body apart, try to fix the individual parts, and then hope to reassemble them into something that would resume normal function. We all know the patient would die. Think about heart transplant surgery and what it takes to keep the body alive and functioning during the operation. In this illustration, we can see that a doctor must consider the whole, even while treating a discrete part, and that there are serious impacts to the whole because of any intervention.

Some of our more complex projects are beginning to resemble the kinds of systems interactions and integrative designs that connect with this example. We are finding many more situations where constituent subsystems and parts have little meaning or verifiable function until assembled into the whole system or a computer-based simulation of that system. Examples might include the most advanced concepts in satellites, unpiloted airplanes, or computer networks that have high degrees of automation and artificial intelligence, even to the point of autonomous decision making and operation.

The complex project manager adopts a different kind of thought process that involves disciplined systems thinking with an acute awareness and sensitivity to the underlying assumptions that are presented within a specific problem or project. There are many valuable techniques that can be employed to discern those assumptions, to assess their implications, and to identify alternative definitions of the problem, assumptions, and possible solutions. Tony Proctor among many others, provides an excellent summary of creative problem solving techniques, including methods for lateral thinking that facilitate the challenging of constraints, paradigms, and assumptions. These are important tools and techniques for all team members to employ.

Using such techniques, a skilled complex project management team directs their focus on a deeper issue. For at the root of many incorrect or misapplied assumptions, there are fundamental contradictions or paradoxes that cannot be overcome by conventional reductionist thinking. Many assumptions are planted at what appears to be the boundary of conflict between two or more contradictions. Fred Smith and FedEx saw an unchallenged assumption, a paradigm that constrained a whole world of intelligent people. FedEx chose to reverse the assumption with a twist of integrative, holistic thinking that said there is a viable business case for shipping a package from any one place in the United States to any other place in the United States *and* doing it overnight. They saw the paradox. They took an assumed "either-or" constraint, inserted "and" instead, and with some hard work along the way they created a new industry. Complex project managers understand the nature and need for the practice of paradoxical leadership—seeking and finding the paradoxes—those contradictions that serve as signposts to important breakthroughs. The breakthrough is initiated by challenging the contradiction, and fulfilled in finding a creative way to simultaneously satisfy what once appeared to be mutually exclusive constraints. Solving a riddle that poses an apparent contradiction is a metaphor for this type of thinking.

Leadership through values, vision, and principles. In his book *Principle-Centered Leadership*, Stephen Covey discussed the idea that much of true leadership is exercised by communicating a vision and a plan that appeals to the values of people through principles. Principle-based leadership provides a solidly anchored reference frame that serves as both a sure foundation and a navigation aid for decision making. As a foundation, guiding principles communicate security and confidence to team members, much like a handrail or ladder might do on a steep mountain trail. As a navigation aid, guiding principles give clarity to position and heading, just as the earth's magnetic field would convey through a compass and as the constellations would reveal through a sextant. The latter metaphor is useful by extension to point out that truly sound principles are transcendent; they hold true no matter where you are or whom you are with. This metaphor further illustrates that principles have within them what is needed, such as a stable magnetic field, where some form of tool or technique or understanding may also be required, such as a compass, in order to derive something of value.

In complex environments, we are often faced with one of those paradigms that need to be broken. Many project managers think as if every problem has a solution for which there is a paved road or high-speed rail that will get them there. To the informed complex project manager, there is a whole new set of perspectives and skills, and a clear realization that much of what is required involves exploration and "living off the land"—that is, creating what is needed from what the local environment provides at that moment.

Correspondingly, much of traditional project management training provides the equivalent of a driver's license, with an emphasis on how to do many things that have been done many times before and for which a lot of standards and road signs are in place. Complex project management training, on the other hand, amounts to something equivalent to multi-climate survival training, where a lot of knowledge is required, but where wisdom, discernment, and good judgment are most important. Complex project managers read the environment, regard the terrain, and understand how to eat, breathe, and live on the move through the unknown and unexplored territory to the next waypoint on their journey. They do not know all that they know through book knowledge or formal directed learning, but through knowing the principles of where to find water, food, and shelter, and how to determine what direction to head in and how to navigate along the way. Complex project managers guide and are guided by principles because principles give them both a firm foundation of reliable knowledge and the ability to adapt that knowledge readily to changing or radically different circumstances. Principles equip, enable, and empower leaders to handle the unknown.

Sense-making leaders makes sense. In maintaining the connection with the model of principle-based leadership and the explorer metaphor, another key attribute of effective complex project managers is their multi-paradigm adaptive leadership style. They recognize that some circumstances call for a conventional ready-aim-fire approach. What sets them apart is that they also know that under completely different circumstances, a fire-ready-aim approach is needed and is much more effective. Conventional thinkers are smirking and mocking in response to that idea. However, researchers such as Kurtz and Snowden, Snowden and Boone, and Palmer, Dunford, and Akin have long studied and validated that leaders who adapt their behaviors, styles, and modes of leadership to the situation at hand are much more effective than leaders who expect those being led to adapt to their dominant style of leadership.

Consider a disaster response team that is dealing with a disaster they never trained to handle. Disasters do not allow time to think or coordinate. Either responders know what to do or they are paralyzed with inaction. Under those circumstances, the only effective approach is for the responders to do what they know to do, react to what they sense, and then identify the next course of action: fire, ready, aim. Leaders in radically complex environments sometimes need to take action first, and make sense of the situation afterward.

Even in less challenging and risky environments, the notion of floating trial balloons or surveying a population for what they might prefer or find acceptable is common practice. A study of how the Japanese auto industry achieved traction in the U.S. market reveals that it was accomplished mostly through trial and error. Japanese automakers, most notably Honda, explored options, made small but well considered investments, and identified by way of exploration the right path and approach for action. Interestingly, as a tangential point, this was a strategy implemented to perfection; however, some highly regarded experts on strategy thought it was not "real" strategy at all. Those individuals were blind to the strategy that defeated them because their internal definition and paradigm held that strategy involved a predetermined destiny directed from an all-knowing supreme leader and carried out faithfully by motivated subordinates. A strategy enacted by a leader who embraces an explorer mindset and leads a team accordingly is indeed a strategy, and one that is likely prevail under many circumstances, particularly those dominated by ambiguity and uncertainty.

Systems and processes to facilitate the discipline of business. In closing, it seems an appropriate time and place to address some other fundamental and often overlooked aspects of management that, because of being overlooked, become obstacles to success in managing complexity. Every business has systems, processes, and a way of doing things that are part of the formula for its success. These systems and processes should rightly represent a framework for business execution that inherently includes standards for behavior and action that contribute stability and predictability to the enterprise. For the same reasons, though, all business systems and processes can over-constrain or under-constrain the behaviors and actions they are intended to control. Even in high performing organizations, there are likely to be some business processes that need to be refined, modified, or replaced. The organizations in today's volatile business environment need to know that the leap into the domain of complexity is extraordinarily risky for those who are not adequately prepared.

For example, an organization that has loose or ambiguous controls in place for financial or schedule management is inviting disaster. Undisciplined management controls lead to unclear expectations, inaccurate reports on performance and current position, and inadequate advanced warning mechanisms that protect the business from critical failure. Similarly, the introduction of new and unfamiliar systems, such as S.A.P., can produce significant temporary disruption and confusion, particularly if combined with the ambiguities noted above. When these fundamental systems and processes fail or falter, the organization loses its ability to sense and see what's happening. Furthermore, when cost and schedule are important to external stakeholders, poor management controls cause them to lose confidence quickly. Complexity makes these problems worse, and sometimes fatal to the project or business. For all involved, life is better if the organization is constantly maintaining or improving its business systems and processes, and ensuring that there is adequate rigor, discipline, and quality in them.

This dilemma becomes even more difficult to deal with where partnering is required. The fundamental issue here is within the premise for selecting a business for collaboration. Companies choose partners who have demonstrated that they have unique skills, tools, and capabilities along with their own company-unique systems and processes to manage themselves effectively and successfully. To ask that organization to change significantly toward becoming at best a second-class copy of another means that they are being asked to change the formula that made them successful. That doesn't sound like a good idea, but neither does operating in partnership with a company that has substantially different systems and processes that make planning, scheduling, budgeting, and performance reporting troublesome, thus jeopardizing the project. Both options have the potential to negatively affect the value contribution of the partner. This is another of those paradoxes that complex project managers must recognize and mitigate based on the specific context of the business situation.

References

P20, line 43. Ashby, W. R. (1956). *An introduction to cybernetics.* London, England: Chapman & Hall.

P21, line 30. Uhl-Bien, M., Marion, R., & McKelvey, B. (2007). Complexity leadership theory: Shifting leadership from the industrial age to the knowledge era. *The Leadership Quarterly, 18*(4), 298–318.

P22, line 6. Hamel, G. (2006, April 26). Management a la Google. *The Wall Street Journal*, p. A16.

P23, line 39. Proctor, T. (2005). *Creative problem solving for managers* (2nd ed.). London, England: Routledge.

P24, line 18. Covey, S. R. (1991). *Principle-centered leadership.* New York, NY: Simon and Schuster.

P25, line 16. Kurtz, C. F., & Snowden, D. J. (2003). The new dynamics of strategy: Sense-making in a complex and complicated world. *IBM Systems Journal, 42*(3), 462–483. and Snowden, D. J., & Boone, M. E. (2007). A leader's framework for decision-making. *Harvard Business Review, 85*(11), 68–76. and Palmer, I., Dunford, R., & Akin, G. (2009). *Managing organizational change: A multiple perspectives approach* (2nd ed.). New York, NY: McGraw-Hill/Irwin.

Chapter 3

Tools for Complex Projects

Kaye Remington and Julien Pollack

If the only tool you have is a hammer, you tend to see every problem as a nail.

—Abraham Maslow

This chapter first defines the differences between a tool or technique, a methodology, and a theory. It then describes the results of some of the research carried out by the author and her colleagues by focusing on the tools, techniques, or approaches developed by senior project managers specifically to address highly complex projects. Selected tools are discussed in more detail. The chapter concludes with a discussion of tools in application.

A Case for Thinking Outside the Tool Box

Maslow's comment is entirely relevant to projects that we might define as complex. It preempts one of the most important findings from our research. That is, managing a complex project successfully requires unconstrained thinking: thinking that embraces more than the standard textbook approaches to project management or the standard tools and methods. We asked senior project managers, who were selected because they had managed high risk, complex projects (judged as such by their key stakeholders), to list the key attributes that enabled their success. Without exception all respondents cited phrases like the ability to "think outside the box"; "flexible approach to management"; "not being constrained by rules"; and ability to "think creatively."

Most standard project management methodologies carry the implicit assumption that the practitioner will use a particular set of tools in a defined order, and that all or most of the tools in the methodology will apply. Complex projects can rarely be managed by applying a standard methodology that has been designed to be used unvaryingly in all contexts. Our research data reveal that tools, techniques, and approaches—and we bracket these three terms together in this context—were selected by experienced project managers as and when the situation demanded, and, if no appropriate tools were available, one was created to fit the purpose. Based on this research data, and supported by mounting anecdotal evidence, the project manager who successfully manages high risk and complex projects appears to be someone who can select from a vast range of tools, methods, and approaches, to ap-

---

ply what is needed, when it is needed. In some cases, this means engaging others who are more experienced with a tool or approach, in other situations, it means being familiar enough with a range of tools and approaches to be able to "move with the moment."

One Size Does Not Fit All: Traditional Approaches versus "Systemic Pluralism"

Differences between individual projects have been recognized for some time. In addition, management research in this field has expanded in the recognition that traditional approaches were not always delivering the best results. Our research suggests that project managers who manage complex project successfully tend to develop their own methodologies and vary these considerably from project to project. The most productive methods appear to be based on the concept of systemic pluralism. "How do we handle it? Well it's difficult ...There isn't one single answer." Systemic pluralism requires two things from practitioners: that project managers recognize the systemic nature of projects and that they adopt a pluralist approach to the tools and methods they apply. That means applying many different tools and approaches and being alert to the need to change tools and approaches as the project complexity develops or changes.

The idea of systemic pluralism was developed as part of the systems field, under the banner of critical systems thinking, a branch of systems thinking which emphasizes theoretical and methodological pluralism. Authors such as Midgley, Mingers, and Flood & Jackson all discuss the development of critical systems thinking and pluralist ideas in the systems, operational research, and management science fields. Discussed in more detail in other chapters of this book, most projects can be more readily described as complex adaptive systems than as simple systems. Complex projects vary dramatically in form and character, exhibiting many different characteristics and aspects of systemicity. A single complex project may even demonstrate multiple kinds of systemicity, with various parts of the project showing markedly dissimilar characteristics and behavior. Differences in systemicity will almost certainly vary considerably within any program or group of interrelated projects.

For those projects that can be described effectively as simple systems, where the outcomes of the project can be so well defined that fully predetermined control is possible, standard or traditional project management tools and processes are very efficient. However, in more complex contexts, where ambiguity, uncertainty, or lack of trust prevail, there will be aspects of the project for which control, in the sense of total predetermination of outcomes, is unlikely or even impossible to achieve. These parts of a project, or subprojects, may benefit much more from approaches based on both systems thinking and multidimensional approaches. In fact, faced with the pluralistic nature of the projects themselves, project managers have no choice but to adopt a pluralistic approach to practice that means drawing flexibly and dynamically from a range of tools and approaches in order to deliver satisfactory outcomes. When implementing a systemic and pluralistic approach the manager must first identify the nature of the complexity; then like an artist, select from the palette of tools, those tools that will provide a variety of perspectives, reveal the layers of complexity, and make the project manageable.

Defining Tools, Methodology, and Theory

Defining tools, methodology, and theory is problematic because these words are used in different ways and in different contexts. Therefore, for the purpose of this chapter, functional definitions will be used. From a purely functional perspective, philosophy and theory can be seen as providing a formal conceptual framework for examining the world, an explicit perspective through which the world can be viewed. Likewise, paradigm is broadly defined as "...a world view, spanning ontology, epistemology, and methodology...," "...based on a set of fundamental philosophical assumptions that define the nature of possible research and intervention." Readers interested in a more thorough exploration of the ontology of paradigms should refer to Kuhn. Complexity theory itself comprises a broad group of ideas, models, and predictive descriptions about how complex systems behave.

Also from a functional viewpoint, a methodology can be seen as a structured set of guidelines for the improvement of the effectiveness of a system or project. It develops within a particular paradigm and embodies particular philosophical and theoretical principles. However, methodology differs from theory and philosophy in that it contains practical guidelines. Checkland placed methodology as the middle ground between philosophy and technique, containing elements of both, while "...a technique tells you 'how' and a philosophy tells you 'what', a methodology will contain elements of both 'how' and 'what.'" Here, methodology is considered to be "... the logos of method...." It provides the principles on which the method is based, and can be considered "...a higher-order term than method and, indeed, than procedures, models, tools, and techniques, the use of all of which can be facilitated, organized and reflected upon in methodology."

Tools, approaches, and techniques are the most practical part of the hierarchy, and they tend to make little direct reference to theory or philosophy. However, they are often created under, or associated with, particular theories or philosophies. For instance, PERT and Gantt charts are both associated with the way of thinking embodied in project management and can be linked to positivist and realist philosophies. Tools, approaches, and techniques generally involve a series of clearly delineated steps. Because of this, it is possible to create clear standards for their use, while this is significantly more difficult for methodologies. According to Mingers and Mingers and Brocklesby, tools are specific activities with well-defined purposes. A tool can also be an artifact, such as computer software, that can be used to perform a particular technique. Use of tools can "... lead to an end point without the need for reflective intervention...," however, reflection on tools, in relation to theory and methodology, can be useful in learning from past mistakes and improving future performance.

The Relationship Between Tools, Methodology, and Theory

One popular way of looking at the relationship between tools, methodology, and theory, is to think of them as a hierarchy. In this kind of hierarchy, theory is usually thought of as sitting at the top, with methodology below that, with tools sitting at the bottom of the hierarchy (see Figure 3-1). In this kind of hierarchy, the upper layers can be thought of as more philosophical or theoretical and distanced from the mess of practical application. By contrast, the lower levels are never as "clean," requiring actual engagement with pragmatic necessity and providing a context where theoretical claims can be tested. Many different practitioners and researchers have found it useful to view this relationship as a hierarchy with different levels of abstraction.

The upper levels in this hierarchy constitute the conceptual basis and intellectual context for the increasing practicalities in the lower layers. The upper layers provide a basis against which consistency can be judged. These philosophical and theoretical aspects provide the "why" for methodology. Methodology can be thought of as specifying "what," while tools and techniques specify "how." We can "...learn more about these tools by reflecting on their links to methodologies, or about methodologies by reflecting on their links to theory."

The practical world of the lower layers plays a different role in this hierarchy. A theory that bears no relationship to the real world of practice is not of much practical value. For theory to be valuable it must enable action, it has to be applied and tested in the real world. Testing the real-world efficacy of the practice provides justification for statements made in the realms of theory and philosophy. Practical application of the lower layers can be used to test the validity of claims made in the upper layers, resulting in either validation of claims or the need to reassess and rework statements about the nature of the world. The lower layers can be thought of as a feedback system for the upper layers.

For Midgley, thinking of this relationship as a hierarchy suggests that theory and philosophy are given special value and thought of as incontestable. He argues that such a hierarchical relationship precludes the idea that practice itself '...may signal a philosophical inadequacy.' However, it is clear that in practice theory and philosophy are often challenged based on practical experience. Midgley argued that philosophy, methodology, and tools should be viewed as mutually supportive.

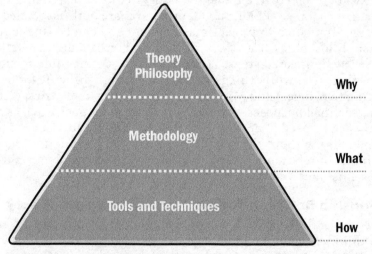

Figure 3-1: A hierarchical relationship between the theoretical and practical

Methods can generally be thought of as an interrelated series of tools, used in practice to achieve a specific purpose. Methods may include representational guidelines, such as modeling techniques, and procedural guidelines, which describe how work is to be conducted. To Paton a method is constructed to deal with an individual situation. It is particular and individual. Methodologies "...provide us with logic to help us construct a method from a given set of tools and techniques." Methods can be thought of as the practical output of the combination of methodologies and tools (see Figure 3-2).

Finding Tools that Suit the Nature of the Project Complexity

Although we found many different tools in use, it was apparent that only some were relevant to complex projects, some were only relevant at particular times in the project life cycle, and some were relevant to one type of projects but not others. One of the tasks we set for ourselves, was to try to discover which tools were relevant, to what kinds of complex projects and when. However, we first needed a frame to define a complex project. As other writers in this book demonstrate, definition of a complex project is highly problematic. The definition is influenced by perception and context. Perception of the complexity of a project is influenced by prior experience, personal capabilities, and the key stakeholders who are involved in making the judgment—their political agendas, cultural needs, and their own abilities to perceive an issue as complex. For example, in earlier research, we found that many sponsors did not perceive the complexity of the project in the same way that the project managers understood it. Some project managers felt they had to simplify the complexity in order to facilitate communication with a sponsor.

From our interviews with senior project managers, we collated a range of tools and approaches used, most of which differed from standard tools and methods found in project management textbooks. We then analyzed the tools and approaches to discover the characteristics of the perceived complexity each tool or approach addressed and the stage of the project to which they were relevant. This, coupled with an extensive literature search, led to a classification of complexity types for projects, based on the source of complexity. With the exception of the fourth category, which we included to account for a particular source of complexity associated with time, this work extended the works of several other authors. The four categories or dimensions, which are based on the source of

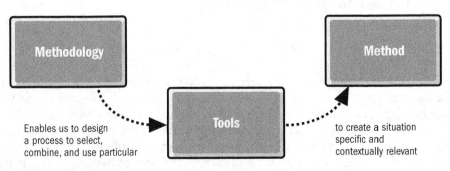

Figure 3-2: The derivation and design of methods

complexity and may constitute a tool to assist stakeholders in identifying the nature of complexity, are as follows:

Structural complexity—derives from a classical view of complexity based on the structure of information pathways. The source of structural complexity is many interrelated and interdependent activities. Complexity, particularly in the form of non-linear feedback, can arise due to complicated organizational and approval pathways as well as in huge work breakdown structures with myriads of activities that might interact.

Technical complexity—derives from technical or design challenges that are more severe than anticipated and in particular, problems that might not yield a solution within the time available.

Directional complexity—was viewed as a type of complexity that arose from unclear or unshared goals or goal-paths. Although this is most common at the beginning of a project, it can arise at any time due to changes of direction resulting from technical or environmental change.

Temporal complexity—was coined in response to projects that appeared to be unduly sensitive to unpredictable changes over time, due to the volatile nature of the internal or external environment. Even if the nature of the change could be anticipated, knowing when the environmental or organizational impact might occur, what form it might take and its potential impact on the project can be hard to predict. Temporal complexity increases with the duration of a project.

The classification proved to be a very useful tool because it can assist project managers and other key stakeholder to identify or anticipate the source of complexity and the approaches that might best address the complexity. Some tools and approaches apply to the whole of the project, others to specific phases, and others to specific dimensions of complexity.

It should be noted that although other classification systems include attributes such as uncertainty, we argue that categories or dimensions of complexity can have behavioral consequences, such as uncertainty, ambiguity, and loss of trust, which exacerbate perceptions of complexity. Thus, with the exception of directional complexity, uncertainty is treated as a consequence in this model, rather than a cause.

Whole of Project Tools and Approaches
Tool for Mapping the Complexity

A tool emerging from our classification project has proved to be useful in helping key stakeholders recognize when a project is more than just complicated. Based on this knowledge, choices can be offered to key stakeholders about whether to proceed, how to proceed, and what tools and approaches might be useful and when they can best be used. An example provided by the authors was a remote area medical facility. Being able to identify and agree upon the nature of the complexity and the expected level of complexity at the beginning of each phase of the project encouraged key stakeholders to monitor and control the project based on the nature of the expected complexity. It enabled them to make appropriate adjustments to the project's organizational structure, key role definitions, and procurement systems as the project progressed through a temporally unstable landscape. As the assessment of complexity is based on perception, it is important that any tool captures the combined perception of the stakeholders. This in itself helps to stimulate dialogue about what contributes to the complexity of the project that, without such a tool, might not occur. As mentioned previously, earlier research revealed that although many project managers understood that the project was more than just difficult, their key stakeholders, such as owners and sponsors did not. This tool assists in structuring the kind of dialogue that is necessary if the project manager is to be given the kind of support needed for a complex project.

System Anatomy Tool

One project approach that stood out in the research was the "system anatomy," which is now referred to as the integration centric development (ICD) approach, and was developed by the team at Ericcson, for a telecommunications rollout that spanned many countries. The challenge was integrating implementation in vastly different cultural settings by geographically distributed and often isolated teams, with different local work practices. The solution was to contain the master planning and communication documents to a one-page "anatomy" diagram that is constructed by key stakeholders. This document became the focus of all communication, control, and monitoring. Essentially the approach allowed central control of key elements and local control of work practices that could be developed locally to suit the particular context; including availability of labor and resources and cultural and political needs.

Time-Linked Semi-Structures

Another project tool, titled Jazz or time-linked semi-structures was derived from observation of projects managed in the entertainment and design industries where time to performance (or market) is often the critical driver in an atmosphere of highly interlinked creative team activity. Particularly in the theatrical world, there are also very tight economic drivers and high levels of competition for those all-important opening night reviews. More of a theoretical model than a tool, as such, this approach supports maintenance of a dynamic balance between a more formal structure at one extreme and the more chaotic environment needed to optimize creativity. The reference to Jazz derives from the improvisational nature of jazz music, which is created "on the spot" without a prescribed score or plan. However, jazz, as a musical form, is guided by a non-negotiable framework that constrains what the soloist can play at any time. As the bassist Charles Mingus said "You can't improvise on nothin.' You gotta have something.'" The structure in the projects we observed was provided by a schedule, highlighting nodal points only, such as design or production meetings, and very clear role definitions that were well communicated and respected by all concerned. Around that structural spine or "time-linked semi-structure" the projects hovered near "the edge of chaos"—the hypothetical point where creativity and associated learning are like to be greatest.

Tools to Address Specific Aspects of Complexity
Earned Value

One tool that addresses complexity is earned value management. Although this tool is part of the mainstream of project management tradition, our research suggests that it is still under-utilized as a tool. Earned value management is particularly useful in projects exhibiting high structural complexity and is indeed often applied in large engineering and defense procurement projects. Where high-level structural and technical complexity exist the most effective procurement options may be in the form of alliances or partnerships. However, successful alliances or partnerships depend on maintaining high levels of trust. For an alliance or partnership to work, all transactions must be completely transparent to all partners in the alliance. Transparency requires demonstration of rigorous monitoring and control. Earned value management assists in communicating transparency and maintaining trust in alliances or partnerships. If sensibly applied, it is one of the most effective ways of keeping track of the value of what has been delivered within a specified time frame compared with projected delivery and expenditure.

Problem Structuring and Soft Systems Thinking Tools

Unclear or unshared goals or goal paths may exist in the absence of technical barriers or may exist before technical barriers have been discovered. Particularly, if the relationships are conflicted or where political agendas are unstated, high levels of complexity may result. Associated with this can occur a loss of trust and willingness to cooperate or work together. What is referred to as directional complexity occurs most frequently at the beginning of a project. If it is not addressed fully at the beginning, lack of clarity breeds loss of trust. Often larger goals are shared, for example, "we want to reduce customer complaints," but the goal paths to achieve the overarching goal are unclear or unshared by the various levels of the organization charged with delivering the goal. Our research in the defense industries indicated that more often than not senior management understood the goals but the project personnel or industry partners, either did not understand, or had a different interpretation, of the goal or goal paths. Although directional complexity is probably the easiest to address given experienced facilitators using a raft of problem structuring and soft systems thinking tools, it is often not addressed adequately because people either do not recognize its presence or tend to ignore it in favor of leaping into what they believe is the meaning of the project. A number of soft systems thinking tools can be applied with great effect to clarify and share goals and goal-paths.

Summary of Tools for Complex Projects

The table below summarizes some of the tools and approaches used by expert practitioners to address different dimensions of project complexity.

Complexity in Combination and Tools

The reality is that when a project is complex it exhibits several dimensions of complexity over time, if not all at once. Each dimension of complexity requires different tools and in some projects, a vast range of tools must be used in parallel. Even an apparently simple project can go very wrong if the nature of the complexity is not

Dimension	Source of Complexity	Tools to be Considered
Structural	High levels of interconnectedness and codependency between activities or organizational complicacy, resulting in unclear or redundant communication and approval pathways.	High level monitoring and control tools, including earned value management, procurement via partnerships, flexible procurement options, program management tools, OR tools, complex systems-based risk tools.
Technical	Design or technical challenges that are extreme or for which no solution is apparent within the time available	Clear role definition, procurement via partnerships and alliances, value management, "hands-off" management control approaches, creative thinking tools, integrating tools facilitating "rich" communication
Directional	Unclear or unshared goals and goal paths; covert or conflicted objectives; cultural barriers, language and communication barriers; covert agendas	Soft systems thinking tools, appreciative enquiry, trust building exercises, value management, problem-structuring tools.
Temporal	Shifting and unpredictable landscape over time; uncontrollable scope changes; uncertain political, regulatory, technical environments over the life cycle of the project	Parallel processing tools (multidimensions in series), environmental scanning, problem structuring and problem analysis tools, change management tools focusing on team motivation.

recognized. In addition, the nature of the complexity can change over time, as in the case of the area medical facility discussed above. It is also important to note the potential impact of one dimension of project complexity on another and the effect that intersection has on choice of tools and approaches. A project that initially presents few technical challenges can become highly problematic with a change of goal path when client requirements change. A structurally complex project might suggest the use of high level project control tools, however if there are technical challenges control needs to exercised in such a way that solution finding is not stifled too early in the project. This kind of situation requires a phased use of tool with approaches, like Jazz, that encourage rich communication, rather than overt control. If directional complexity is also present, enough time must be allowed to achieve understanding and alignment using soft systems thinking tools.

In reality, however, particularly with mega projects, such as large construction and engineering projects, a myriad of projects and interests intersect, each at different stages and exhibiting different dimensions of complexity. In an intercity rail upgrade project, for example, temporal complexity was expected due to the duration of the project (over 10 years), the possibility during that time of a change of government (which might mean cancellation of the project), and the probability of significant advances in technology during the project life cycle. This is coupled with high structural complexity due to the size of the project, the number of railway stations involved, limited access to tracks and stations, the complicated approval pathways involving government and commercial entities and the potential for bottlenecks due to shortage of specialist expertise. Technological challenges also abound, associated with how to address the number of bridges, tunnels, and stations that have existing heritage orders when few alternative tracks are available. However, the most challenging aspects relate to the directional complexity involved in aligning goals, addressing and monitoring conflicting requirements of the many stakeholder groups. Tools are only helpful in these kinds of projects if they form part of a philosophy and methodology that support a systemic and pluralistic approach and if they are able to be used and applied in a timely manner, by people who are competent in their usage.

Conclusion: Tools Are Just Tools

It is important to recognize that managing a complex project is a higher order management activity and should be treated and resourced accordingly. A discussion of tools is not complete without addressing organizational and individual capabilities. Tools in themselves are useless without the appropriate level of capability. Most important is the capability of the governance team in identifying the nature of the complexity associated with a project, ability to identify the tools or approaches needed, ability to identify the skills and competences to apply the tools, and the willingness to ensure that the right people are engaged to deliver the project. Our data strongly suggests that the project managers who manage complex projects successfully are like artists, selecting the most appropriate tools and approaches from their very large palettes and working with those tools to produce the color, form and texture appropriate to the work in hand. However, they also behave like scientists in their ability to select, analyze, and synthesize empirical data, and like politicians in their ability to influence and manage a network of relationships. Tools are, in the end, just tools.

Bibliography

P29, line 9; P30, line 12; P33, line 23; P35, line 8. Helm, J., & Remington, K. (2005a, May), Adaptive habitus: Project managers' perceptions of the role of the project sponsor. *Proceedings of EURAM Conference*, Munich, Germany and Helm, J., & Remington, K. (2005b). Effective sponsorship, project managers' perceptions of the role of the project sponsor. *Project Management Journal, 36*(3), 51–62.

P29, line 22. Crawford, L., & Pollack, J. (2004). Hard and soft projects: A framework for analysis. *International Journal of Project Management, 22*(8), 645–653. and Pollack, J. (2007a). Multimethodology in series and parallel: Strategic planning using hard and soft OR. *Journal of the Operational Research Society. 60*, 156–167.

P30, line 7; P33, line 33. Turner, J. R., & Cochrane, R. A. (1993). Goals-and-methods matrix: Coping with projects with ill defined goals and/or methods of achieving them. *International Journal of Project Management, 11*(2), 93–102. and Payne, J. H., & Turner, J. R. (1999). Company-wide project management: The planning and control of programmes of projects of different type. *International Journal of Project Management, 17*(1), 55–59. and Shenhar, A. J. (2001). One size does not fit all projects: Exploring classical contingency domains. *Management Studies, 47*(3), 394–414.

P30, line 13. Remington, K., & Crawford, L. (2004, August). Illusions of control. *Proceedings of IRNOP VI Project Research Conference*, Turku, Finland. and Smith, C. (2007). *Making sense of projects: Theory, practice and the pursuit of performance.* Aldershot, UK: Gower Publishing, p. 22.

P30, line 21. Midgley, G. (1996). What is this thing called CST? In R. Flood & N. Romm (Eds.), *Critical systems thinking: Current research and practice,* (pp. 11–24). New York, NY: Plenum Publishers. and Midgley, G. (2000*). Systemic* *intervention: Philosophy, methodology, and practice.* New York, NY: Plenum Publishers.

P30, line 22; P31, line 16. Mingers, J. (1997a). Multi-paradigm multimethodology. In J. Mingers & A. Gill (Eds.), *Multimethodology: The theory and practice of combining management science methodologies* (pp. 1–20). Chichester, UK: John Wiley & Sons. and Mingers, J. (2003). A classification of the philosophical assumptions of management science methods. *Journal of the Operational Research Society, 54,* 559–570.

P30, line 22; P36, line 5. Flood, R., & Jackson, M. (1991). *Creative problem solving: Total systems intervention.* New York, NY: John Wiley & Sons.

P31, line 10. Healy, M., & Perry, C. (2000). Comprehensive criteria to judge the validity and reliability of qualitative research within the realism paradigm. *Qualitative Market Research: An International Journal, 3*(3), 121.

P31, lines 11, 18, 35; P32, line 11. Mingers, J. (1997b). Towards critical pluralism. In J. Mingers & A. Gill (Eds.), *Multimethodology: The theory and practice of combining management science methodologies* (pp. 407–440). Chichester, UK: John Wiley & Sons, p. 429–430.

P31, line 13. Kuhn, T. (1962). *The structure of scientific revolutions.* Chicago, IL: University of Chicago Press.

P31, lines 18, 35; P32, line 6. Mingers, J., & Brocklesby, J. (1997). Multimethodology: Towards a framework for mixing methodologies. *Omega, International Journal of Management Science, 25*(5), 489–509.

P31, line 19. Checkland, P. (1981). *Systems thinking, systems practice.* Chichester, UK: John Wiley & Sons, p. 162.

P31, line 23. Checkland, P. (1999). Soft systems methodology: A 30-year retrospective. In P. Checkland & J. Scholes, (Eds.), *Soft systems methodology in action* (pp. A1–A65). Chichester, UK: John Wiley & Sons, p. S36. and Checkland, P. (2002). Thirty years in the systems movement: Disappointments I have known, and a way forward. *Systemist, 24*(2), 99–112.

P31, line 26; P36, line 35. Jackson, M. (2000). *Systems approaches to management.* New York, NY: Plenum Publishers, p. 11.

P31, line 38. Rosenhead, J. (1997). Foreword. In J. Mingers & A. Gill (Eds.), *Multimethodology: The theory and practice of combining management science methodologies* (pp. xii–xiv). Chichester, UK: John Wiley & Sons, p. xiii.

P32, line 6. Fitzgerald, B., & Howcroft, D. (1998). Towards dissolution of the IS research debate: From polarization to polarity. *Journal of Information Technology, 13*(4), 313–326. and Ragsdell, G. (2000). Engineering a paradigm shift? An holistic approach to organizational change management, *Journal of Organizational Change Management, 13*(2), 104–120.

P32, line 13. Jackson, M. (1999). Towards coherent pluralism in management science. *Journal of the Operational Research Society, 50*(1), 19.

P32, lines 23, 26; P36, line 35. Midgley, G. (2000). *Systemic intervention: Philosophy, methodology, and practice.* New York, NY: Plenum Publishers.

P33, line 2. Midgley, G., Munlo, I., & Brown, M. (1998). The theory and practice of boundary critique: Developing housing services for older people. *Journal of the Operational Research Society, 49*(5), 467–478.

P33, lines 4, 6. Paton, G. (2001). A systemic action learning cycle as the key element of an ongoing spiral of analyses. *Systemic Practice and Action Research, 14*(1), 95–111.

P33, line 12. Remington, K., & Pollack, J. (2006, December). *Complex infrastructure projects: a systemic model for management*. Paper presented at ANZSYS Conference, Sydney, Australia. and Remington, K., & Pollack, J. (2007). *Tools for complex projects*. Aldershot, UK: Gower Publishing.

P33, line 12; P34, lines 27, 39; P35, line 24; P36, line 38. Remington, K., & Pollack, J. (2007). *Tools for complex projects*. Aldershot, UK: Gower Publishing.

P33, line 33. Baccarini, D. (1996). The concept of project complexity—A review. *International Journal of Project Management, 14*(4), 201–204. and Williams, T. (2002). *Modelling complex projects*. Sussex, UK: John Wiley & Sons.

P33, Figure 3-2. Paton, G. (2001). A systemic action learning cycle as the key element of an ongoing spiral of analyses. *Systemic Practice and Action Research, 14*(1), 99.

P35, line 15. Lilliesköld, J. (2003, November). Coordinating dependencies in complex system development projects. *Proceedings of the IEEE Engineering Management Conference, IEMC '03*, pp. 400–404. and Taxén, L., & Lilliesköld, J. (2005, March). Manifesting shared affordances in system development: The system anatomy. *Proceedings of ALOIS, Second International Conference, Limerick, Ireland.* Available at http:www.alois2005.ul.ie/. and Lilliesköld, J., & Taxén, L. (2006, October). Operationalizing coordination of megaprojects: A workpractice perspective. *Proceedings of IRNOP VII Conference*, Xi'an, China, pp. 574–587.

P36, line 10. Bjørkeng, K., Clegg, S., & Pitsis, T. (2009). Becoming (a) practice. *Management Learning, 40*(2), 145–159.

P36, line 12. Lendrum, T. (1998). *The strategic partnering handbook* (2nd ed.). Sydney, Australia: McGraw-Hill.

P36, line 42. Pollack, J. (2007b). The changing paradigms of project management. *International Journal of Project Management, 25*(3), 266–274.

Checkland, P., & Howell, S. (1998). *Information, systems and information systems: Making sense of the field*. West Sussex, UK: John Wiley & Sons.

Checkland, P., & Scholes, J. (1990). *Soft systems methodology in action*. Chichester, UK: John Wiley & Sons.

Midgley, G. (1990). Creative methodology design. *Systemist, 12*, 108–113.

Midgley, G. (1997). Mixing methods: Developing systemic intervention. In J. Mingers & A. Gill (Eds.), *Multimethodology: The theory and practice of combining management science methodologies* (pp. 249–290). Chichester, UK: John Wiley & Sons.

Chapter 4

Strategic Management: Developing Policies and Strategies

Christoph Loch and Frederick C. Payne

What Is Complexity?

We are adopting a strict definition of complexity, in order to focus our discussion on developing policies and strategies. Complex projects have many parameters and variables with many interactions, or, more formally, collections of components and activities that are "made up of a large number of parts that interact in non-simple ways...[such that] given the properties of the parts and...their interactions, it is not a trivial matter to infer the properties of the whole."

In other words, complexity is not the same as size: a large project may not be complex if it can be divided into pieces that can be worked through separately without interacting with one another; in this case, one just puts many teams in parallel, who each proceed without having to take into account what the others do. The management challenge is still relatively simple. Second, complexity is not the same as uncertainty and project risk (stemming from novelty). If we know that an activity may take two days if the weather is good and up to five days if the weather is bad, we can prepare ourselves for it, for example, by having a buffer in the plan. *Complexity fundamentally has to do with interactions.*

It is well known that complexity may be caused by the technical system of many interacting physical components. However, complexity may come from multiple sources:

- **Technical complexity:** interactions of many system components cause interdependencies among many tasks in the project.
- **Actor complexity:** Many stakeholders are interested in the project, possibly emphasizing different dimensions and wanting contradictory outcomes, and the stakeholders may influence one another
- **External complexity:** The project may touch multiple market segments, be influenced by regulations in multiple regions or domains, be affected by standard defining bodies such as ISO, or face multiple competitors.

There may be complexity on each of these dimensions separately, (such as multiple mutually influencing stakeholders), but complexity may also arise from interactions *across* dimensions: technical features may win or antagonize, or even solidarize, stakeholder groups, or actors may influence regulatory changes. This cross-domain complexity may be just as damaging as well-known types of complexity, but initially be overlooked by management.

Take implementing an Enterprise Resource Planning (ERP) tool as an example. The stakeholders come from every corner of the organization and are familiar with what they have today. They all legitimately want something better in the future, but are reluctant to give up anything that they currently have for the greater good of the organization (actor complexity). All dimensions of running a business must be blended into one ERP system; program delivery feeds accounts receivable/payable, which feeds payroll, and so on (technical complexity). The finance part needs to meet regulatory requirements and timekeeping needs to meet local employment laws for each business in each country implementing the ERP system (external complexity). In this example, the strategy needs to emphasize a single approach with enough flexibility but blueprinted and agreed upon early in the process, and the policy must be to achieve the blueprint without undue interruption.

How Complexity Makes Project Management Difficult

Complexity causes two fundamental difficulties: First, it causes **causal ambiguity**, which means that that many different actions and parameters interact, so the effect of actions is difficult to assess: any action has multiple effects, and any observed effect has multiple possible explanations. Even when, in principle, everything in the project is "deterministic" and COULD be foreseen, it is just impossible to consider all cause-and-effect relationships, which makes the project unpredictable: "It's not difficult to anticipate the position of ONE tree, but you can't map a million of them, so you are likely to run into one of them."

Second, complexity causes **interaction uncertainty**, again even if in principle, every event might be deterministic and foreseeable. A typical feature of complex systems is that the overall problem has to be partitioned into pieces in order to be manageable. Thus, individuals or departments are assigned pieces of the problem, coordinated by a system architecture with defined interfaces. These individuals act locally to do the best they can with ("optimize") the pieces of the problem for which they are responsible. However, because of the complex interactions among subproblems and variables, the individuals influence one another, and while they may be aware of the influences, they often cannot fully consider them in their local decisions. As the component designs evolve over time, ongoing problem choices in other groups make the requirements for a particular group inherently unstable. The interactions themselves cause uncertainty for the individual.

As an example, take the development engineer for the air intake of a car's climate control system. This engineer had been constructing a particular component for more than a year, based on design assumptions (such as the available space) that were formally written down and "frozen" at various design reviews. A combination of technical complexity across car projects (because the intake system was shared by several models) and actor complexity (because manufacturing and prototyping of the final plastic part was performed by a supplier) came from the strategic positioning of the project. It was out of the control of the project engineer, but nevertheless it forced him to cope with 18 changes (each requiring him to negotiate design and tooling changes with the part supplier), many of them based on elements beyond his horizon, which thus had no obvious logic. As a result, he experienced severe stress and ultimately took an extended sick leave.

These two fundamental challenges caused by complexity make traditional project planning inadequate: planning, no matter how thorough, cannot hope to successfully anticipate all interactions and causal ambiguity. They force management to either strategically structure projects differently, or adopt more flexible methods of management policy.

What Project Management Can Do in Principle
Reduce Complexity: Decouple and Modularize

The most radical response to complexity is to *leave out* a few features, or market segments, or countries with different regulatory regimes, in order to get (at least the first version of the project) under control. Reducing the variables reduces complexity. A less radical and widely discussed tool to reduce complexity is *modularity*. A modular system is one with few and well defined interfaces cutting across the modules (component groups) and functions of the product. For example, software modules are subroutines that have a clear interface for evoking them. In car development, modularization comes in the form of mechanical "chunks" with clear interfaces to the rest of the car. For example, a car engine is developed largely independently of the body.

Modularity, in effect, reduces complexity itself by dividing the complex system into several smaller subsystems, which do not, or barely, interact. Why does not everyone build modular systems, if they are so helpful? The answer is that the design restrictions imposed by modularity reduce system performance and compactness, especially for products incorporating new technologies that are not yet fully understood. In particular, modularization limits the search space of the design team, which may result in a suboptimal solution. Suffering these performance disadvantages may well make a product uncompetitive. Thus, modularity is not always an option.

Freeze Components

It is an important architectural choice as to what should be optimized for the system and what components and interfaces are less important. Such "secondary" system elements may be fixed at some point during the development process. Freezing specifications stops short of segmenting the design (or reducing complexity itself, as modularization does). It defines which optimizations across interfaces have precedence over other optimizations. Holding some components and interfaces fixed reduces the size of the part of the design system that contributes to complexity.

Take the example of developing an integrated entertainment system (CD, radio, personal entertainment module, TV, GPS, and links to the phone) as part of a new car model. After a long "back and forth" about the best operating system (OS) for the software, the team had to settle on one (freeze the decision), although the choice was not the one with the highest performance (this was hotly contested). However, without the freezing, the many other components of the project had no chance of converging to a design in a timely fashion.

Some luxury car manufacturers have traditionally given design and feature decisions more emphasis than decisions regarding production issues. As a result, feedback loops from production back to product elements of the design process are limited. This eliminates complexity, at the expense of production cost.

Experience plays an important role in freezing decisions. An organization developing a next generation product, based on a well-known architecture and well-understood technologies, can predict many aspects of the system's performance. The organization can strategically choose in advance ranges of design parameters that are likely to yield high performance. Thus, many parameters can be frozen (i.e., ranges do not need to be considered) without trading off performance. In contrast, when freezing is used in novel projects, it is often not understood what performance is sacrificed; rather, the freezing is defensive in order to get the project's progress under control.

Control-and-Fast-Response

Control-and-fast-response is a useful and interesting approach to complexity that follows a different mind-set than established project management. Weick and Sutcliffe discussed what high-reliability organizations, such as a nuclear power plant or an aircraft carrier, must do to guarantee a reliable functioning of a very complex system. Reliable operation must be guaranteed (almost at all cost) because much is at stake. A striking example is the operation of an aircraft carrier:

> . . . you have six thousand people crammed into tight spaces away from the shore on a 1,100-foot, 95,000-ton floating city run by an overburdened 'city major.' Within those tight spaces on a carrier, you also have people working with jet aircraft, jet fuel, nuclear reactors, nuclear weapons, an onboard air traffic control system, refueling and re-supply from adjacent ships that are moving, a surrounding battle group of seven to nine ships that are supposed to protect the carrier but that can themselves also be dangerous obstacles in fog or high seas and unpredictable weather.

People on a carrier cannot afford to be wrong, or lives will be lost. This is a huge challenge because the system is so complex—the different parts of the carrier are tightly coupled, and impact one another, and the individual components constantly change, because, for example, of human error, equipment failure, or changing weather conditions. "Safety is elusive because it is a dynamic non-event—what produces the stable outcome is constant change rather than continuous repetition. To achieve this stability, a change in one system parameter must be compensated for by a change in other parameters." Yet, accidents rarely happen.

Weick and Sutcliffe recommended that the organization develop what they call "mindfulness." This refers to "the combination of ongoing scrutiny of existing expectations, continuous refinement and differentiation of expectations based on newer experiences, willingness and capability to invent new expectations that make sense of unprecedented events, [and] a more nuanced appreciation of context and ways to deal with it."

Mindfulness includes a number of "soft skills," such as a policy of preoccupation with failure, reluctance to simplify, sensitivity to operations, commitment to resilience, and deference to expertise. In our language of "systems," mindfulness means the ability to know precisely what the "in control" target state of each component of the system is, to detect even small deviations from the target state, and to quickly react to them and contain them so that they do not spread to other components of the system, causing a major problem there. In other words, mindfulness represents control-and-fast-response: We prevent deviations if possible, and if one occurs, we need a policy to contain it immediately.

Control takes the form of preoccupation with failure, or ever paranoid and pervasive monitoring. For example, aircraft carriers conduct foreign-object-damage walk-downs on deck several times a day to prevent small objects (such as bolts or trash) from being sucked into airplane engines. In the constant chatter of simultaneous loops of conversation and verification, "seasoned personnel do not 'listen' so much as they monitor for deviations with a policy of reacting instantly to anything that does not fit their expectations of the correct routine."

When a slight deviation is discovered, even if it seems inconsequential, corrective and, if necessary, drastic action is taken. For example, a seaman on a nuclear carrier reported the loss of a tool on the deck. All aircraft aloft were redirected to land bases until the tool was found, and the seaman was commended for his action—recognizing a potential danger—the next day at a formal ceremony. Commitment to resilience means the ability to have a policy that substantially deviates from established routines, and to modify those routines, in order to mitigate the deviations before they escalate out of control.

Control-and-fast-response embodies a different mentality from traditional project management: It admits that there is a wide "state space" of influence factor configurations out there, which contains many nasty surprises, and therefore we insulate the system from this state space and keep it iron-fisted at the state that we know works. Compared to traditional project management, the emphasis is not on planning contingencies but on mutual adjustment of the system elements (such as ground crew, pilots, and ship operations) to bad news that emanates from different system elements, in order to keep the system in the control state, or to minimize deviations from it before they escalate. This relies not only on planned routines but also critically on a willingness to improvise (resilience) if that particular combination of circumstances has not been foreseen. Moreover, because of system complexity, it is not possible to anticipate all system constellations.

Control-and-fast-response in the way described by Weick and Sutcliffe differs from our topic because it is directed at ongoing processes. Projects are, by definition, directed at new activities (or at least activities having some novel aspects). Thus, it becomes more difficult to stay in the "green area of control." However, control-and-fast-response and mindfulness are highly relevant to project management for two reasons. First, they provide a good discipline of knowing as much as possible and reacting to deviations that are not required for learning about the path toward the goal. Second, mindfulness helps to alert us to the problems of complexity, the interactions among multiple system parts, as a major source of risks. Mutual adjustment and resilience are highly applicable in project management. The lessons from control-and-fast-response are to carefully assess what one knows, and where one can make system changes without being worried about catastrophic changes; venturing out of this safe traditional zone into unchartered waters should be done cautiously, expecting the worst, and with a fallback option. Thinking back to the ERP example, here a control-and-fast-response approach to what the project subteams are allowed to do makes sense with the project plan as a base line; any unilateral deviations from the plan may cause havoc spreading throughout the project because of the many interactions.

It takes a bit of personal risk to reputation to venture outside of an agreed upon and thus legitimized plan. If it does cause cascading problems, it may reflect reck-lessness, and the person taking the initiative is blamed. However, sometimes oppor-tunities for creativity do exist, so if done successfully, taking the initiative yields a positive result of "what can be done when thinking outside of the traditional proj-ect management box" or the "iron triangle of death—cost, time, and scope." The challenge is the judgment of what risks are acceptable—it is fundamentally a judg-ment because complex systems are, by definition, difficult to predict. This is where project strategy can help, by diagnosing complexity as well as its justification, then helping the actors to make judgments with a holistic view.

Small Steps and Controlling Variability

There are two lessons from control-and-fast-response directly applicable to, in-deed often named in, project management: first enforce tight coordination among all parties, by forcing every actor to identify the other actors with whom they in-teract, and to regularly communicate and to consider their mutual effects on one another. Thus addressing the most critical interactions this way may be enough to reduce ambiguity and mutually imposed rework enough to make the project viable.

Second, large steps into the red out-of-control state are likely to not work out; it may be better to make small steps, control variability, and iterate yourself forward in quick cycles. Iteration and learning may be more promising than planning and control. Alternatively, one may undertake several parallel trials and see which one works best (if the trials are informative and van be performed cheaply).

The Role of Strategy

Strategy has a very important role to play in shaping the complexity of the projects that an organization undertakes. Strategic decisions determine what types of projects are chosen, and they affect the overall complexity of the organization's tasks directly by influencing how much the projects themselves interact (for exam-ple, because one project is a proof of concept for another, or the market reputation of one influences another).

All too often, an inherent appetite for "more revenue" becomes the dominant determinant of project selection, or "What we bid upon is what we make." The complexity of the resulting portfolio is rarely considered—but this is dangerous: In-viting the complexity of pursuing many projects in parallel may very well be appro-priate in a rich economy where increased market share is the predominant strategic goal, but does it really offer a strategic advantage over one's competitors? Or should the organization *reduce complexity by undertaking fewer projects*?

For example, General Motors Corporation in 2009 had 7 brands totaling 87 different vehicles available in the United States alone, not to mention the Vauxhall, Opel, and Holden brands in Europe, Asia, and Australia. Was this self-created complexity generated around an increased market share strategy really necessary? Does consumer demand really require such a level of complexity? Marketing studies show that variant proliferation may be a symptom of an underlying weakness of the brand.

However, the extreme answer, "strategy should reduce, or at least limit, complexity" is too narrow and in many cases wrong. Complexity of a strategy makes it harder to copy it, and complex projects may have a better chance of achieving uniqueness, and thus differentiation and competitive advantage. Platform strategies with a modular design approach typically become feasible when the products in the category have become mature, and thus prone to cost competition. Complexity may well be the price to pay for having something novel to offer.

For example, the Joint Tactical Radio System (JTRS) is planned to be the next generation voice-and-data radio used by the U.S. military in field operations after 2010. Launched with a Mission Needs Statement in 1997, and a subsequent requirements document in 1998 (which has been revised several times), JTRS is a software-defined radio that will work with many existing military and civilian radios and their associated waveforms. The Government Accounting Office reported, "Over the past decade, the Department of Defense (DOD) has undertaken a major transformation of its military operations—one that will rely on network centric communications to improve force information sharing, collaboration, and situational awareness and, thereby, enable more rapid and effective decision-making and speed of execution on the battlefield. The Joint Tactical Radio System (JTRS) program, initiated in 1997, is a key effort in this transformation. By capitalizing on emerging software-defined radio technology, the program plans to develop and procure hundreds of thousands of JTRS radios, which are expected to interoperate with existing radio systems and provide the warfighter with additional communications capability to access maps and other visual data, communicate via voice and video with other units and levels of command, and obtain information directly from battlefield sensors."

In other words, this program is loaded with several types of complexity: technical because thousands of radios will have to work together and with other communication media in real time under varying circumstances. Actor complexity because having many users also means having many stakeholders. And external complexity because battlefield technology changes, budget availability changes with political tides, and external technology constraints change because consumer electronics change so fast (the time elapsed since the program's start, 1997, is an eternity in electronics). All of this complexity has not been recklessly imposed but reflects the wide-ranging benefits that the JTRS program is hoped to bring.

Still, the question arises whether it could have been tackled in smaller sequential and iterative portions in order to alleviate the daunting complexity, which certainly has made itself felt in many symptoms of management difficulties. The GAO report continues,

Although JTRS offers the potential to address key communications shortfalls and significantly improve military capabilities, the program has encountered a number of problems, including unstable requirements, immature technologies, and aggressive schedules, which have resulted in significant cost increases and delays. In August 2003, we reported that the lack of a strong, joint-management structure presented significant challenges to the program's ability to control costs currently estimated to total about $37 billion. In response, Congress directed DOD to strengthen program management, and in February 2005, DOD established a Joint Program Executive Office (JPEO) to manage the JTRS program and its various components. Following JPEO's assessment of the program, the Defense Acquisition Board directed JPEO to come up with a plan to restructure the JTRS development effort—a plan that DOD approved in March 2006. Given the criticality of JTRS to DOD's force transformation, Congress directed GAO to continue its ongoing review of the JTRS program.

The recent restructuring of the JTRS program appears to put the program in a better position to succeed, by emphasizing an incremental, more moderate risk approach to developing and fielding capabilities. The incremental approach reflects the military services' most urgent priorities for a mobile, flexible communications and networking capability and defers the development of some of the more challenging requirements to later increments. Deferring these requirements will allow more time to mature critical technologies, integrate components, and test the radio system before committing to production. DOD expects that JTRS program management through the JPEO and other structural changes will improve oversight and coordination of standards and development of the radios. The centralized management structure is also empowered to manage development costs, which are expected to total US$2.1 billion more than originally projected between fiscal years 2006 and 2011. In addition, the restructuring attempts to facilitate information-sharing and competition by ensuring government purpose rights to contractor-developed products.

Over the longer term, the program faces several key management and technical challenges. For example, although the new joint management structure for JTRS is a significant improvement over the previous fragmented program management structure, joint development efforts in DOD have often been hampered by an inability to sustain requirements commitments and funding support from the military services and other department stakeholders.

This discussion implies that determining the value of a project cannot be determined exclusively on margin, revenue, budget, and strategy, but on building a longer than one year growth path (possibly multiple paths) that will surmount competition and have a reasonable chance of success even if it does not retain the entire original strategic intent. Having a path of success includes external value generation potential as well as internal execution capability. Thus, strategy should determine the strategic portfolio on not only financial or market criteria alone but complexity, and the risks associated with it should be part of the selection criteria. This implies directly that the complexity of the projects, and the entire portfolio, should be tracked. Moreover, an operating strategy should ensure that the policies, capabilities, structure, and processes are put in place to deal with the complexity that the portfolio requires. In the following, we discuss both principles for the strategy of complex projects.

Traditional Project Selection Criteria

Project selection criteria need to address portfolio balance as well as attractiveness and viability of the individual projects.

Balance refers to the holistic view of the portfolio as whole: Are the projects complementary in covering the company's business needs, or are they excessively concentrated on one need? For example, is there a *risk balance*, are there mostly moderately safe projects and just a few high-risk undertakings, or is the portfolio too conservative or too risky? Is there a *balance of market coverage*—do all important market segments receive project support or are projects too focused on one sector? Is there a balance between products and services? Other balance questions cannot be posed generically but must emerge from the strategic challenges of the organization.

Project attractiveness refers to the requirement that each project should be above a minimum attractiveness hurdle in its own right—no matter how good the strategic balance, a project portfolio composed of "dogs" cannot create value. Many useful criteria are used in companies; examples are listed in the following. Not all of them are weighted equally and in the end, some may be ignored completely. If they are all at least considered in the project selection process, everyone knows exactly where the project stands, the perceived benefits to be derived, and the ultimate priority of the project within the portfolio. The criteria are as follows:

- **"Business case" criteria:** Expected revenues, market share, financial returns, versus investments, time to market, usage of scarce resources, and risk (technical as well as market).
- **Other long-term consequences of the selection:** Fit with the strategic direction of the company, durability of the competitive advantage created, involvement of preferred suppliers, partners, government entities, etc., and thus strengthening of the organization network position.
- **Interests of the employees**
- **Impacts on community and environment**
- **Desire to maintain high business standards and ethical guidelines**

Widen the Set of Portfolio Criteria

These balance and attractiveness criteria are well known and widely used. However, all of these criteria are "business content" focused, but they neglect the project execution process (with the exception of the usage of scarce resources). Our discussion on the dangers of complexity suggests that complexity is a major risk item in the execution process, and thus should be monitored and mitigated appropriately. Therefore, project complexity should be incorporated in the portfolio dimensions at both levels.

Complexity at the portfolio level. How much complexity is introduced by the composition of the portfolio? Complexity has to do with the number of variables and their interactions. Thus, we can operationalize this criterion in the following way: How many interactions are inherent in the portfolio? These correspond to the cross-domain complexity dimensions mentioned earlier:

- **Technical interactions.** Some interactions are positive, for example, a project acts as an enabler for others, perhaps by providing a common platform or by building components that are used by other projects. Other interactions are negative, for example, the technical solution developed because of the needs for one project degrades the functionality available in another project.
- **Resource interactions.** Projects compete for the same scarce resources (project personnel, specialists, management attention, building, marketing, channel capacity, manufacturing, etc.), and so allocating resources to one project deprives other projects.
- **Market interactions.** Projects may be complementary, for example, strengthening a common brand, or one building acceptance for the other. Projects may also cannibalize each other if they are directed toward similar needs and customer segments.
- **External interactions.** Projects may cannibalize each other in stakeholder "tolerance" ("we have allowed you to do project A, so now you can't also do project B"), or compete for shared regulatory quotas.

The complexity implied by the entire portfolio should be, at a minimum, estimated by counting the interactions. Once the management team has a feeling for the potential for cross-project interactions, it can ask itself whether this portfolio is manageable, or whether it is so unwieldy that controlling the important interactions looks unfeasible or very management-heavy—in this case, it risks producing bad surprises and jeopardizes the success of individual projects. Think about this as "risk management at the portfolio level:" project level risk may "average out" over many projects, but complexity compounds itself over many projects. In this case, management might consider simplifying the portfolio in order to reduce complexity-induced risk. Conversely, if the complexity of the portfolio significantly enhances its value potential, management might consciously decide to pay the price, which implies putting resources with the right competencies and capabilities in place to deal with the complexity at the project management level.

Problems result if the business management does not realize the burden that portfolio complexity places on the projects. In this case, aggregate strategic plans are de facto unrealistic and not explicit and project management may be blamed for interaction-caused execution problems that are really caused by complexity at the portfolio level and outside the control of the project managers.

Many years ago, one of the authors was working in a business that had a few portfolios; we will mention two here that describe interaction-caused execution problems. First, I was heading-up a portfolio that was focused on break-through novelty-based product development while another portfolio manager was dealing with derivative products coming off a huge "cash cow" base. My mission was to use advanced technology to achieve future cash cow products. The derivative oriented portfolio manager's mission was to continue the cash cow business as long as possible, introducing smaller size, adding capabilities, and so on. I hired a premier ASIC designer to work on our break-through projects. This designer was the envy of the derivative-oriented portfolio manager since the ASIC designer's capabilities could make his projects smaller and more capable faster. You see where this is going. . . . The battle was on; both of us saw our portfolios as being of high priority for the company. I can admit now, that if it wasn't for the cash cow business, I would not have had a portfolio to manage! The derivative-oriented portfolio manager would probably admit now that if we did not engage in novelty-based product development, that his portfolio would have been unsustainable over the years.

It was not until we collectively recognized that an aggregated view of our strategic portfolio plans was not working and that we really needed to engage our interactions across the dimensions. Then it became evident as to how we needed to operate. As for the ASIC designer, I explained to the project manager within my portfolio the need to continue the cash cow business for the time being and we lent him out to the derivative oriented portfolio manager's projects part time and as appropriate brought him into the novelty-based product development team on a full-time basis.

Portfolio balance is about not only the interactions inherent across portfolios but also the policy prescribed by the overall organization where the portfolios reside. The policy component of a project management system describes senior management's perception of the strategic role of project management for the organization (the ultimate portfolio).

1. Strategic importance of project management
2. Organizational commitment to project management
3. Overall maturity of organizational project management

Complexity at the project level. Complexity is also caused at the project level, from technical, stakeholder, or external variables that interact. Again, this needs to be diagnosed at the outset in order to be prepared for problems that are not caused by management problems or classical project risk, but by the ambiguity stemming from overlooked or unexpected interactions. A diagnosis at the outset helps the project management team to prepare, proactively by putting communication and coordination mechanisms in place, but also in a contingency spirit by agreeing on procedures that are triggered with conflicts and interaction related problems do occur.

A diagnosis can happen directly by identifying and counting the critical influence factors on the three domains of technology, actors, and external and constructing a design structure matrix that illustrates interactions among the influence factors. This is discussed further in the following. Another tool that allows identifying complexity is the Diamond Approach, which characterizes the prospective project on the dimensions of novelty (the amount of work that the organization has not done before), pace (the urgency and deadline tightness), complexity (the number of not only components but also subsystems), and technology (the amount of novel technologies that will be used). Complexity is an explicit element of the diamond approach, which helps to identify key project management challenges at the outset, and to monitor it throughout the project life cycle.

Integration With Project Execution

Strategy sets the context and the tone. If complexity, and especially its roots stemming from the portfolio level, are not recognized and incorporated in project execution tools, then project and portfolio managers are sent into minefields studded with traps that they have not been warned about. It may certainly make sense to consciously engage in a complex project portfolio if the strategic benefits of the complexity are worthwhile. Then project execution must be equipped for dealing with the consequences.

This incorporates a diagnosis system, as described previously, and coordination and risk management systems that can absorb and manage the cross-project interaction problems that complexity imposes. A key tool in representing and communicating complexity is the design structure matrix (DSM). It was first proposed in engineering by Steward and further developed as a management tool by Eppinger, Whitney, Smith, and Gebala.

The DSM maps interactions among pieces of a project in matrix form, by listing which task needs input from which. Here, it can be adapted to represent the key sub-teams per project and list the interactions among parties across the projects (use a separate DSM to map complexity within a project).

Figure 4-1 presents a brief example of an application of this tool. Say, for simplicity of illustration, that each party listed (A through D) is one project. In the figure, impacted projects are listed in the columns, and impacting projects along the rows. Crosses (x) mark dependencies. Project B is sequentially dependent on project A, as the impact goes only one way; for example, project A produces information that project B needs, or project A addresses a customer base that task B should not duplicate. Projects B and C are independent. Projects C and D impact each other—that is, they might require mutual information input, or rely on a common platform that is a compromise between them. Thus, they are coupled (interdependent). The matrix suggests an ordering of the project: A, then B in parallel with C and D, the latter two being performed in a closely coordinated way.

To see interactions across the system, actor, and external level, consider the following example. A company that develops ink jet and laser technologies for offering total coding and printing solutions. Each solution combines multiple technologies, such as ink, laser, encoding, tracing, identification, or technologies in characters, letters, and graphs (technical complexity). In order to have any reusability and parts

	A	B	C	D	
Project A	A				A-B: Sequential
Project B	X	B			B-C: Independent
Project C			C	X	C-D: Coupled
Project D	X		X	D	A-D: Sequential

Figure 4-1: Example of a design structure matrix, DSM

commonality at all, solutions represent compromises of varying the business practices of different customer industries, for example, a solution must work on different surfaces and materials that their products will print on, such as paper, plastic, metal, and fibers (actor complexity). Finally, the various customer industries may have standards and legal requirements that may cause conflicts, such as pharmaceutical material requirements that clash with cost requirements in a different industry (external complexity). The most important ones of these interactions can be represented in a portfolio DSM.

Using the DSM as a tool, senior management can put the following steps in place to ensure a systematically applied policy of managing complexity rather than simply suffer the consequences of "crept up" complexity. This needs to happen both at the portfolio level (steps 1-4) and the project level (step 5).

1. Diagnose portfolio complexity (ideally, complexity should be "designed" but this seems elusive at the outset, so start by diagnosing the complexity that is there). Graphically show the existing complexity in a DSM that represents the key interactions across projects.
2. Make the business case for complexity. Which interactions are fundamentally implied by the business or the technology, which are decisions (such as component sharing, projects addressing the same customers), and for these, what is the business case? What is the value offered by doing it this way?
3. Identify the correction loop. What can we do to eliminate or reduce interactions that are not sufficiently valuable (e.g., by modularization of the projects, organizational reassignment of interacting projects to the same team)?
4. Communicate and explain the complexity, make the interacting parties public (e.g., DSMs with a focused representation of key interactions), so the teams are (a) prepared and informed and (b) are accountable for managing those interactions.
5. Put in place project management systems that enable the teams to deal with the complexity levels (within and across projects) that they face. Project level complexity and tools for managing it are discussed in Chapter 9.

Enabling the organization to manage complexity also involves leadership that is willing to make and support these diagnosis and decision tools (and the processes implied by them), for if it is not recognized as a top-down approach, the chances of success are minimized. Leadership should recognize that complexity is not a level but a continuum and should develop strategies that are nonconflicting and policies that can incorporate the full breadth of possibilities. If complexity is put on the agenda in its benefits and costs and managed as part of project portfolio decisions rather than just lamented over, project managers can become more effective.

The usual disclaimer applies: Diagnosis and decision tools do not replace judgment and courage to take (inevitably risky) decisions. The tools help to make decisions based on better information, but they will never make the decision because information is never complete and unambiguous. The critical management responsibility remains.

References

P41, line 6; P42, line 19. Simon, H. A. (1969). *The science of the artificial* (2nd ed.). Boston, MA: MIT Press, p. 195.

P42, line 19. Kauffman, S. A. (1993). *The origins of order: Self-organization and selection in evolution.* New York, NY: Oxford University Press, p. 42.

P42, lines 22, 24. Loch, C. H., & Terwiesch, C. (2002). The Circored project A & B, INSEAD case 06/2002-5040, Teaching Note.

P42, lines 28, 35. Van Zandt, T. (1999). Decentralized information processing in the theory of organizations. In M. Sertel, M. (Ed.), *Contemporary economic issues* (Vol. 4, pp. 125–160), London, England: MacMillan.

P42, line 28. Loch, C. H., & Terwiesch, C. (2007). Coordination and information exchange. In C. H. Loch & S. Kavadias (Eds.), *Handbook of new product development management* (pp. 315–345). Oxford, UK: Butterworth Heinemann/ Elsevier.

P42, line 35. Thomke, S. H. (1998). Managing experimentation in the design of new products. *Management Science, 44*(6), 743–762.

P43, line 16; P47, line 13. Ulrich, K. T. (1995). The role of product architecture in the manufacturing firm. *Research Policy, 24*(3), 419–440.

P43, line 27. Ethiraj, S. K., & Levinthal, D. (2004). Modularity and innovation in complex systems. *Management Science, 50*(2), 159–173.

P43, line 28. Ulrich, K. T., & Ellison, D. J. (1999). Holistic customer requirements and the designselect decision. *Management Science, 45*(5), 641–658.

P44, lines 19, 30, 36, 42; P45, lines 16, 21, 37. Weick, K. E., & Sutcliffe, K. M. (2001). *Managing the unexpected.* San Francisco, CA: Jossey-Bass.

P46, line 29. Sommer, S. C., Loch, C. H., & Dong, J. (2009). Managing complexity and unforeseeable uncertainty in startup companies: An empirical study. *Organization Science, 20*(1), 118–133.

P47, line 7. Larreché, J.-C. (2008). *The momentum effect.* Boston, MA: Harvard Business School Press.

P47, line 10. Rivkin, J. W. (2000). Imitation of complex strategies. *Management Science, 46*(6), 824–844.

P47, line 11. Miller, R., & Lessard, D. L. (2000). *The strategic management of large engineering projects.* Boston, MA: MIT Press. and Shenhar, A., & Dvir, D. (2007). *Reinventing project management: The diamond approach to successful growth & innovation.* Boston, MA: Harvard Business School Press.

P47, line 20; P48, line 37. U. S. Government Accounting Office. (2006, September). Report to U.S. Congressional Committees. *Defense acquisition, restructured JTRS program reduces risk, but significant challenges remain.* (Publication No. GAO-06-955). Available from http://www.gao.gov/htext/d06955.html, p. 1.

P49, line 5. Cooper, R. G., Edgett, S. J., & Kleinschmidt, E. J. (2001). *Portfolio management for new products.* Cambridge, MA: Perseus Publishing.

P49, line 14. Loch, C. H., & Kavadias, S. (2011). Implementing strategy through projects. In P. W. G. Morris, J. K. Pinto, & J. Söderlund (Eds.), *The Oxford handbook on the management of projects* (pp. 224–251). Oxford, UK: Oxford University Press.

P51, line 16. Cooke-Davies, T. J., Crawford, L. H., and Lechler, T. G. (2009). Project management systems: Moving project management from an operational to a strategic discipline. *Project Management Journal, 40*(1), 110–123.

P51, line 35. Shenhar, A., & Dvir, D. (2007). *Reinventing project management: The diamond approach to successful growth & innovation.* Boston, MA: Harvard Business School Press.

P52, line 10. Steward, D. V. (1981). *Systems analysis and management: Structure, strategy and design.* New York, NY: Petrocelli Books.

P52, line 11. Eppinger, S. D., Whitney, D. E., Smith, R. P., & Gebala, D. A. (1994). A model-based method for organizing tasks in product development. *Research in Engineering Design, 6*(1), 1–13.

P52, line 16. Loch, C. H., & Terwiesch, C. (2000). Product Development and Concurrent Engineering. In P. M. Swamidass (Ed.), *Encyclopedia of production and manufacturing management* (pp. 567–575). Dordrecht, Netherlands: Kluwer Academic Publishing.

Loch, C. H., De Meyer, A., & Pich, M. T. (2006). *Managing the unknown: A new way of managing high uncertainty and risk in projects.* New York, NY: John Wiley.

Mihm, J., & Loch, C. H. (2006). Spiraling out of control: Problem-solving dynamics in complex distributed engineering projects. In D. Braha, A. Minai, & Y. Bar-Yam (Eds.), *Complex engineering systems* (pp. 141–157). Cambridge, MA: Springer/NECSI.

Pich, M. T., Loch, C. H., & De Meyer, A. (2002). On uncertainty, complexity and ambiguity in project management. *Management Science, 48*(8), 1008–1023.

Chapter 5

Fear of Flying

Stephen Carver and Harvey Maylor

Introduction

Evidence from many studies has shown that the majority of programs and projects fail to meet one or more of their objectives. Indeed, the criticism of many levels of portfolio, program, and project management (PPPM), in many spheres of human activity, does lead to the question as to why anyone would want to take such a role with the prospect of failure so present.

This failure has been attributed to many causes. The analysis of one major program was typical in that the cause of "poor program management" was cited as the most influential. However, the report provided little by way of insight into precisely what aspects of program (or project or portfolio) management were poor. It was deemed enough to point in the general direction, and then walk away. Given the very particular nature of the challenges faced in this program, such analysis was clearly incomplete.

Such a generic consideration of PPPM is unlikely to be successful not least due to the lack of universality in practice as to what constitutes a portfolio, program, or project. Further, post-rethinking project management, the need to consider particular characteristics of situations that would lead to an intelligent 'fit to context' approach has been established. In practice, this means that to achieve success, organizations and individuals need to be able to appropriately respond to the challenges of each situation.

One way to describe the context for a particular activity is to consider its managerial complexity or difficulty. If it is known then a suitable response in terms of process is required and the level of managerial effort could be established in principle, along with the selection of the task manager. However, matching to context does require that we are able to describe the landscape of challenge that each context brings.

This chapter charts our journey from the naïve question that formed our initial research efforts, "what makes projects difficult to manage?" We found managerial complexity to have both structural and dynamic elements, and there to be a large number of possible concepts or elements of complexity. Having determined our own grounded classification, re-visiting the literature demonstrated that these concepts or elements could easily be grouped in any number of ways. In terms of progressing the discussion, an integrative classification is suggested. The classification provides a conceptualization of the experience and challenge of managers. In communicating this to senior managers, we have successfully used the analogy of flying to explore the requirements of portfolio, program, and project (PPP) managers under different conditions of managerial complexity. The analogy raises some useful questions for both senior managers and researchers. Finally, and following from this, we note that while "pilot" still ranks as one of the more desirable professions, the role of project, program, or portfolio manager currently doesn't appear to have the same cachet, despite the growth in the number of people holding these important roles. This lack of inherent desirability of the PPPM profession is entirely reasonable given published project success rates. So, is there really a "fear of flying?" We examine the lessons for the PPPM profession(s) and senior managers of this challenge.

The Accidental Profession

"If your organization asks you to get involved in a project, best advice is run away, run away, run away!"

Adams

In the authors' combined 50 years of teaching, consulting, and practice in the field of project management, it is a sad reflection that many students and prospective practitioners approach the subject with high levels of negativity, confusion, and even suspicion. The response from many professionals in the area to the question, "How did you end up as a PPPM?" will often be along the lines of "I didn't duck fast enough." Indeed, if one considers the levels of success being experienced by projects in many sectors, this is understandable. The Standish Group reported appallingly low project success rates (32% in 2009, not significantly different from the first study in 1996). Avoidance of projects would seem to be a sensible career move.

With a global recession and tightened fiscal constraints, the fear of being involved in projects should be heightened. However, the popularity of project work is undiminished, with burgeoning membership of professional associations and the continued march of 'projectification.' For the future, if success levels were to improve, such negative mental associations could change. A key question then for professional bodies and educators then, is how such professionals should be developed, so that positive and reinforcing cycles of better performance leading to better professional image, can be established. This was one of the key issues facing the rethinking project management network that ran from 2004–2006.

Rethinking Project (and Program and Portfolio) Management

The starting point for the rethinking project management network was the consideration of the relationship between theory and practice. There were many challenges to the theoretical basis for PPPM knowledge to accompany the litany of challenged project performance in both the national and professional press.

The network concluded that the development of twenty-first century practitioners would have to be different from twentieth-century practitioners. For instance, the network noted that twentieth-century project management was associated with

the heavy-handed and unintelligent application of apparently omnipotent methodologies and software. These viewed projects as hard, definite, and closed systems in
which defined activities would take place with the objective of delivering an end
product. This was inconsistent with the reality experienced by so many practitioners, often exacerbating feelings of helplessness rather than of self-actualization and
control. In program management, the work of Pellegrinelli, et al. noted one management approach (Managing Successful Programmes, the UK Office of Government
Commerce programme management standard) that led to a view that following its
standard methodologies "was often more a matter of compliance than conviction."

The change in the objective for the development of practitioners was identified as being from "trained technicians" to "reflective professionals." This echoed
voices within the project management literature who encouraged a move away
from standardized, process-driven methodologies, or "one size fits all," to a more
situational approach. This requires an understanding of the situational drivers that
would require an approach to be amended or tailored to the specific needs of that
particular portfolio, program, or project.

Understanding the Managerial Context

Our starting point for providing *A* descriptor of the managerial context (not *THE*
descriptor) was the recognition by a number of scholars that there was a lack of
frameworks that could be used to describe key dimensions and characteristics of
project complexity. Some had been defined a priori, but none had a grounded empirical base.

Our study asked project managers the question, "What makes a project complex
to manage?" One of the findings was that practitioners did not distinguish between
complex and *complicated* or *difficult*. Of the aspects that practitioners defined as
complex, we noted that academics are wont to discount these factors as "merely
complicated." Complexity science did not appear to have had an impact on the language of practice. Complexity as propagated within "complexity theories," is about
patterns of behavior of system of interrelated elements that are nonlinear, dynamic,
emergent, etc. Such conceptualization is very different from the common usage of
the term complexity by managers.

Once we describe the dimensions of complexity from this original study, we
will show how these evolved by integration with the current literature into an approach to describing not the complexity (as this is a contentious construct) but the
complexities of a particular context. It is a small point but one that we have found
to be very effective in moving from the generality of complexity, to a more specific
discussion about a particular cause or type of complexity. Further, we demonstrate
how this provides a useful conceptualization for managers. In particular, we show
how there are two key complexities—structural and dynamic—and the categories
of concepts that constitute each.

The analogy of flying is used to describe four different combinations of structural and dynamic complexity and its application is demonstrated by the use of
examples. This analogy has been found to be useful in working with practitioners
and their organizations in creating greater clarity in the dissemination of project

complexity concepts. Finally, we explore the requirements of PPP managers under different conditions of managerial complexity.

Stage 1—Being MODeST

The original paper was the result of an identified gap in the literature for a grounded framework of managerial complexity. A multistage empirical study was carried out to show how project/program managers perceived managerial complexity by asking, "What makes your project/program complex to manage?" The results established a grounded model of structural managerial complexity - the MODeST model (Figure 5-1), where the dimensions of **M**ission, **O**rganization, **D**elivery, **S**takeholders, and **T**eam evolved as high-level headings for groups of characteristics. The groups again represented clusters of 132 identified concepts.

While the graphical representation shows these as apparently independent elements, this is not the case. For instance, the organizational setting would have an impact on the resources available, and the objectives on the process used. However, as a starting point, this provided what we termed the **structural** elements of complexity—they could be captured at any point in time (typically before, during, or after a piece of work) as a perceptual measure or indicator of managerial complexity.

However, further analysis of the data from the study indicated that there was an additional dimension of complexity, as well as the structural, and that was the **dynamic**. The dynamic dimension resulted when the elements of structural complexity were not stable and changed over time. For example, when the organization is restructured during the lifetime of the project/program or the stakeholders underwent significant change and/or shifted their positions. This multidimensional framework not only leads to a multiplicative complexity effect but also further complicates the conceptualization of project complexity itself.

For each element, there are 20 or more questions to assess that element, and examples of each are shown in Table 5-1.

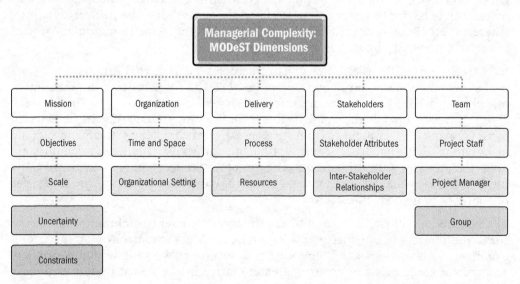

Figure 5-1: Dimensions of perceived structural managerial complexity

Stage 2—Being Comprehensive

The MODeST framework was a useful starting point for the discussion about complexity in project management. However, it was clear that this failed to integrate a significant body of work that had been undertaken elsewhere. The clustering process that had led to MODeST, would work just as well, with the already provided high-level categories. This held the potential of a much bigger prize—to be able to integrate elements of the literature into a framework that could be applied (and therefore used for comparative purposes) in both practice and research applications.

The most common high-level categorizations of complexity were identified as:

- Scale: how big is the task being undertaken;
- Uncertainty: the level of unknowns in the task;
- Pace: the time required for delivery compared to the 'natural' time that the task would take; and
- Socio-political: the interactions with and between different parties associated with the task.

Consistent with the earlier findings, each of these could be shown to have both structural (initial or snapshot conditions) and dynamic (changing) elements, though this dynamic element was the least well developed in the literature.

The change to categories is described in Geraldi, Maylor , and Williams. The 132 previously identified complexity concepts were successfully mapped to the new high-level categorizations and 8 new concepts from the literature were added. The result was a highly comprehensive instrument for assessing complexities, which comprised 140 questions.

However, while 140 elements ticked the box for comprehensive, it failed on usefulness! The production of a reduced instrument is now complete and being used by a number of organizations at the outset and key checkpoints in their process for all PPP work, not just projects. In addition, one organization is in the process of revising its approach to risk to include the assessment of complexities as a key feeder

	Structural Dimension	Dynamic Dimension
Mission	Are the requirements clear?	How frequently do the requirements change?
Organization	Is there a mismatch between the matrix structure of the project and the department structure of the organization?	Is there ongoing organizational restructuring that affects the project?
Delivery	How well does the project team understand the project management methodology?	Is a new project management methodology being introduced?
Stakeholders	How many stakeholders are there?	Are the stakeholders changing?
Team	Are the team members motivated?	Is the level of motivation of team members changing?

Table 5-1: Examples of assessment questions for managerial complexity

to their risk management activities. This is the phase where, as identified by the rethinking work, the theory is intended to inform practice.

One strand that has progressed in parallel with the development of the complexities instrument is the evaluation of the implications of certain complexities for managers—their skills and requirements—and is described in the following section.

Stage 3—Trying To Be Useful!

The work that we describe here was undertaken with a firm belief that the first stage in helping to solve some of the challenges of delivery is to provide a conceptualization for practitioners that assist in gaining a common language and understanding. In this we have gone from the concrete (the experience of practice) and abstracted the key elements of what makes tasks complex to manage (structural and dynamic factors). This work has had some success in providing a set of attributes or complexities that can assist in that common language and understanding.

In order to progress the discussion, we first started with the main categories of complexity, structural and dynamic. Assessment of the overall level of each category allows the placing of a task within the matrix shown in Figure 5-2. We will return to the means of assessment later. For now, the approach allows tasks to be located according to their complexities and hence allow different approaches to their management to be situationally assessed.

Having created the model it can be used to discuss the complexity of various projects/programs.

As can be seen in Figure 5-3, **Type A** is a project exhibiting low levels of both structural and dynamic complexities. This is the well-bounded project, with well-defined requirements and understood route to delivery. The stakeholders are likely to be known and to operate within defined and understood structures. The level of change is low, discouraged, and actively managed where it does occur. Key issues

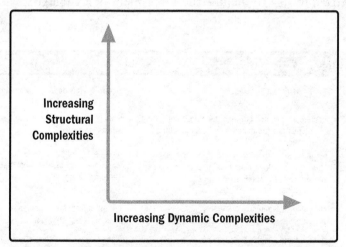

Figure 5-2: Combination of structural and dynamic complexities

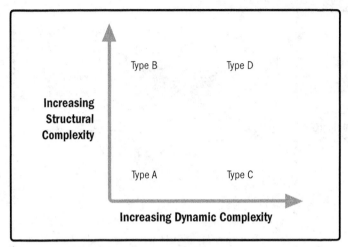

Figure 5-3: Tasks and complexities

here involve structured control in a largely stable environment. Traditional project management methodologies appear to be well suited to this type of activity.

Type B, while having high levels of structural complexity, exhibits low levels of dynamic complexity. An example of this type of project is the development of an oil field, where there are many projects (oil platform, oil pipeline, gas pipeline, oil/gas receiving facilities, etc.) that are linked together and form what might be considered to be a program or portfolio. While the combination of these projects is structurally very complex, each individual project can be seen to be a relatively "simple" element and be managed accordingly. The dynamic complexity of this combination of projects is low due to the extreme care taken to specify and plan early in their life cycles and then to impose very strict control regime on any changes. Key issues here involve structured coordination in a largely stable environment. Application of traditional program or portfolio management methodologies appears to be well suited to these types of tasks, and the use of traditional project management within the constituent projects.

Type C has high levels of dynamic complexity but relatively low structural complexity. These projects may not be particularly large in scale but are likely to have ill-defined or rapidly evolving requirements, stakeholders, underpinning technologies, or political environments. Conventional project management methodologies are increasingly unlikely to be applicable the higher the dynamic element of complexity becomes. In their place, faster and smaller incremental planning and action stages may be used, and more flexible resource structures and processes may be required.

Type D has the highest levels of both structural and dynamic complexities. Like type B it may be considered to be a program or portfolio of smaller linked projects with some but not necessarily all exhibiting type C characteristics. Within the overall environment for the program, there will be a much greater level and acceptance of fundamental uncertainty and emergence (as for type C) may extend over a longer period of time and with greater levels of importance or impact for the organi-

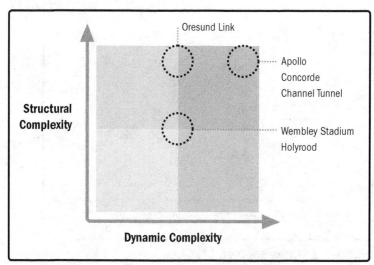

Figure 5-4: Placement of tasks in the complexity domain

zation. Key issues here involve fluid coordination in a dynamic environment. Type D tasks are currently challenging established and evolving project and program methodologies and paradigms.

The main implication of this very high-level classification is that it is possible to establish the location of a task, and then consider the implications for the organizational and individual response to the particular level and type of complexity.

For example, the assessment of the managerial complexities of major pieces of work, puts DII[1] in the top category of having very high structural and very high dynamic complexities. Other major projects (that had significant overruns) include Holyrood and Wembley Stadium, but these are not in the same league complexity wise. For type D, normal rules of planning and action don't hold, and as a result, expectations that projects would run like a much less complex piece of work are misguided. As the scale of a project grows, the number of interfaces between elements of the system increases exponentially. These elements themselves are changing and have an impact in unpredictable ways on other parts of the system. The impact of one change on the system will be disproportionate to the magnitude of this change.

Reflections on the Use of the Typology

There is little that is totally predictable in PPP work, and complexity assessments should reflect this. For instance:

1. Shell's Sakolin project: Initially, this was a project with a high level of structural complexity but relatively little by way of dynamics (i.e., type B). However, in 2004, the Russian government effectively seized control of the assets of the project. The result was a major increase in the dynamic complexity—effectively shifting this to type D. The result of this shift was a fundamental change in the requirements of the management of the project—from requir-

---

[1]DII is one of the largest IT infrastructure programs undertaken in Europe, with the brief to integrate the U.K. Ministry of Defence's 300+ legacy IT systems into one platform.

ing people who could deal with scale, to requiring people who could deal with a broader range of complexities.

2. The launch of mobile phone texting in a major U.K. telecommunications company was seen as a type A project—well contained and presenting a new product that, it was believed, would make a limited impact on the phone market. The resulting uptake caused significant issues for network operators who struggled to provide the necessary bandwidth to deal with the volume of nonvoice traffic, and phone makers, who had only included limited texting capability in new phones. The resulting success took the project to type D, and required a fundamental rethink of the approach, governance, management and extent of the impacts.

Assessing the complexities, whether at this high level or using the four categories of both structural and dynamic elements, requires consideration of TIPS:

Temporality—the assessment is only valid now, as demonstrated by both examples.

Interactive—it is affected by the actions and inactions of the manager—it is not independent of what they do. For instance, imposing a rigid process on a situation where there was a high degree of dynamic complexity, is just likely to make the situation more difficult to manage.

Position in work breakdown structure is important—there will be different complexities at different levels. Tasks are not homogeneous and tasks within one level will exhibit different complexities.

Subjective—the assessment is entirely subjective – it is based on the judgment of an individual and can reflect both knowledge and ignorance of a situation (I know it is complex because I've done this before; I think this is complex because this is the first time I am attempting it).

Implications of Assessment of Complexities

There are many areas where the assessment of complexities would assist in the discussion of how the task could be managed. These include:

1. The nature of the processes or systems required to run the task;
2. The amount of time and effort managing the task will take;
3. The requirements of the task manager.

The Nature of the Processes or Systems Required To Run the Task

In an attempt to define the implications of the complexities for practice, we have seen that Williams was among many who noted that current methodologies and processes have become largely trapped within the structural scale dimension. That is, they are reasonably good at handling anything large, but as soon as anything with pace, socio-political, uncertainty, or any dynamic challenge comes along, they are far less effective. This is just one of the insights from this work and provides some explanation as to the poor levels of success being achieved by organizations in the project work, despite the widespread application of current methodologies and processes.

The Amount of Time and Effort Managing the Task Will Take

For example, we encountered a Nobel Prize winning scientist from one of Scandinavia's top institutes. He had just been awarded millions of Euros from the European Union to conduct a research project involving more than 15 institutes and companies from more than 10 countries. We asked this scientist, "How are you going to manage this as principal investigator?" His response was "I have a spare afternoon once a month to take care of this." The communications and IP issues alone were going to take more time than this to manage, but when we were challenged as to how much time and effort we expected it to take, we had to rely on rough percentages, settling on "between 5% and 10% of the overall effort." This figure had no calibration, and certainly nothing that was even vaguely acceptable to the scientific mind! An assessment of the complexities of the task would have at least provided a qualitative guide to the extent of the task of management.

The Requirements of the Task Manager

The examples provided earlier illustrated that the notion of one size fits all applies just as poorly to the selection and development of the task manager as it does to the selection of the process. In exploring the requirements of the task manager, there have been some useful contributions to this (International Project Management Association [IPMA], Global Alliance for Project Performance Standards [GAPPS]), but nothing that has engaged the conversation with senior managers as successfully as the analogy we are about to describe.

Flying

"I've never known an industry that can get into people's blood the way aviation does."

Robert Six, Founder and CEO Continental Airlines

As established at the beginning of this chapter, reports suggested that few projects succeed completely, and if they arrive at all, they are often late and overbudget. Of those that are completed, many fail to deliver the benefits they promised. In short, if projects were civil aircraft we would be living in a world where jumbo jets regularly fall out of the skies. Airport runways would be strewn with wreckage and passengers waiting endlessly in lounges would be rightly terrified of the prospect of boarding the plane.

What if managing projects were rather more like flying commercial passenger airplanes? The requirements for each are immediately comparable; the flight (project) arriving safely (project delivered) on time (on schedule) and with the fuel load provided (resource or cost). In addition, the manner of its delivery is appropriate to consider, without surprises. Exciting delivery is not a requirement.

Similarly, the comparison between take-off and project initiation is relevant. Just about anyone can initiate a project, and data from pilot training simulators show that most people can get a plane off the ground. Landing the plane (project) is rather different. There is a saying among pilots that:

"A good landing is where everyone walks away unharmed.
A really good landing is where we can use the plane again."

Aspect of Flight	Project Comparator
Pilot	Project manager
Airline	Project organization
Cabin crew	Project team
Passengers	Stakeholders
Air traffic control	Program/portfolio management
Instruments	Performance indicators
Flight plan	Plan
Fuel	Budget
Flight time	Timeline
Airspace	Project environment/culture
Flying rules	Systems/methodologies
Weather	Risk
Accident investigation	Post-project review

Table 5-2: Flight/project analogies

Projects can be delivered 'at any cost', but it is a really good manager that can ensure that the team wants to work together again. Further aspects of commercial flight and their project comparators are shown in Table 5-2.

No one would let an untrained pilot fly an aircraft full of passengers. Yet in many companies the selection and training of suitable project managers is still an assumed (rather than taught) professional skill. A good commercial airline pilot is a trained professional whose entire focus is to ensure that the flight is as well planned and executed as possible. They go to great lengths to ensure that the flight goes smoothly within a high reliability environment. In the project environment, methodologies/check lists and governance systems are utilized to ensure a similar modus operandi.

Pilots do not take off without doing the necessary preparation: planning (flight plan); reviewing checklists (preflight checks); conducting risk management (weather); and employing constant monitoring and control. They instill confidence in others by always appearing calm and in control and communicate clearly and factually. Their training is to plan and then have a back up the plan. They enhance their skills in flight simulators (project risk/contingency/scenario planning) and optimism (which might lead to optimism bias) is largely eliminated by their systems of work.

While flying, an autopilot flies the plane leaving the pilot to intervene only if they choose or events occur that are outside certain established parameters (or the pilots need flying hours). The comparison with established organizational project and control systems is an interesting one. Here we see that 'management by exception' is well established in flying, but less so in project work.

Like project managers, pilots are acutely aware that if the flight ends in disaster they will "arrive at the scene of the accident first...and at speed." Similarly, many project disasters have reputational and/or financial consequences. Pilots have to sign off aircraft before take off (project launch/project charter) knowing that some systems may not be fully functional. *In* extremis they can refuse to sign if they think that the level of risk is too high. In many organizations, project managers are not given any choice in the matter and are sometimes misled about the status of the project that they are expected to fly—small wonder then that in such cultures "smart people avoid projects."

Air space is the environment in which projects fly, and it is divided into two types: controlled and uncontrolled.

Controlled. Here, all flights fly within strict air corridors controlled by air traffic control. It is known as instrument flight rules (IFR) and pilots are carefully tracked and monitored by controllers on the ground to ensure that flights are correctly prioritized and collisions are avoided. An added advantage of IFR is that the pilots can 'fly blind' through clouds or at night relying on the controllers to keep them from harm's way.

In our project analogy, these flights will be flown according to 'rules' which in organizations are the project procedures, methodologies, and governance (sponsors/steering groups, etc.). These rules ensure that projects are controlled in a standardized way such that whole programs can safely be coordinated.

Uncontrolled. Here, the pilots are largely free to fly as they like but have to ensure their own safety by "looking out the windows." In the civil aviation world, this is known as visual flight rules (VFR). As long as pilots avoid the airspace controlled by IFR, they may largely make their own decisions as to how and where to fly.

In the project world, VFR applies to smaller projects (often run within a single department) where air traffic is light and complex tracking and coordination systems are not required. It should be emphasized that the pilots (project managers) still need flying skills but they largely have to assess the risks for themselves and realize that flying blind is extremely hazardous. It is usual for pilots to submit a VFR flight plan that outlines their intended flight time, course, and destination. If they fail to arrive, their hope is that someone will come out to look for them and/or clear up the wreckage.

Once structural complexity increases the more numerous and interrelated flights within the airspace lead to a requirement to prioritize and control them so accidents or collisions do not occur. In flying, air traffic control has this responsibility and in projects, portfolio, or program management. They will ensure that projects are only allowed to take off if the runway is clear (resources are available), and that they have a place to land (handover and deliver benefits).

It is important to note here a professional distinction: air traffic controllers are not required to be pilots. Rather, their task is to establish and control air corridors where projects can be tracked, given guidance, and prioritized for takeoff and landings. It is interesting to note that sometimes air traffic controllers look after several flights at once and similarly some managers will often find themselves members of several steering groups. The world's air traffic control is made up of many integrated national systems, and likewise divisional/global organizations should have a common project system/language that allows interdivisional programs of projects to be undertaken successfully.

One of the greatest concerns for pilots is the weather—in project terms "risk." They typically go to considerable trouble to study forecasts, and when flying, will often use radar or visual information to avoid turbulence or thunderstorms that could make the flight "eventful." Likewise, project managers should use weather (risk) forecasting methods to ensure that risks are identified, avoided, or controlled thus ensuring as smooth a flight as possible. While forecasts and a weather eye can help avoid the worst weather conditions, there is always the possibility of other unforeseen events—in project terms "the unexpected." Pilots must be capable of dealing with events that were neither planned nor forecasted. Like the pilot, project managers can only achieve this if they have the rest of the systems under control and they are correctly trimmed. Severe weather often leads commercial pilots to fly longer routes (using more valuable fuel) in order to ensure a smooth flight. Project managers do likewise but sometimes budget or time constraints mean that the flight has to fly through turbulence.

Finally, the analogy draws on the use of accident investigation in the development of more reliable and resilient processes, people, and technology when it does all go wrong. The world of commercial flight appears to have learned the lessons well of its accidents, with the results that today, it is safer to fly than to cross the road in most countries. While such learning is embedded successfully in systems of flight, project systems are far less successful at learning. One major U.K. government department noted recently that "lessons learned review" were no longer carried out and had been replaced by "lessons identified reports." The reason was simply, 'we have realized we don't learn.'

As with all analogies, flight has its limitations. As Winter and Sczepanek noted, this provides one view, not the only view. The focus has been on the development and role of the manager (civil pilot, fighter pilot, air traffic controller [ATC], or war-room commander). The analogy may extend and enlighten other roles, for instance, that of the crew (project team) or perhaps the most important individuals—the passengers (stakeholders), without who the flight would have no objective.

Application of the Flying Analogy

By combining the flying analogy with the task, it is now possible to create a tool for analyzing and teaching complexity within the project and program environment. It should be emphasized that this is a simplified model that only establishes high/low parameters; however, as a platform for initial conceptualization, it has been found to be valuable.

As can be seen in Figure 5-5, four generic types of management have been proposed.

Type A—the civil pilot. A commercial airline pilot model fits well with the established traditional project methods and mindset. Once a flight has been planned, dynamic change is positively managed out of the venture as far as possible. The objective is to arrive at the chosen destination, on time, on budget, and with as few deviations to the plan as possible. It is an environment of risk avoidance, planning, procedure, and compliance.

Type B—air traffic controller. The air traffic control model is applied to ensure co-ordination of several projects. The objective is to orchestrate a system to

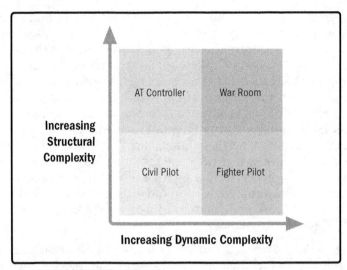

Figure 5-5: Generic types of management

minimize any conflicts between flights and to maximize the utilization of given airspace. To enjoy the benefits of the system, all flights have to adhere to the prescribed systems or avoid the designated air lanes. It is an environment of risk avoidance procedure, coordination, and governance.

Type C—the fighter pilot. A fighter pilot needs all the planning skills of a commercial pilot but takes off on a mission with the expectation that the dynamic complexity of the flight will be high "a plan seldom survives the first contact with "the enemy." The mission objective is clear but nothing is more important than the pilot retaining fluidity of thought and action. It is an environment of risk acceptance, frameworks, and tactical initiative.

Type D—the war-room commander. A fighter pilot alone is ineffective and soon dead. To maximize the strategic advantage of the fighter pilot, it is vital to have a system that not only identifies and coordinates "friendly" (internal) flights but can also track "enemy" (external) flights such that the system can adapt to the dynamically challenging environment. In this case, the focus is on looking outside the internal environment and predicting, expecting, and accepting high levels of change. It is an environment of risk acceptance, systems, and strategic initiative. In addition, the war room commander will have all the other types of activities ongoing.

Implications for Organizations

We presented this analogy to many project managers and then asked, "So what kind of project manager are you—fighter pilot or airline pilot?" Over 80% responded as fighter pilot.[2] Whether the perceived glamour of the fighter pilot or the reality of their work as having a high degree of dynamic complexity guides this view, is not clear. Either way, from an organizational perspective, this is a challenge, as the

---

[2]We are not presenting this as scientific evidence, rather an observation that we found interesting and believe to be worth exploring further.

preference for known or stable delivery in most organizations would suggest that it is more likely that 80% of projects would require the attributes of airline pilots. The implication for those organizations is clear: They need to provide the context (analogous to ATC) in which projects can work to be more like airline flight. The level of dynamic complexity can be assessed and should be managed. Further, the role of the civil pilot project manager needs to be encouraged and rewarded. As one senior manager recently commented, "We have too many fighter pilots who get rewarded for being fighter pilots in a war. The problem is that if there isn't a war to fight, they go out and start one."

For the other roles, while the application of program and portfolio management standards and processes may be effective for large-scale tasks, there are other complexities that need to be considered. For instance, where the high levels of complexity are due to socio-political challenges, pace, or fundamental uncertainties, the standards and generic process models appear ineffectual. The assumption that the adoption of standards will improve delivery is therefore to be challenged.

Lastly, the analogy of war room operations is most useful, and the practices of wartime leaders like Sir Keith Park in the Battle of Britain, do require some further exposition – there is much there that modern leaders could take from the way that both the structural and dynamic complexities were 'managed.'

Conclusions

At the beginning of this chapter, we noted that a rational mind would avoid taking the role of a project manager. However, the reality is that this has been a growing arena for management activity and its popularity appears to be undiluted by published success rates. Using the flying analogy and reflecting on the growth of project management, perhaps we are now seeing the limits of visual flying rules; the skies are now so crowded with projects that a different kind of project manager (the commercial pilot) and rules for flight (IFR) need to be employed. The evidence of so many crashes surely requires this.

So, why would someone take on the role of a project manager? The personality profile for pilots, published by the Air Line Pilots Association International may give a clue. "Pilots are inclined to modify their environment rather than their own behavior. Pilots need excitement; a 9-5 job would drive most pilots to distraction." Indeed, a participant at a recent project management workshop noted similarly that despite working in an environment where the customer didn't know what they wanted and changed their mind frequently, their own senior managers undermined them at every opportunity and their team were demoralized and ready to quit, they wouldn't change their job for the world. Fear of flying? Doesn't look like it to us!

References

P57, line 9. National Audit Office (NAO). (2009). *Major projects report.* London, UK: National Audit Office.

P57, line 16; P58, line 43. Winter, M., Smith, C., Cooke-Davies, T., & Cicmil, S. (2006). Directions for future research in project management: The main findings of a UK government-funded research network. *International Journal of Project Management,* 24(8), 650–662.

Heading, line 14. Davis, J. C. (1984). The accidental profession. *Project Management Journal*, 15(3), 6.

P58, line 17. Adams, S. (1996). *The Dilbert principle*. New York, NY: HarperCollins.

P58, line 25; P66, line 27. Standish Group. (2009). *Chaos report (application project and failure)*. Boston, MA: The Standish Group International Inc.

P58, line 40. Koskela, L., & Howell, G. (2002). The underlying theory of project management is obsolete. *Proceedings of the 2002 PMI Conference*, Seattle, WA.

P59, lines 6, 9. Pellegrinelli, S., Partington, D., Hemingway, C., Mohdzain, Z., & Mahmood, S. (2007). The importance of context in programme management: An empirical review of programme practices. *International Journal of Project Management*, 25(1), 41–52.

P59, lines 13, 21. Shenhar, A. J. (2001). One size does not fit all projects: Exploring classical contingency domains. *Management Science*, 47(3), 394–414.

P59, line 19. Xia, W., & Lee, G. (2004). Grasping the complexity of IS development projects. *Communications of the ACM*, 47(5).

P59, lines 23, 27; P60, line 27. Maylor, H., Vidgen, R., & Carver, S. (2008). Managerial complexity in project based operations: A grounded model and its implications for practice. *Project Management Journal*, 39(S1), S15–S26.

P61, line 10. Baccarini, D. (1996). The concept of project complexity: A review. *International Journal of Project Management*, 14(4), 201–204.

P61, line 11. Williams, T. M. (1999). The need for new paradigms for complex projects. *International Journal of Project Management*, 17(5), 269–273.

P61, line 13; P65, line 35. Williams, T. M. (2005). Assessing and building on project management theory in the light of badly over-run projects. *IEEE Transactions in Engineering Management*, 52(4), 497–508.

P61, line 15. Geraldi, J. G., & Adlbrecht, G. (2007). On faith, fact and interaction in projects. *Project Management Journal*, 38(1), 32–43.

P61, line 18. Xia, W., & Lee, G. (2005). Complexity of information systems development projects: Conceptualization and measurement development. *Journal of Management Information Systems*, 22(1), 45-83.

P71, line 32. ALPA (2010), *Personality Profile of Airline Pilots*, Washington, DC: ALPA Int. – The American Union for Airline Pilots, p.1.

Chapter 6

The Impact of Complexity on Project Cost and Schedule Estimates

Dale Shermon

Introduction

This chapter provides advice for management and senior practitioners about how their projects' complexity will influence their cost and schedule estimate. The thought that budgets need to be defined early with confidence is worthy of serious discussion, setting realistic, justified budgets earlier in a project's life cycle will greatly ease the financial processes of the project. An attitude of "entry-ism"[1] when establishing the cost and time budget at a politically acceptable level, rather than an appropriate level, will pave the way to financial problems which will emerge later in the life cycle. The estimating methodology of parametrics being a function of size, productivity, and complexity as independent variables and effort (and therefore cost) as a dependent variable is discussed.

The top-down parametric estimating process involves a number of steps including data gathering, normalization, determining cost estimating relationships (CERs) using statistical analysis, testing a hypothesis, and finally applying the model. Historical trend analysis (HTA) is an application of parametric estimating in the context of business case (BC) approval including economic analysis (EA) in the form of investment appraisals (IA) and affordability. To exemplify these principles cost growth in defense programs is the topic and a case study for this chapter.

The Business Case

Engineers and designers have had brilliant ideas; throughout history, they have created products and systems that have changed the world. Initially, hardware and more recently software systems have transformed our world and have even enabled us to travel beyond our world. However, none of these innovations would make it off the drawing board without the benefit of a business case. In early years, there was an informal understanding between people that investors would recover their

---

[1] The phenomena in projects of setting the budget low to get approval and then growing the budget once accepted.

capital or investment because of an innovation. Nevertheless, currently this business case is a more formal affair. Investors seek a business case that determines the return on investment (ROI), internal rate of return (IRR), net present value (NPV), cash flow, etc.

It is not just the private sector that requires this level of analysis. The public sector will also stipulate a number of hurdles, gates, or milestones through which a project must successfully navigate or cross before the program has a release of public funding. In some cases, these obstacles to funding will require a business case to be generated or a similar type of justification to precede the launch or kick-off of a project.

This can be mystifying for the engineer or designer who can see nothing more than the brilliant innovation or system that they have nurtured like a loving parent from an inspiration into a fully engineered design. It can be difficult to persuade some of these geniuses that their "baby" is not going to leave the drawing board until a business case has been established. They are so blinded by the brilliance of their creation that in some instances they never make it past the drawing board stage because they are unable to articulate the benefit and value to the wider population or at least to investors in such a way as to attract investment.

On the other side of the business case, the investors are rightfully skeptical about any or all cases that they review. Many investors fund projects, which promise high returns, just to find that the project absorbs more and more funding without any sign of the return that was envisaged. Now this is not necessarily the fault of the engineers. Engineers, by their very nature are optimistic people. Engineers need to be optimists. They are challenged by difficult, tricky, complicated problems to solve; if they were easy, it would not require an engineer. Such people wake every morning and go to work with a "can do" attitude, no setback is going to stop them from solving the complex problems of the day.

It is also these optimists who are asked to estimate the cost and schedule of projects!

It is therefore little wonder that many projects are blighted with cost overruns and schedule slippages. The engineers' optimism at the bidding stage will inevitably mean that they will consider all projects achievable and conceive a solution to the most difficult problems at the outset, which in reality will not be the final solution.

So how do project managers of complex project ensure that they do not suffer the frustrations of inadequate budgets and unrealistically short program durations?

Estimating and Parametrics

There are three recognized estimating techniques: analogy, analytical, and parametric. At different times in a project's life cycle, these estimating techniques are appropriate. At the earliest point of the project's life cycle, when the budgets are being set, the parametric estimate is the most appropriate methodology.

Parametric estimating provides an estimate of cost and schedule based upon a historical database of past projects, which have been normalized. This database has then been analyzed to determine the technical design and performance characteristics that are cost and schedule drivers. From this point, a hypothesis needs to be tested, and a statistical analysis can be conducted to prove that hypothesis. The results of this testing is a set of algorithms known as cost estimating relationships (CER) and schedule estimating relationships (SER) that represent the database of past projects. To demonstrate accuracy of the estimating relationships they can be used to predict those historical projects based upon their historical parameter values. These CER and SER can then be put to new usage with future projects parameter values to determine the cost and schedule of future complex projects.

Typically, parametric models will contain hundreds if not thousands of CER algorithms. They are combinations of lower level models that are brought together to form the big picture. It is common for the core algorithm to consider independent variables of size (e.g., volume, weight, Software Source Lines of Code [SLOC]), productivity (e.g. variation from industry norm, tooling, labor skills), and complexity (e.g., technology, application, environment). The complexity aspect of a parametric model will be considered later in this chapter.

Why is this useful? A parametric model is not optimistic (or pessimistic); it is just a representation of the past which can be used to predict the future. Using a parametric model to set the budget for a complex project will ensure that the budget is adequate and the schedule realistic. Because it is a top-down methodology, nothing is omitted or duplicated. Figure 6-1 shows the difference between top-down and bottom-up estimating methodologies with the parametric advantage occurring when there is little information, which is generally the case at the start of a complex project. It is possible to estimate the cost of new complex projects without the need to 'tease' an estimate (staff hours, material, and other direct costs) out of a designer or engineer.

But, has the problem just been moved from one area to another? Although the estimate is not coming from the engineer or designer, we will need them to quantify the parametric inputs, which represent the likely solution to the complex problem they have been set. We will require their view of the performance or design

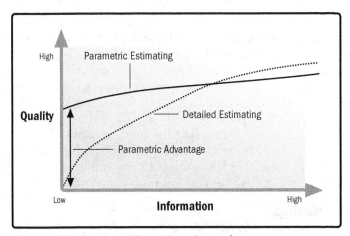

Figure 6-1: Parametric estimating advantage

parameters, which are the cost and schedule drivers. Again, these could be biased or optimistic.

So how does a project manager of a complex project ensure that the parameters are free from optimism?

Capability and Design

There is often a misconception that it is possible to estimate the cost (and schedule) of a set of capabilities or requirements. Project sponsor's often have a desired capability that they wish to acquire often expressed in terms of a set of requirements and a need for an indication of the cost and delivery date. For example, I have a need to transport and contain a gin and tonic, what is the cost?

Now the problem here is that cost cannot be related directly to the capability or requirement. The requirement needs to be interpreted into a design, and it is the design which is given a cost and delivery date. In my example, the design envisaged could be a plastic cup and hence the cost would be less than one cent or penny. The naïve project manager would accept this as a realistic budget for the complex project.

A common problem is that the engineer's optimism that a simple solution is sufficient does not become reality. The plastic cup becomes a lead crystal glass because the solution is always a glass of some description and the plastic cup was never going to be a satisfactory design. The cost consequences are many multiples of what the original budget was conceived to be, but by this time, nobody can remember why the estimated cost (of the glass) and budget (of a plastic cup) are so far apart?

The problem is not requirements creep; this can be managed by a project manager by monitoring changes or alteration to the requirements. Here, the problem is conceiving an early immature design when only the requirements are articulated. Therefore, we toil for many days and nights to accurately predict the budget for the wrong design. This example is very simple, when the level of deviation between initial and final design is translated into complex real life projects there are serious financial consequences.

Advanced application of parametrics will include an extension to the cost and schedule parameters into the requirements space. It is possible to create a knowledge base or expert system, which will compare the capability and the proposed design early in a project life cycle, when a complex project is having its budget set. In a more practical example of a complex project, it would be possible to avoid the highly accurate cost and schedule estimate of a 20,000-ton aircraft carrier, which would be completely incapable of satisfying the requirement to fly 70 aircraft from its flight deck. An advanced parametric model would highlight the need either to increase the size (displacement) of the aircraft carrier, and thus the budgeted cost, or to reduce the capability or requirement (number of aircraft).

Parametric Estimating

There is a number of commercial parametric cost estimating models available or it is possible to create and research your own. This section will consider the option to build your own parametric model and then we will review a commercial system. As already stated a parametric model can contain thousands of variables or cost drivers. This example will be a multiple variable model that can be applied across many projects at a high level early in the project life cycle.

The steps in creating a parametric cost model are as follows;

1. Determine the requirements for a parametric cost model and the return on investment (ROI)
2. Determine the boundaries and assumptions
3. Gather historical data of past relevant projects including cost, schedule, technical and design data
4. Normalize those data for currency, economics, quantities, production rate, units of measurements (metric or imperial)
5. Identify likely cost drivers (independent variables)
6. Formulate a hypothesis regarding the independent variables and the cost or effort (dependent variable)
7. Test the hypothesis statistically to determine its significance
8. Document the cost estimating relationship for future usage.

In this simple parametric case study there has been a database created and normalized. In this example, aircraft data have been normalized to U.S. dollars ($) at constant 2006 year of economics and reduced to the theoretical first piece (T_1) of the production run. The T_1 is theoretically the first item of a production quantity, which exhibits the learning phenomenon and is therefore the most expensive. The first hypothesis considers the increase in cost with the increase in weight (see Figure 6-2). This is a reasonably intuitive hypothesis, if something is larger then it will require more raw materials and more processing hence more labor content, therefore "the more the system weights the more it costs."

However, this simple hypothesis is not likely to satisfy all the historical data points or projects. These will be a level of 'noise' in the data, which means that the line of best fit does not go through all the historical projects. In statistical terms,

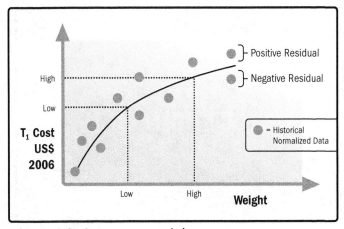

Figure 6-2: Cost versus weight

this is considered a random error term, which can be represented as a positive or negative residual.

If these residual figures are plotted against another variable, for example a performance characteristic, then a second parameter becomes part of the cost estimating relationships. In many systems, the residual can be plotted against a time axis (see Figure 6-3) and it becomes apparent that there is a relationship over time. This can be most likely explained as representing the technology influence isolated from the overall weight effect. As time passes, technology becomes more complex.

This addition to the CER can be justified with the hypothesis that as time passes the complexity of the systems increases. It now becomes apparent that newer systems will cost more than older systems, after their weight has been normalized out of the data. If you consider this hypothesis for many systems, it is true. For example, in the early days of aircraft, they were made from wood, canvas, and wire. This has evolved through to today when the technology is more advanced in term of materials and manufacturing processes adopting composites, electronics, and software.

Figure 6-3 in turn will have residuals, which can be calculated, plotted, and statistically analyzed and rationalized with hypothesis to develop the CER further. A parametric model does not need to be difficult to understand, but the number of CERs will grow to accommodate more hypotheses observed in the real world. These hypotheses are nominally the cause of residuals and explain why one simple CER will not completely model the cost of a complex project.

When a parametric cost model is used to normalize the cost there are a number of CERs that are applied. One of these submodels is the technology maturity model. Figure 6-4 shows graphically the theory behind this model based upon a constant industry or operating environment. Naturally, if the industry or operating environment is changing the maturity of the technology will change.

The hypothesis behind this model predicts that as time progresses, technologies are assumed to mature. This is explained in terms of market forces. Due to market forces, immature technologies are expensive owing to the limited number of sup-

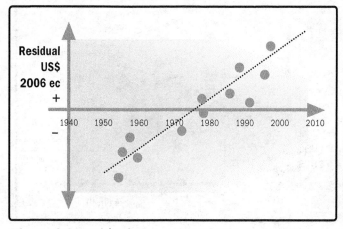

Figure 6-3: Residual cost versus time

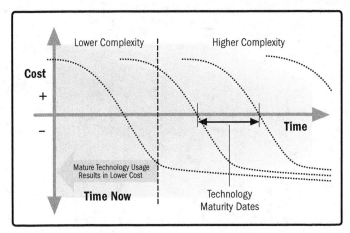

Figure 6-4: Technology maturity model

pliers of the new material and providers of manufacturing processes. This lack of availability resulting in higher costs due to the demand and the model would generate a positive cost penalty. As time progresses, more suppliers join the market and provide the material and skills. Competition ensures that the costs are reduced, resulting in the application of a cost benefit.

Part of the problem in complex defense projects is that mature technologies are seen as less capable. The services (navy, army, air force) constantly want to move to the next technology to ensure superiority on the battlefield. Equipment would be cheaper if the current generation of equipment were reordered with existing mature technology. However, the admirals, generals, and wing commanders desire the next generation of equipment not the present.

Accuracy

Before there is too much excitement about our ability to predict the cost of a complex project, let us consider the obvious question. How accurate is a parametric model? To determine the relative accuracy, a data set was employed containing more than 90 fighter aircraft. The approach was to normalize the cost and technical data. Costs were normalized against currency, economics, and quantity. The technical data were normalized for metric (kg) versus imperial (lbs) and other such anomalies.

After normalization, the fighter aircraft data were subjected to the analysis process and a simple parametric model was created. The historical projects then had their costs predicted based upon this parametric model. To assess the accuracy of this technique, the predictions were plotted against the historical data and the coefficient of determination (R^2) calculated through a series of the graphs.

Figure 6-5 provides a graphical visualization of the fighter aircraft accuracy. A simple, core CER based upon just the weight of the systems provides a poor model ($R^2 = 0.23$). There is an immediate increase in accuracy when the complexity of the systems, indicated by the time dependent residual, is added to the CER ($R^2 = 0.87$). This complexity represented the increase in the level of technology introduced over

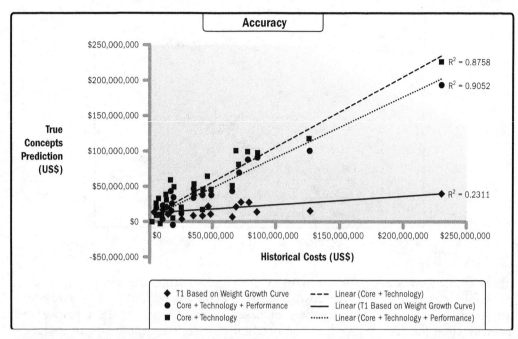

Figure 6-5: Historical cost versus predicted cost

time. Finally, the correlation of the historical costs and the prediction of the CER is refined further ($R^2 = 0.90$) with the introduction of a performance variable, which will predict the cost most accurately. This model will be used as the basis of a case study at the end of this chapter.

Historical Trend Analysis

There are a number of commercial parametric models on the market, which can be used to estimate cost. One of the oldest models has an independent variable term or cost driver called "manufacturing complexity" or complexity for short. The complexity occurs because of comprehensive normalization. The model has numerous submodels and CERs that result in a final representation of the core elements of the product. Complexity is a technology index and, if the technology is constant, it can indicate productivity. This complexity variable leads to many different applications of the parametric cost model including supplier assessment, cost as an independent variable (CAIV), predictive earned value management (P-EVM), and historical trend analysis (HTA). The latter application is useful in the context of predicting the cost of complex projects and setting the correct budget early in the project life cycle when little information is available.

Daryl Webb published a series of papers looking at complexity over time. Manufacturing complexity of structure (MCPLXS) is the result of product calibration using the PRICE H model. Webb conducted a series of system level calibrations grouping the systems into product types and plotted the resulting complexity over time as seen (Figure 6-6). In the analysis, there was a consistent upward trend in military systems.

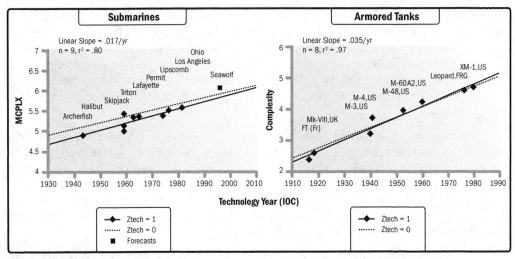

Figure 6-6: Complexity over time

This approach was made easier with the introduction of the PRICE knowledge management systems, which enabled the consistent storage, retrieval, and analysis of system level programs, such as the future U.K. aircraft carrier.

However, although most systems demonstrate a trend, not all systems follow an upward trend. Commercial aircraft have become more complex as time has passed, but they have a flat or declining complexity over time when reviewed by aircraft type (Figure 6-7).

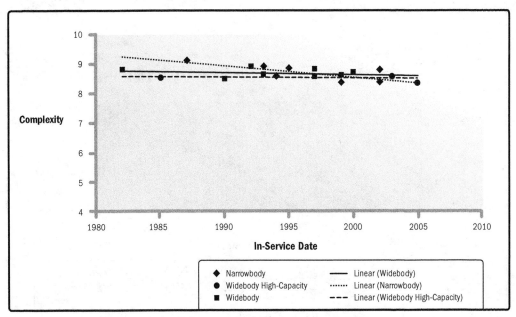

Figure 6-7: Commercial aircraft complexities by aircraft type

This picture changes when analyzed by manufacturer (see Figure 6-8) and provides an indication of the possible reason for this lack of upwards trend. The duopoly achieved by supplier A and supplier B provides for very competitive environments, one in which productivity is key to survival. As the complexity parameter is an indication of both a technology index and productivity, it is possible to deduce that the productivity in the commercial aircraft environment is divergent to the technology increase.

This phenomenon is not just limited to the commercial parametric model. Philip Pugh also observed a HTA. When considering the unit production cost (UPC) of a system, divide it by a size parameter, such as total unit weight (tons). This cost per unit weight exhibits a strong trend when considered over time. He plotted the historical UPC per unit weight of various complex projects on log-linear graph and observed a growth in system cost over time. Although the trend analysis appeared to be linear, they are curves due to the choice of axis.

This cost per unit weight versus time discovery was implemented by Pugh in the algorithms in the family of advanced cost estimating tools (FACET) model produced by QinetiQ.

Why use the whole weight of a system in a complex project? It would seem logical that any cost growth would be limited to certain subsystems, rather than the whole system? For example, in a destroyer, the significant weight is in the hull and super structure. Surely, this part of the ship, welded steel, has been the same for the last 50 years. If anything, the cost of this part of the system has reduced due to modular construction and other manufacturing techniques. The real cost growth in a complex project has been in the radar, communication, propulsion, and navigation systems. Perhaps the focus should be on these rather than the overall cost density.

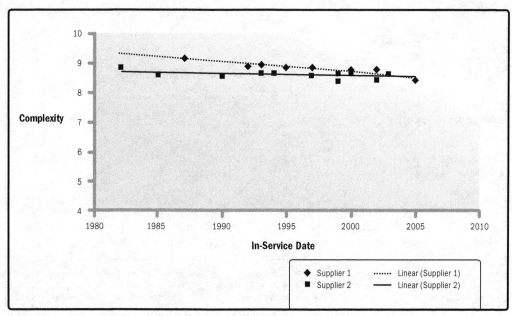

Figure 6-8: Commercial aircraft complexities by manufacturer

Case Study

As an example of how parametrics cost estimating can be applied on a real complex project, a parametric estimate will be considered for the Lockheed Martin (F35) Lightning II or Joint Combat Aircraft (JCA).

The current assumptions[2] for the F35 have been taken from public domain sources

- Empty weight = 13,300 kg
- Length = 15.67 m
- Height = 4.33 m
- Wingspan = 10.7 m
- Crew = 1
- Total installed power = 11,472 kw
- Production quantity = 3,181
- In-service date = 2012

These technical and programmatic details have been used to estimate the production cost of the F35 aircraft, although the development and in-service cost could just as easily have been determined using parametrics. For production, the weight based CER for this parametric cost model is based on the following analysis (see Figure 6-9).

This follows the earlier hypothesis that the systems cost more due to their weight. The error in this relationship is the residual, which needs to be explained by some other independent variable. The relationship between the in-service date (ISD) and residual costs can be seen in Figure 6-10, which shows an influence with the passing of time.

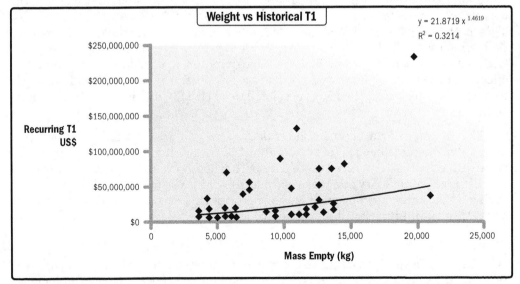

Figure 6-9: Aircraft weight versus time

---

[2]This case study was prepared in 2009.

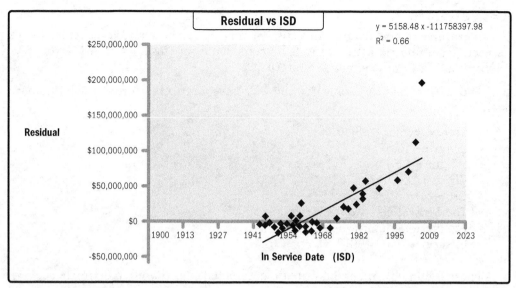

Figure 6-10: Residual versus time

If the F35 parameters are used in this parametric model, it is possible to derive a theoretical first piece (T_1) of US$147 million that will become a unit production cost of US$135 million based on the 2010 economic conditions.

A recent General Accountability Office (GAO) report updated the F35 production cost and stated a figure of US$131 million in (out-turn) costs. As the majority of the program extends beyond 2010, this figure would be reduced when considered in constant 2010 economics.

In an alternative commercial parametric model, it is possible to determine the complexity parameter of fighter aircraft and extrapolate the HTA until the F35 ISD. This methodology is presumed more accurate due to the greater level of normalization, which is applied to the raw data. As discussed, there are a number of models within a parametric model such as technology maturity, schedule effects, quantity effects, etc., leading to increased normalization. When the resulting complexity is used to predict the cost, the F35 is predicted to be US$132 million at 2010 economic conditions.

The accuracy of the approach reflects the data that are required. It follows that more information is needed for the commercial parametric model. The complexity versus time approach required more data both when normalizing the cost to derive the historical complexity and when estimating. If this estimating technique is to be applied at the early, preconcept stages of a project this need for more programmatic and technical information should be considered.

Summary

With the help of this chapter, it is possible to summarize the influence of parametric estimating on complex projects. Not all complex projects experience an increase in complexity in parametrics terms. There are nondefense projects, for example commercial aircraft, which experience a neutral or reducing complexity. It is speculated that this is caused by the rate of productivity reduction exceeding the level of technology growth.

It would seem that the historical trend analysis (HTA) of a complexity parameter could result in an increased degree of accuracy when applied to fighter aircraft. The results would indicate that utilizing a commercial parametric model is an efficient approach to normalizing raw cost data prior to extrapolation of the complexity into the future.

The assumptions for the F35 case study predict the UPC to be in the range of US $132 million to $135 million at 2010 economic conditions. At the early stage of a complex project, an accuracy of 20% is a good outcome and in this case in line with the current authority figures.

Finally, it is recognized that this initial case study demonstrates that parametrics has a place in the initial assessment of complex projects. However, this is only one project type, fighter aircraft, but it is equally applicable to other complex projects in the space, land, and sea domains. Parametrics as an approach to set early complex project budgets is equally applicable in non-defense domains, if realistic budgets are desirable and business cases are going to be successful. Parametrics can be deployed to helping to set realistic budgets for complex projects and safeguarding the project manager.

References

P77, line 4. Shermon, D. (2009). *Systems cost engineering*. Aldershot, UK: Gower. ISBN: 978-0-566-08861-2.

P77, line 5. International Society of Parametric Analysts. (2008). *ISPA Parametric Estimating Manual*. Retrieved from http://www.ispa-cost.org/newbook.htm

P80, line 7. PRICE Systems. (n.d.). *PRICE H or TruePlanning for hardware from PRICE systems*. Retrieved from www.PRICESystems.com

P80, line 18. Webb, D. (1990). Cost complexity forecasting historical trends of major systems. *Journal of Parametrics, 10*(4), 67–95.

P81, line 3. Shermon, D. (2002). Knowledge management in parametrics. *Cost Engineer, 40*(3).

P82, line 9. Pugh, P. G. (2007). *Source book of defence equipment costs*. ISBN: 978-0-9556258-0-0.

P82, line 17. Qineti, Q. (n.d.). Family of Advanced Cost Estimating Tools (FACET). Retrieved from www.qinetiq.com/home/products/facet__the_family.html

P83, line 5. F-35 Lightning II. (n.d.). In *Wikipedia*. Retrieved from http://en.wikipedia.org/wiki/F-35_Lightning_II. and Lockheed Martin. (n.d.). F-35 Lightning II program update and fast facts. Retrieved from www.lockheedmartin.com/data/assets/aeronautics/products/f35/F-35FastFacts.pdf

P84, line 4. Government Accountability Office. (2010). Join*t strike fighter: Significant challenges and decisions ahead*. Publication no. GAO-10-478T. Washington, DC: Government Accountability Office.

Chapter 7

Beyond Competence: Developing Managers of Complex Projects

Lynn Crawford and Ed Hoffman

Introduction

Considerable attention and development activity has been devoted over the last 20 years to determining and codifying, in standards and certification programs, the knowledge and practices that are considered necessary for competent performance of project managers. Although not explicitly stated as such, these efforts are essentially geared toward threshold competence represented by minimum standards for project management knowledge and practice considered necessary for effective workplace performance. Further, they are primarily designed for management of single or stand-alone projects for which goals and methods can be well defined. On such projects, minimum standards for knowledge and practice can provide a shared vocabulary and assist in achieving a relatively consistent level of performance for a majority of project management practitioners. However, the adequacy of these mainstream practice standards, knowledge guides, methodologies, and recommended best practices in addressing the experienced complexity of projects, has been increasingly questioned by both researchers and practitioners.

While the terms "complex" and "complexity" are now widely used to describe projects and the problems and challenges people experience in project environments, the actual meaning of the terms is rarely made explicit. Some organizations attempt to categorize the projects in their portfolios according to their degree of complexity but complexity is not a single construct so such categorization systems, in practice, are based on multiple attributes, such as scope, clarity of goals and objectives, and level of ambiguity and uncertainty.

Projects are inherently uncertain and unpredictable as they require decisions to be made in the present concerning events that are to occur in the future. Determination of success or failure is often ambiguous as it is judged by stakeholders from different perspectives. While the level of uncertainty and ambiguity in projects contributes to perceptions of complexity, it is arguably people who introduce the complexity to projects, and on this basis, all projects are to some extent complex. As Snowdon said, "if you "walk up to an aircraft with a box of tools in your hand, nothing changes" but "when a rumour of reorganisation surfaces: the complex human system starts to mutate and change in unknowable ways; new patterns form in anticipation of the event."

These challenges of projects have been exacerbated in recent times by advances in communication technologies and evolving societal values that have progressively eroded the illusions of command and control upon which standards for project management competence have been built. A fundamental premise of good project management has been the ability to plan, establish clear project boundaries, and exercise control to predictably achieve expected results. As pace, permeability, visibility, accountability, and stakeholder diversity increase, control becomes more elusive. It is hardly surprising, therefore, that mainstream standards and certifications for project management are being challenged on the basis that they are linear, rational, and change averse and often either fail to reflect or are in direct conflict with the real dynamics of projects. Satisfaction of threshold or minimum standards for knowledge and practice in management of projects can be considered a hygiene factor for effective performance in project management roles. However, as the Engineering and Physical Sciences Research Council (EPSRC) funded Rethinking Project Management Network recognized, there is a need for a change of focus from trained technicians to reflective practitioners.

A number of factors have focused attention on the need to move beyond threshold performance to development of more dynamic competence especially for senior practitioners required to manage the more challenging projects or programs. One factor is that with advances in communications technology, both success and failure are far more visible and, especially in the case of public and high profile projects, subject to media scrutiny. Consequently, there is greater pressure on performance and less latitude for people to learn from their mistakes. Another factor is that organizations worldwide are realizing that their competent and experienced staff are retiring and leaving a vacuum because for the last forty years they have been failing to "develop their own."

Until around 1970, organizations had taken much of the responsibility for developing a skilled workforce through a tradition of on the job training, coaching, and mentoring. Those experienced employees who are currently on the verge of retirement, began work about 40 years ago, at the time when organizations, under the influence of economic rationalism, were reducing their workforce numbers and putting pressure on academic institutions to produce work ready graduates. Senior staff, at that time, were required to work harder and no longer had the time, or the responsibility, to coach and mentor new recruits. Therefore, current senior staff have not had the opportunity to learn through personal experience how to transfer their knowledge. Attempts to fill this gap through training in mentoring and coaching can only provide a partial solution.

So, while there is "significant growth in project work" resulting in a need for more managers of projects, organizations have not invested in succession planning and are facing the challenge of losing their most experienced employees. Hence, there is simultaneously increased demand for experienced senior project managers and reduced supply.

It is, therefore, not surprising that a number of organizations are looking for ways to fast track the development of people capable of managing an increasing number of challenging and complex projects. To do this they need to look beyond project management competence as defined in current standards and certification programs, to ways of rapidly developing higher levels of expertise that will underpin superior performance.

Professional Competence and Beyond

Competence is a term that "has different meanings, and ... remains one of the most diffuse terms in the organizational and occupational literature." Dictionary definitions of competence include "power, ability or capacity (to do, for a task etc.)" and "due qualification or capacity, adequacy or sufficiency" to do a task. According to Woodruffe, competency "seems to be used as an umbrella term to cover almost anything that might directly or indirectly affect job performance." There are, however, more specific uses and meanings of the term.

The work of McClelland and McBer Associates in the United States, beginning in the 1970s and reported by Boyatzis in the early 1980s, established what may be referred to as the competency model approach. Followers of this attribute-based approach define a competency as an "underlying characteristic of an individual that is causally related to criterion-referenced effective and/or superior performance in a job or situation." This approach is primarily concerned with behavioral competence but according to Spencer and Spencer specifically encompasses knowledge, skill, and three core personality characteristics—motives, traits, and self-concept.

Inherent in the competency model approach, following in the tradition of McClelland, Boyatzis, and Spencer and Spencer, is the distinction between threshold and high performance or differentiating competencies. Threshold competencies are units of behavior that are essential to do a job, but which are not causally related to superior job performance. Schroder defined a high performance competency as "a relatively stable set of behaviors which produces significantly superior workgroup performance in more complex organizational environments."

The competency model approach has become popular among human resource professionals, and most major institutions now have a corporate competency model that identifies behaviors that are considered to drive superior performance in their organization. The identified behaviors are highly contextual and do not easily form the basis for generic standards for workplace performance.

A far stronger candidate for development of generically applicable standards is the competency standards approach. This approach to competence is promoted in the standards and qualifications frameworks of the U.K. (National Vocational Qualifications [NVQ]), the Australian Qualifications Framework (AQF), and similar frameworks in South Africa and New Zealand. While the competency model or attribute-based approach assumes that identifiable personal attributes will translate into competent performance in the workplace, the competency standards approach assumes that competence can be inferred from evidence of demonstrated performance at a predefined acceptable standard. Under the Australian Competency Standards approach, based directly on the U.K. model, competence is defined as:"the ability to perform the activities within an occupation or function to the standard expected in employment."

Both of the approaches outlined involve assessment of a different aspect of competence. Each approach has both advantages and disadvantages. As Heywood, Gonczi, and Hager pointed out, a comprehensive consideration of both underlying enabling **attributes** and of **performance** "will be the most fruitful."

The model in Figure 7-1 brings together the competency model or attribute based and competency standards (performance based) approaches to competence described earlier and relates it to existing standards and guides for competence in project management roles.

From Figure 7-1, it can be seen that mainstream project management standards and certifications address either or both of the input and output competencies identified. The IPMA 4 level certification model which uses interviews and simulations in assessment and encompasses contextual, behavioral, and technical competences (International Project Management Association [IPMA] offers the most holistic approach for assessment of project management competence currently available. It can still, however, be regarded as providing only a threshold or baseline for competence at each level of certification. This highlights an ultimate limit to standards and certification. The standards development process requires focus on what is required of most practitioners in most circumstances. Standards are inevitably based on the known, on codification of experience of the mainstream of practitioners.

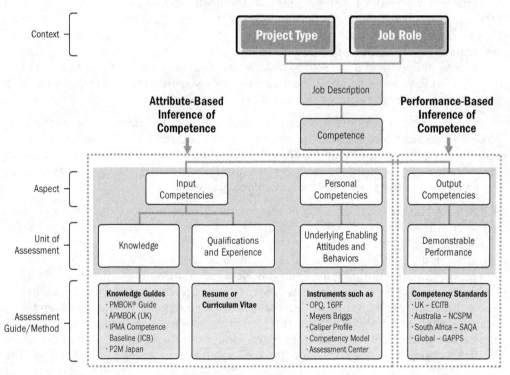

Figure 7-1: Integrated model of competence for project management roles

They delineate the requirements for minimum rather than superior performance in work roles. They can be used to ensure that the foundations are in place but go no further. They do not provide guidance for assessment and development of ability to operate in the largely uncharted and dangerous waters of very complex and unpredictable projects.

Dreyfus and Dreyfus developed a five-stage model, from novice to expert or mastery, that provides a useful basis for explaining the dilemma faced when endeavoring to fast track development of practitioners towards capability to manage very complex projects. The five stages of this model are shown on the left side of Figure 7-2.

As in any profession, standards can only provide a basis for assessment and development to the level of competent performers. According to Dreyfus and Dreyfus, beyond competence is experientially based development of intuitive and holistic behaviors and responses that can be characterized as "expert." Reflection in and upon action, highlighted by Schön, has become accepted as fundamental to higher levels of professional development. Cheetham and Chivers developed a model of professional competence that seeks to integrate reflective practice with competence-based approaches by pointing out that reflection is fundamental to all competency development. Their model also includes meta-competencies, "which come into their own when managers and professionals deal with the complexity of managerial and professional work" and "represent the range of perceptions that exist about an individual's performance as well as focusing on the irrationality and unpredictability of personal feelings." Meta- or trans-competencies exist 'above' other competencies, enabling and guiding their development. According to Cheetham

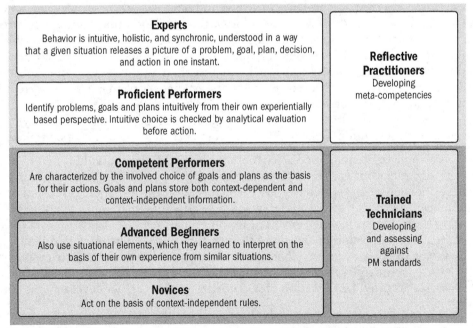

Experts
Behavior is intuitive, holistic, and synchronic, understood in a way that a given situation releases a picture of a problem, goal, plan, decision, and action in one instant.

Proficient Performers
Identify problems, goals and plans intuitively from their own experientially based perspective. Intuitive choice is checked by analytical evaluation before action.

Reflective Practitioners
Developing meta-competencies

Competent Performers
Are characterized by the involved choice of goals and plans as the basis for their actions. Goals and plans store both context-dependent and context-independent information.

Advanced Beginners
Also use situational elements, which they learned to interpret on the basis of their own experience from similar situations.

Trained Technicians
Developing and assessing against PM standards

Novices
Act on the basis of context-independent rules.

Figure 7-2: Summary of Dreyfus & Dreyfus model of skill acquisition as presented and modified for application to project management

and Chivers, meta-competencies may include communication, creativity, problem solving, learning/self-development, mental agility, analysis and reflection. They are dynamic, interactive, and far less amenable to "standardization" than the basic processes and practices considered necessary for management of most projects most of the time. It is considered that meta-competencies are "innate and natural to human beings" and can be learned, but cannot be taught. It is in this realm of meta-competencies that cannot be taught that the challenge lies for fast-track development of managers of complex projects.

Developing Reflective Practitioners

If the meta-competencies required for superior performance can be learned, but not taught, what can individuals and organizations do to fast-track development? The fundamental answer to this question can be traced back to the work of John Dewey who identified the centrality of experience to learning but pointed out that not "all experiences are genuinely or equally educative. Experience and education cannot be directly equated to each other. For some experiences are mis-educative. Any experience is mis-educative that has the effect of arresting or distorting the growth of further experience." For learning from experience to be effective, the learner must be self-aware and have a degree of humility that may be missing in some practitioners especially if they believe and have certifications to attest to their "competence" as project managers. The use of personal experience as a resource in adult learning is well established, but we need ways to "animate" useful learning from experience that will translate into the mastery required to manage challenging projects.

Managing Experiential Learning in the Workplace

Traditionally, development of "expert" practitioners, in the workplace, took many years. In the engineering and construction industry, which has a long history of project-based work and views project managers as key value adding resources, research indicates that it takes 15 years to develop a project manager capable of managing a US$100 million contract, and 25 years for a US$1 billion contract. Potential project managers would be identified in their mid-twenties and developed through "spiral-staircase" career placements. Managers of major projects require both general and project management experience and expertise, so a spiral-staircase development path involves alternating placements between functionally based management roles and management of projects of increasing levels of complexity.

Development is considered a partnership between the individual and the employing organization. Career aspirations and development needs are regularly reviewed and opportunities consciously sought for training, education, and work experiences. Providing structured developmental work experiences is not easy but several studies on staff retention have found employees cite opportunities for development through rotation through projects, functions, and company divisions as a key factor in their decisions about whether or not to stay with their employers. In response, companies like Booz Allen, Mobil, and Citibank were reported, some 10 years ago, as providing rotation opportunities in their career development plans.

Few organizations today have the luxury of confidently planning development of managers over two or more decades. As indicated earlier, the need for "expert" managers is urgent. But even if employers choose to begin now to develop managers for the future, "as a result of globalisation, increasing societal complexity and flexibility, careers have lost their linearity and predictability." New recruits are likely to be Generation Y, who are predicted to switch jobs frequently; however, structured work-based experiences remain central to development of expertise. It has never been easy but compressed timescales and changing societal values require innovative approaches.

Industry/University Alliances, Corporate Universities, and Project Academies

As Dewey said, not all experience leads to beneficial learning. Learners need to be capable of critical reflection so they can interpret their experience and draw upon it selectively as a source of learning and change. Education can assist in developing meta-competencies that facilitate effective learning from experience.

Alliances between corporations and universities are a common feature of what is often today referred to as "talent management." Such alliances take many forms, but typically involve the development, by an academic institution, of subjects or an entire degree, in partnership with one or more organizations, to provide tailored development programs that have academic support and credibility. This makes sense when aiming to develop higher order or meta-competencies.

Some organizations choose to establish "corporate universities." These are owned and operated by companies as vehicles "for the education and development of employees . . . for disseminating an organization's culture and fostering the development of not only job skills, but also such core workplace skills as learning-to-learn, leadership, creative thinking, and problem solving." They do not usually award degrees. It has been suggested that the number of corporate universities in the United States may have exceeded 4,000 by 2010, including some of the earlier initiatives in companies such as Boeing, Motorola, and McDonalds.

Related to this is a trend towards development of what are referred to in some organizations as project academies. They may be stand alone, or part of wider corporate efforts to develop skills across multiple job families. They are not always called project academies, although this term is used by organizations such as Shell and NASA. Their mission is the development of talent to manage the organization's portfolio of projects and programs and encompasses a range of responsibilities and activities including provision of courses, alliances with academic institutions, and structuring of work-based experiences. The importance of this imperative is illustrated by an initiative that resulted in the coming together of representatives of twenty six organizations from Europe, North America, and Asia Pacific, to share their experiences in developing their "academies." The next step was joint development of a process for gathering data to benchmark their development initiatives.

Benchmarking Project Academies: Methodology and Results
Methodology

Data collection instruments were developed by representatives of six organizations and they included 46 questions. These questions were scored 0–5 against a good practice model in terms of both approach and deployment. Eight companies were included in the first stage of data collection and benchmarking. A two-person team of experienced assessors worked with each of the eight companies to complete the assessment, gathering detailed evidence to support conclusions, and returning the results to the organization for verification. Quantitative data collected included organizational characteristics, services provided by the academy, and costs incurred.

Demographics

All companies in the sample are large. Each company employs more than 10,000 people and has annual revenue in excess of US$10 billion. For reasons of confidentiality, industry distribution cannot be detailed, but six different industries are represented. One half of the companies participating consider themselves more than 75 percent project based while about a quarter of the sample consider themselves less than 10 percent project based.

Results

Annual cost of the academy varies across the sample from under US$1 million up to US$15 million. The main categories of expenditure are classroom training, e-learning, and in-role support or experiential learning but the patterns of spending and activity distribution vary by organization.

All but one of the organizations in the sample have clearly defined project related career paths. Five have documented competency frameworks that relate to roles. The highest performing organization continually "scans" the horizon for the requisite levels and numbers of suitably qualified people, in terms of the competencies they require. Most organizations have some form of talent management program including nurturing of graduate recruits and identification and fostering of "high flyers." One organization regularly monitors the needs of the business and changes in the external environment and modifies their activities accordingly. They also use knowledge sharing forums to encourage continuous development of knowledge. Several of the organizations have one or more links or alliances with academic institutions and one specifically encourages two-way research placements.

Experiential Learning

Given the importance of experience to competence development, and particularly to the higher levels of proficiency and expertise, it is interesting that only one of the sample organizations plays a strong role in facilitating the process. Through a leadership development program across the organization, practitioners with high potential, and who are expected to lead higher level or more complex efforts in the near future are identified and provided with a comprehensive development agenda including specific work assignments, supported by technical and leadership training, coaching and mentoring. A developmental program focuses on improving specific leadership behaviors and technical capabilities. A competitive process ensures that the most qualified individuals are selected for this opportunity at the right time in their careers when the learning will have the greatest impact.

Roles and Responsibilities of Project Academies

While the purposes and objectives of project academies differ according to organizational needs and cultures, there are some common roles and responsibilities:

Workforce development. The project academy's foremost responsibility is providing professional development training and experiences for the organization's project workforce. This begins with the identification of competencies, and can include strategies for both formal and informal learning.

Advocacy for practitioners' professional development needs. The project academy can serve as a champion for the project workforce, and advocate for the leadership support and resources necessary to meet its specific professional development needs.

Common vocabulary. In decentralized global organizations, the project academy is uniquely positioned to provide a common framework and standardized terminology for project management. Training courses can serve as vehicles for educating the workforce about the organization's policies, procedures, requirements, and definitions related to project management.

Alignment with corporate strategy. Corporate strategy defines the context in which projects succeed or fail. The project academy is responsible for ensuring that competencies and associated activities are consistent with corporate strategy, goals, and policies.

Alignment with external stakeholders. As with corporate strategy, the project academy is responsible for understanding external stakeholder concerns and requirements (e.g., the standards or certification requirements of project management professional associations), and aligning competencies and associated activities with them as necessary.

Promotion of continuous learning across the organization. By promoting learning at all career stages, the project academy helps to create a community of practitioners who are reflective and understand the importance of learning in project success.

Promotion of institutional knowledge. As with continuous learning, the project academy plays an important role in building institutional knowledge that enables the organization to thrive as projects emerge and retire. Through knowledge sharing activities that bring the organization together, the project academy plays a vital role in ensuring that lessons learned and best practices remain accessible.

Conclusion

Creating a future for project management—as a profession and as an approach to effectively delivering corporate strategy—demands capability that goes beyond minimum standards for competence. To meet this challenge, a number of corporations are taking direct responsibility for developing sufficient people with the right set of skills, experience, and behaviors to cope with the management of complex projects. Development of higher-order expertise, which is required to manage more complex projects, requires opportunities to gain relevant experience. This is supported by the meta- or overarching competencies required to support critical reflection and the ability to learn effectively from that experience. While some organizations are partnering with academic institutions to provide education that will support the development of the required meta-competencies, few are investing in the difficult but vital and rewarding challenge of providing structured work-based experiences, supported by mentoring and coaching, to fast-track development of the talent they need to manage their portfolios of projects and programs.

References

P87, line 15. Cicmil, S. J. K., Cooke-Davies, T. J., Crawford, L. H., & Richardson, K. A. (2009). *Exploring the complexity of projects: Implications of complexity theory for project management practice.* Newtown Square, PA: Project Management Institute.

P87, line 21. Crawford, L. H., Hobbs, J. B., & Turner, J. R. (2005). *Project categorization systems: Aligning capability with strategy for better results.* Newtown Square, PA: Project Management Institute.

P87, line 24. Pitsis, T., Clegg, S., Marosszeky, M., & Rura-Polley, T. (2006). Making the future perfect: Constructing the Olympic dream. In D. Hodgson & S. Cicmil (Eds.), *Making projects critical* (pp. 265-293). London, England: Palgrave.

P87, line 26. Atkinson, R. W. (1999). Project management: Cost, time and quality, two best guesses and a phenomenon, its time to accept other success criteria. *International Journal of Project Management, 17*(6), 337–342. and Atkinson, R. W., Crawford, L. H., & Ward, S. (2006). Fundamental uncertainties in projects and the scope of project management. *International Journal of Project Management, 24*(8), 687–698.

P87, line 29; P88, line 2. Snowdon, D. (2002). Complex acts of knowing: Paradox and descriptive self-awareness. *Journal of Knowledge Management, 6*(2), 100–111.

P88, lines 13, 18. Crawford, L. H., Morris, P. W. G., Thomas, J., & Winter, M. C. (2006). Practitioner development: From trained technicians to reflective practitioners. *International Journal of Project Management, 24*(8), 722–733.

P88, line 15. Herzberg, F. (1968). One more time: How do you motivate employees? *Harvard Business Review, 46*(1), 53–62.

P88, line 18. Winter, M. C., Smith, C., Morris, P. W. G., & Cicmil, S. J. K. (2006a). Directions for future research in project management: The main findings of a UK government-funded research network. *International Journal of Project Management, 24*(8), 638 –649.

P88, line 31; P91, Figure 7-2. Eraut, M. (1994). *Developing professional knowledge and competence.* London, England: The Falmer Press.

P88, line 40. Winter, M. C., Smith, C., Morris, P. W. G., & Cicmil, S. (2006b). Directions for future research in project management: The main findings of the EPSRC Research Network. *International Journal of Project Management, 24*(8), 638.

P89, line 9. Robotham, D., & Jubb, R. (1996). Competences: Measuring the immeasurable. *Management Development Review, 9*(5), 25–29.

P89, line 10. Brown, R. B. (1993). Meta-competence: A recipe for reframing the competence debate. *Personnel Review, 22*(6), 25–36.

P89, line 11. Delbridge, A. (1985). *The Macquarie dictionary (Rev. ed.).* Dee Why, NSW: Macquarie Library Pty Ltd., p. 1651.

P89, lines 12, 13. Woodruffe, C. (1992). What is meant by a competency? In R. Boam & P. Sparrow (Eds.), *Designing and achieving competency* (pp. 16–30). London, England: McGraw-Hill Book Company.

P89, line 15. McClelland, D. C. (1973). Testing for competence rather than for intelligence. *American Psychologist, 28*, 1 –14.

P89, lines 16, 27. Boyatzis, R. E. (1982). *The competent manager: A model for effective performance.* New York, NY: John Wiley and Sons.

P89, line 20. Spencer, L. M. J., & Spencer, S. M. (1993). *Competence at work: Models for superior performance* (1st ed.). New York, NY: John Wiley & Sons, Inc., p. 9.

P89, lines 27, 29. Schroder, H. M. (1989). *Managerial competence: The key to excellence.* Dubuque, IA: Kendall Hunt.

P89, line 43. Gonczi, A., Hager, P., & Athanasou, J. (1993). *The development of competency-based assessment strategies for the professions.* Canberra, Australia: Australian Government Publishing Service.

P90, line 2. National Training Board. (1991). *National Competency Standards Policy & Guidelines.* Canberra, Australia: National Training Board, p. 30.

P90, line 4. Cheng, M-I, Dainty, A. R. J., & Moore, D. R. (2003). The differing faces of managerial competency in Britain and America. *Journal of Management Development, 22*(6), 527–537.

P90, lines 5, 6. Heywood, L., Gonczi, A., & Hager, P. A. (1992). *Guide to development of competency standards for professions.* Canberra, Australia: Australian Government Publishing Service.

P90, line 14. International Project Management Association. (2006). *ICB-IPMA Competence Baseline Version 3.0.* Nijkerk, The Netherlands: International Project Management Association.

P90, Figure 7-1. Crawford, L. H. (2005). Senior management perceptions of project management competence. *International Journal of Project Management , 23*(1), 7–16.

P91, lines 6, 13, Figure 7-2. Dreyfus, S. E., & Dreyfus, H. L. (1980). *A five-stage model of themental activities involved in directed skill acquisition.* Berkeley, CA: Operations Center, University of California, Berkeley for the Air Force Office of Scientific Research (AFSC), USAF. and Dreyfus, H. L., & Dreyfus, S. E. (1986). *Mind over machine: The power of human intuition and expertise in the era of the computer.* New York, NY: The Free Press.

P91, line 12. Cheetham, G., & Chivers, G. (2005). *Professions, competence and informal learning.* Cheltenham, UK: Edward Elgar Publishing.

P91, line 16. Schön, D. A. (1983). *The reflective practitioner: How professionals think in action.* Aldershot, UK: Ashgate Publishing Ltd.

P91, line 17; P92, line 1. Cheetham, G., & Chivers, G. (1998). The reflective (and competent) practitioner: A model of professional competence which seeks to harmonise the reflective practitioner and competence-based approaches. *Journal of European Industrial Training, 22*(7):267–276.

P91, line 24; P92, line 6. Brown, R. B., & McCartney, S. (1995). Competence is not enough: Meta-competence and accounting education. *Accounting Education, 4*(1), 47.

P92, lines 12, 17; P93, line 8. Dewey, J. (1963). Experience and education: The Kappa Delta Pi lecture series. London, England: Collier Macmillan Publishers.

P92, line 21. Brookfield, S. D. (1986). *Understanding and facilitating adult learning.* San Francisco, CA: Jossey-Bass Publishers. and Miller, N., & Boud, D. (1996). Animating learning from experience. In D. Boud & N. Miller (Eds.), *Working with experience* (pp. 3–13). London, England: Routledge.

P92, lines 28, 33. Turner, J. R., Keegan, A., & Crawford, L. H. (2000). Learning by experience in the project-based organisation. *Proceedings of PMI Research Conference* (pp. 445–456), Paris, France. Sylva, NC: Project Management Institute.

P92, line 42. Bernstein, A. (1998, June 22). We want you to stay: Really. *Business Week*, p. 67. and Branch, S. (2010, November 9). You hired 'em, but can you keep 'em? *Fortune*.

P93, line 1. Lo Presti, A. (2009). Snakes and ladders: Stressing the role of meta-competencies for post-modern careers. *International Journal for Educational and Vocational Guidance*, 9(2), 125.

P93, line 2. Kunreuther, F., Kim, H., & Rodriguez, R. (2009). *Working across generations*. San Francisco, CA: Jossey-Bass.

P93, line 22. Meister, Jeanne C. (1998). Ten steps to creating a corporate university. *Training & Development*, 52(11), 38.

P93, line 25. Meister, J. C. (2006). Corporate universities: What works and what doesn't. *Chief Learning Officer*, 5(3), 28-70.

Part 2

With Researchers and Students in Mind

Chapter 8

Human Behavior and Complexity

Terry Cooke-Davies

Why Human Behavior Matters

Human behavior, as mentioned in Chapter 1, is potentially both a significant source of complexity in projects, and an effective antidote to it.

Perhaps this is intuitively obvious, since both specific research studies and more general reviews of the research literature demonstrate or assert the primary significance of managing people effectively in delivering successful project results. Indeed, on the basis of more than two decades of research, teaching, and consulting, Dennis Slevin and Jeffrey Pinto asserted, "Project managers who take the time to perfect their skills in the critical areas [of leadership, motivation, communications skills, team building and so forth] continue to demonstrate that successful project management depends first and foremost on our ability to effectively manage the human resources for which we have been made responsible."

More recently, a research project led by Dr. Svetlana Cicmil and partially funded by Project Management Institute investigated the implications of complexity theory for project management practice. Cicmil et al. concluded that project managers deal with project complexity by utilizing standard project management tools and techniques in combination with a set of alternative skills and competencies that are not codified or captured in the conventional recommendations of good practice.

These skills and competencies, however, are notoriously difficult to hone, and there is considerable evidence that organizations in many industries that undertake complex projects are faced with a shortage of skilled people in both professional and craft categories. In Chapter 11, Lynn Crawford and Ed Hoffman share their insights on the development of skilled professionals, but this present chapter will pull together research not only from within the sphere of project management literature, but further afield from the general management literature, from social psychology, and from the study of cognition in its various aspects.

Many of these skills and competencies are concerned with relationships between either people or groups of people or different aspects of human behavior that arise from nonrational or irrational behavior that seems to be endemic to the human condition. Indeed, as scientific attention turns to a more accurate understanding of the internal world of human beings through advances in fields such as psychology and neuroscience, a new basis of understanding is being developed in which the reflective leader can base his or her skills and competencies.

That is not to say that these advances open up completely new aspects of leadership. Projects have always been delivered by people working together and leading and motivating them to align their efforts behind the project goal has always been an important task for the project manager. But such is the pace of these developments coupled with the increase in what could be called the "human and cultural dimension" of many complex projects. An effective project manager of today must master these "soft" skills, and have profound insight into their own cognitive processes, as well as recognize how this plays into their leadership of the people who they are leading.

If human behavior is indeed pivotal in the unfolding of complex projects, then we cannot afford to ignore what has been discovered about humankind in the course of the past decades. As the headline of a review of one of Howard Gardner's books in *The Economist* once put it, "Might the proper study of management be man"?

For projects, perhaps, the right place to start investigating the "behavior of (hu) mankind" is at that place where projects become concretized in contractual relationships—in relationships on projects.

Relationships on Projects

The study by Cicmil et al. observed that "An effective project manager is a participant in … process of relating, continuously engaged in emergent enquiry into what they are doing and what steps they should take next and reflexive in thinking about the quality of their own participation in complex processes of relating in their local project situation."

Apart from the general run of daily interpersonal relationships, projects involve certain formal power-relationships that crucially contribute to the context within which behavior is played out on projects. Perhaps the most salient of these is the relationship between the "buyer" of the output of a project and the "seller" who manages the resources necessary to deliver that output. An international study of communications between the buyer's project sponsor and the seller's project manager in 100 IT projects provides some interesting insights into the gap between good practice and general practice in this particular aspect of behavior. The study demonstrates that project performance is greatest when there is a high degree of collaboration between the buyer and seller, and the sponsor and project manager work together in partnership, with the project manager empowered to take appropriate decisions. The study also demonstrates, however, as has been shown in numerous other research studies, that such behavior is not commonplace. There is a critical need on even the most straightforward projects for alignment of interests between principal and agent, for the use of both structure and informality in communications, and for the provision of trustworthy quantitative data for analysis where required by the principal.

With more complex projects, the potential for difficulties arising from relationships becomes even more problematic, with multiple layers of hierarchy involved in some version of a principal-agent relationship, as illustrated in Figure 8-1.

The illustration is taken from a paper discussion of two specific kinds of undesirable behavior—delusion and deception—that combine to result in projects that are "over budget, over time, over and over again." These two sets of behaviors and the problems that they cause on complex projects will be considered in more detail. However, before leaving the problem of managing relationships, it is as well to deal with a specific behavioral aspect of relationships—the question of "identity" or, in its most extreme expression, "tribalism."

People seem to like to belong to groups, whether they are rotary clubs, church congregations, Girl Scout troops, supporters' associations. The reasons for joining these groups are many and varied, and indeed, may be inadvertent or resisted. How many people want to become asylum seekers, or a persecuted minority? However, once one "belongs" to a group, a human tendency seems to lead us all to distinguish between the "in-group" to which we belong and the "out-group" to which we do not belong. In his book, *Irrationality*, Stuart Sutherland observed that, "if the member [of a group]'s attitudes are biased in one direction, simply by interacting together their attitudes become even more biased in the same direction." In other words, any differences of attitude between specific groups that are party to a particular project are likely to harden as the project progresses. This tendency for the attitudes of a defined group to become extreme has been named by Irvin Janis as "Groupthink" (after its use in George Orwell's influential novel *1984*). Although there is some evidence in recent years that more is at stake in group dynamics than Janis claims, managers of complex projects can expect the attitudes, norms, and behavior of different parties to the project to call for high levels of expertise in managing intergroup relationships.

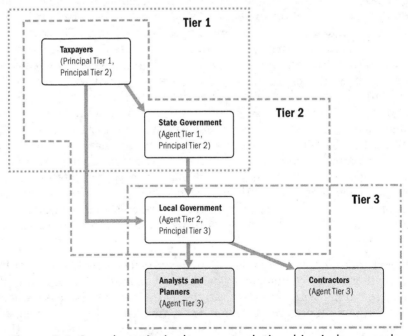

Figure 8-1: Complex principal—agent relationships in large-scale infrastructure projects

But what of these attitudes, norms, and behaviors?

Understanding Human Behavior

In 2002, one of two people who shared the Nobel Prize for Economics was a Princeton University professor of psychology named Daniel Kahneman. He was awarded this honor for having integrated insights from psychological research into economic science, especially concerning human judgment and decision making under uncertainty. The official press release for the prize states that, "Kahneman's main findings concern decision-making under uncertainty, where he has demonstrated how human decisions may systematically depart from those predicted by standard economic theory. Together with Amos Tversky (deceased in 1996), he has formulated prospect theory as an alternative, that better accounts for observed behavior. Kahneman also discovered how human judgment may take heuristic shortcuts that systematically depart from basic principles of probability. His work has inspired a new generation of researchers in economics and finance to enrich economic theory using insights from cognitive psychology into intrinsic human motivation."

With these words, the world of economics recognized that when it comes to making economic decisions, such as happens frequently in the world of complex projects, human behavior is not always rational. Kahneman and Tversky demonstrated through an impressive body of experimental evidence, that a person's attitude to risk depends on the "frame" through which the risk is viewed. People are more willing to entertain risk in order to avoid "loss" than they are in order to increase what they already stood to "gain."

Examining the same phenomenon through the lens of the emerging discipline of "neuroeconomics," Benedetto de Martino and his colleagues at University College London gave experimental subjects a decision task to perform while they were in a functional magnetic resonance imaging (fMRI) scanner. They demonstrated not only that the results of the experiment were entirely consistent with prospect theory, but also that different parts of the subjects' brains were involved depending upon which of the two decision frames they were presented with. A particular region of the brain known as the orbital and medial prefrontal cortex (OMPFC), which is known to mediate emotional responses, showed activity that rose in correlation with a subject's propensity to be susceptible to the particular frame in which their decision was taken. This led the researchers to speculate that, "that more 'rational' individuals have a better and more refined representation of their own emotional biases that enables them to modify their behavior in appropriate circumstances, as for example when such biases might lead to suboptimal decisions. As such, our findings support a model in which the OMPFC evaluates and integrates emotional and cognitive information, thus underpinning more "rational" (i.e., description-invariant) behavior."

For project managers leading major complex projects, this has at least four implications: (1) there is a psychological aspect to the management of risk that needs to be considered along with all quantitative and qualitative risk assessment techniques; (2) if human beings are irrational about risk, then there may well be other aspects of human behavior that are not rational; (3) if the degree of "irrationality" exhibited in decision making is related to how individuals integrate emotions into their decision-making processes (of which more later) then "emotional intelligence" is particularly important to the managers of complex projects; and (4) if the "frame of reference" through which a risk is viewed fundamentally influences someone's willingness to take risks, then the "frame" through which someone views other aspects of a project might influence other aspects of their behavior.

In the remainder of this section, different insights from social psychology and its related disciplines will be explored, before moving on to consider the importance of "frames" or "viewpoints" when understanding context.

Quirks of Thinking

In 2003, in an article in the *Harvard Business Review* titled "Delusions of Success," Daniel Kahneman and Don Lavallo stated "in planning major initiatives, executives routinely exaggerate the benefits and discount the costs, setting themselves up for failure." In this article the authors of the paper cited three main causes for this failure: "optimism bias" reinforced by "attribution errors" and the "illusion of control," anchoring and competitor neglect.

Each of these factors highlights a different aspect of human nonrationality of which the manager of a complex project needs to be aware, both with regard to his or her own mental processing, and to that of project team members. There is, of course, a thriving industry of self-help books and training courses led by charismatic figures all of which could be characterized as popular psychology, or "pop-psych." It is an industry that has dealt superficially and/or pragmatically in "how to" tips for getting by in the face of these and other idiosyncrasies of human behavior. For the aspiring manager of complex projects, however, the skills and competencies must go much deeper. Research in the field of social psychology has identified many "quirks" of human nature that belie the rational nature of human behavior that has been assumed not only by economists (as has already been seen), but also by project management practitioners and the developers of project management tools and techniques (See Chapter 1).

There are few people who have not at some time or other experienced in their own lives, the drive toward irrational behavior or faulty reasoning, when under the influence of strong emotion. Love, euphoria, frustration, envy, or anger (to name but a few) can lead us astray from the paths of reason and rational thinking. Strong emotions bring about physical changes to the human body, such as increased heart rate, raised blood pressure, or a dry mouth, but they also make us see the world in a distorted way. The well-known Victorian fable by Robert Louis Stevenson, *Dr. Jekyll and Mr. Hyde*, pushes this notion to extremes. However, the general truth that emotion leads to both a loss of control and a greater propensity to irrational and antisocial thinking has been clearly demonstrated in a most dramatic way by examining the decisions about "safe sex" taken by teenage boys when in a state of arousal.

For example, in a series of imaginative experiments, male students at University of California at Berkeley were asked to predict how they would react to a range of propositions involving sexual activities when aroused. They first answered these questions in their normal state, and then, with the aid of graphic stimulation, answered similar questions while in a state of arousal. The results were dramatic. The students in their rational state proved themselves quite incapable of predicting just how they would react when in a state of arousal. In every case, when aroused, the students predicted that their willingness to engage in a variety of slightly unusual sexual activities would be nearly twice as high (72%) they had predicted when they were "cold." Of particular interest in the context of managing projects was the result of five questions about whether or not they were willing to indulge in immoral activities: When they were aroused, they predicted their propensity to be more than twice as high (136%) than they had predicted in their cold state.

As Ariely said "Every one of us, regardless of how 'good' we are, underpredicts the effect of passion on behaviour." And passion, of course, includes emotions such as anger, frustration, or elation just as it does sexual arousal.

As cognitive neuroscience starts to supplement the results of experimental psychology with the observed activity of the brain obtained from PET scans and fMRI images, a picture emerges of the way that emotions and other brain functions that are not accessible to human consciousness combine with reason to motivate and direct all human decisions and behavior. For example, Paul Wason's experiments in the 1960s on "confirmatory reasoning" revealed the human tendency to look for and select evidence that supports a particular hypothesis, rather than that which contradicts it. As has already been seen in the case of prospect theory within the past decade or two, neuroscientists such as Antonio Damasio and Antoine Bechara have demonstrated the intense activity of those parts of the brain that process, control, and integrate emotions while purely rational decision-making tasks are being undertaken. It appears that our apparently "rational" activity of decision making is actually strongly influenced by emotional activity that introduces a whole series of biases into the process.

This isn't to deny the strong impulse that people feel to base their decisions on rational grounds, rather it is to emphasize that much of the processing that is taking place in our brains is happening beneath the surface of our conscious minds—like much of an iceberg lies beneath the surface of the sea in which it is floating.

As a result of this part-conscious and part-preconscious processing, we are all prone to a number of errors in terms of our decision making, for example: seeing patterns and meaning in data that is actually random; drawing unsupported conclusions from incomplete and inconclusive data; seeing what we expect to see when the data is actually ambiguous or inconsistent; seeing what we want to see (along the lines of Wason's experiments) and expressing "optimism bias"; and being hard to persuade to change our views or beliefs.

Each of these five habits is well attested in research, and a brief description of each is appropriate.

Seeing Patterns and Meaning in Data That is Actually Random

When people look at the moon with the naked eye, they can see patterns that make up the face of the "man in the moon" and when looking at Mars through a telescope, it is possible to make out a series of "canals." Gamblers claim that they experience hot and cold streaks in random rolls of the dice and alter their bets accordingly.

Of course, this isn't all bad. The ability to spot patterns is highly beneficial to humankind in numerous ways. This ability can often lead to discovery and advancement. However, coupled with this useful intuitive ability, we do not seem to possess the same intuitive understanding of numerical probability. In an elegant experiment, Kahneman and Tversky illustrated this lack of intuitive understanding with a simple experiment. Subjects were told that in a certain town there are two hospitals. The larger of the two has an obstetrics ward that has an average of 45 births per day while the smaller of the two averages only 15. Over a period of one year, roughly as many boys are born as girls. Subjects were asked which of the two hospitals would have more days on which 60% of the births are boys. Most of the subjects thought that there would be no difference. In fact, male births will be 60% of all births on about twice as many days in the small hospital as in the large one.

The same fallacy is at work when considering any sequence of random occurrences in order to understand the "gamblers' streak" problem. Consider, for example, the likelihood of all "heads" turning up when a coin is tossed, say, five times in a row. The likelihood of that happening is one chance in 32, since there are 32 possible combinations of heads or tails (one half multiplied by itself 5 times). There is exactly the same chance of the sequence being TTHHT, THTHT, or any other possible sequence of 5 results, even though intuitively people tend to regard the notable sequence of five consecutive heads (or tails) as less likely than any other.

On the other hand, if the sequence is changed to 10 tosses of the coin, there are 1,024 possible sequences, of which all heads is only one. This leads to the formulation of what is known to the general public as "the law of averages," but which is referred to by statisticians as "the law of large numbers"—the larger the population, the more likely it is that the statistical average will be achieved.

This is perhaps related to another observation of the general limitations of human cognition, which is the failure to appreciate the exponential nature of consequences involved in "positive feedback loops." As was shown in Chapter 1, a failure to appreciate systemicity is cited as one of the major causes of complexity on projects, and certain kinds of systemicity involve escalating consequences similar in kind to the deafening "feedback" heard when a microphone is placed in too close a proximity to a loudspeaker in an amplified circuit. Just as people have a tendency to see patterns where none exists, there is also a seeming incapability of recognizing the presence of the alarming nature of geometric progression (of the kind that produces compound interest).

Try this simple "thought experiment:" imagine an ordinary sheet of paper, of the sort that you place into any office printer, say 8.5 x 11 inches, or A4. Imagine that you fold it in half, mid-way along the longer side, and then repeat this. Imagine yourself repeating the action 30 times more. Before reading on, try to estimate how thick the resulting folded stack of paper would be. You might estimate that it would be more than 10 meters thick, perhaps even more than 100 meters. But most people are totally shocked to learn that the resulting stack would in fact be nearly 400,000 kilometers thick. In the same way, the escalating impact of systemic imbalance is not intuitively obvious to most people working on projects.

None of this means that the managers of projects need to be qualified statisticians, but it does mean that when basing judgments on apparent patterns of occurrence, they need to exercise caution before deciding whether a particular phenomenon forms part of a pattern, or is a random happening.

Drawing Unsupported Conclusions from Incomplete and Inconclusive Data

It is not only natural, but also laudable, to seek evidence that confirms something that we hold to be true. If, for example, a project manager believes a member of his or her team is a fast and effective worker, each time that team member works fast and effectively, or is told by a colleague about the work that has been done fast and effectively, the project manager will consider his or her belief to be well founded.

If we are to hold anything to be true, it is necessary that we can cite confirmatory evidence that it is, indeed, the case. Unfortunately, on their own, isolated instances and credible anecdotes are not sufficient to support the case conclusively. At best, such evidence only suggests that our belief may be true, which is a long way short of providing proof that it is a valid belief.

Let us call the admirable team member Albert. We should also recognize that the belief that Albert's work rate is actually a belief about how fast and effectively Albert carries out his work in comparison with a control group, let's say his teammates. Now, in order to prove conclusively that the belief is grounded, it is necessary to note not only times (a) when Albert's work is fast and effective, but also times (b) when Albert doesn't work fast and effectively, (c) when other team members work fast and effectively, and (d) when other team members don't work fast and effectively. The belief then turns out to be well founded if the proportion of Albert's work that he does fast and effectively is greater than the proportion of the other team members' work that they do fast and effectively. In effect, for many of us, our belief is based on an excessive reliance of data in only one out of four possible segments.

There is a great deal of literature about how well people evaluate the kind of information in assessing the presence or strength of relationships of which Albert's work rate is simply an example. Gilovich reported on the basis of eight separate citations that although people sometimes perform such tasks accurately, there are as many or more occasions when they perform poorly. The problem appears to be an excessive reliance on data that confirms our beliefs (i.e., a and d) and, in many cases, simply the data (a) that positively confirms our pre-existing beliefs.

Paul Wason, for example, carried out extensive research during the 1960s to demonstrate that when people can choose what evidence they gather to support or refute their beliefs, they more often than not seek evidence that confirms their beliefs, rather than challenges them. Wason's experiments, involving the choice of cards to turn over in order to prove whether a particular "rule" is or isn't valid, are interesting in that it is not likely that the subjects will have any desire for the hypothesis to be true or to be untrue. Simply, there is a human tendency to seek evidence that confirms our hypotheses, rather than challenges them.

Seeing What We Expect To See When the Data Is Actually Ambiguous or Inconsistent

There is a third "quirk" of thinking that, like the two prior ones described previously, seems to be a function of human cognitive processing, rather than any willful or self-seeking activity. "Anchoring" is the name given to another well-researched phenomenon that demonstrates the mind's unfailing tendency to "anchor" calculations and estimates to some baseline that it has previously established. It has been suggested that the actual mechanism of anchoring is similar to the well-observed phenomenon of "imprinting" in the brains of birds and animals first described so convincingly by 1973 Nobel Laureate Konrad Lorenz. Whether or not this is so, what is indisputable is that once the idea of a particular number has been planted in a human mind, it will be taken as a reference point for subsequent calculations and estimates, regardless of whether or not there is any logical connection between the anchored number and the subsequent calculation. This has far-reaching consequences for anyone involved in "high-level" or "order of magnitude" estimates and, when coupled with optimism bias, suggests that underestimating costs or delivery dates is an almost innate human tendency against which one must be constantly on one's guard.

Seeing What We Want To See

Each of the three foregoing "quirks" contributed in some way to the "delusions of success" identified by Lovallo and Kahneman, but the particular cognitive error that received the greatest attention in their article was what they referred to as "optimism bias." They asked their readers to "consider a survey of 1 million students conducted by the College Board in the 1970s. When asked to rate themselves in comparison to their peers, 70% of the students said they were above average in leadership ability, while only 2% rated themselves below average. For athletic prowess, 60% saw themselves above the median, 6% below. When assessing their ability to get along with others, 60% of the students judged themselves to be in the top decile, and fully 25% considered themselves to be in the top 1%." Other experiments also confirmed the tendency of people to be over-optimistic about their own ability to control events.

Resisting Learning

In view of these quirks of thinking, it is hardly surprising that managers of complex projects find that they have a difficult time coping with the complexities of people's behavior.

Indeed, the work of Lovallo, Kahneman, Tversky and others adds weight to the work of Chris Argyris and his colleagues during the 1980s and 1990s. Argyris concluded that "Professionals embody the learning dilemma: they are enthusiastic about continuous improvement—and often the biggest obstacle to its success." Argyris observed that executives strive to remain in unilateral control, to maximize "winning" and minimize "losing," to suppress negative feelings and to be as "rational" as possible. In view of this, they tend to use their intelligence to "reason defensively," and as the prior discussion has shown, they have an extensive cognitive armory to provide them with whatever evidence they need to support their views "rationally." This helps them to avoid the "doom loop" of bad feelings that threaten to engulf them once they stray too far from their comfort zone, and are confronted with the serious possibility of their own personal failure.

Argyris' work points to another dimension of the human aspect of leading complex projects, one that has not been given its due weight in recent years—the context in which complex projects take place, especially the business context.

Attribution Errors

Many of the quirks of thinking described result in well attested "attribution errors" that are acknowledged by psychologists and underpinned by rigorous research and that are not given the attention they deserve in project management formation or literature. These include:

- **Self-serving bias**: The tendency to take the credit for success, and blame external factors for failure.
- **Self-centered bias**: The tendency for an individual contributor to take a disproportionate amount of credit for the outcome of group effort.
- **Egocentricity bias**: The tendency to exaggerate the importance of one's role in past events.
- **False consensus effect**: The tendency to believe that most people share one's opinions and values.
- **Assumption of uniqueness**: The tendency to overestimate one's uniqueness.
- **Illusion of control**: The tendency to exaggerate the degree of one's control over external events.
- **Hindsight bias**: The tendency to retrospectively overestimate the probability of past events occurring.
- **Self-righteous bias**: The tendency to regard oneself as having higher moral standards or greater moral consistency than others have.
- **In-group/out-group bias**: The tendency to view members of the group to which one belongs in a more positive light than members of groups of which one is not a member.
- **Base-rate fallacy**: The tendency to neglect population characteristics and prior probabilities when making probabilistic inferences.
- **Conjunction fallacy**: The tendency to regard the conjunction of two events as more probable than either of them occurring singly.

The Neurological Basis to Persistent Habits

Not only are these habits ones that we are all prone to, but they stem from cognitive processes that are usually quite helpful in making sense of and participating in the everyday world around us. Without the ability to recognize patterns, for example, Fleming would not have discovered penicillin, Semmelweis would not have introduced the practice of antisepsis, and Darwin would not have drawn conclusions that led eventually to his theory of evolution by means of natural selection. It is the "unforeseen consequences" (to borrow a term from system dynamics) of humankind's habitual use of these abilities that persistently creates for us the difficulties of complexity and nonrational behavior that have been described in this chapter.

As cognitive neuroscience gains more ground in understanding the patterns of usage of energy in the brain (in the form of oxygen and blood sugars), there is also evidence emerging that responding in a habitual manner is actually the most energy-efficient response for the brain to take to any particular situation with which we are confronted. The brain uses an inordinate proportion of the total energy produced by our bodies (20% to 60%) relative to its proportion of our total body weight (~2%). In view of this, it is an entirely appropriate survival strategy for the brain to operate in general using the lowest possible amount of energy consistent with the task in hand. Higher order cognitive processing calls for unsustainable use of large amounts of energy, whereas habit or conditioned reflex uses much less.

It is hard to overstate the importance of these findings, although there is a great deal of research yet to be done before the precise linkage between the neurological aspects of energy use and the cognitive aspects of human decision making and interpersonal behavior are well-understood. As a working hyothesis, Roth suggested that project managers should recognize that 90% of all tasks are likely to be performed by 1% of the neurons in the brain (reflexes and reflex-like responses) and 99% of the tasks are carried out by 10% of the neurons in the brain (more or less automized responses). Furthermore, the remaining 90% of the brain's neurons are reserved for complex non-routine tasks such as dealing with novel cognitive, emotional, and motor problems, especially with respect to social interaction and communication.

Getting To the Truth of a Situation

As has already been stated, in *Delusions of Success*, Lovallo and Kahneman blamed the kind of cognitive errors that have been explored so far in this chapter under "quirks of thinking" for the failure of so many initiatives in business which, by extension, can be readily seen to add to the complexity of projects.

In responding to this article, however, Bent Flyvbjerg wrote to the *Harvard Business Review* stating that the research that he and his colleagues had carried out, while supporting the presence of "optimism bias" in large infrastructure projects, suggested that what he called "strategic misrepresentation" (lying, to you or me) played a greater part in the failure of these complex projects to deliver their promises. Flyvbjerg wrote,

> Lovallo and Kahneman underrate one source of bias in forecasting: the deliberate 'cooking' of forecasts to get ventures started. My colleagues and I call this the Machiavelli factor. The authors mention the organizational pressures forecasters face to exaggerate potential business results. But adjusting forecasts because of such pressures can hardly be called optimism or a fallacy; deliberate deception is a more accurate term. Consequently, Lovallo and Kahneman's analysis of the planning fallacy seems valid mainly when political pressures are insignificant. When organizational pressures are significant, both the causes and cures for rosy forecasts will be different from those described by the authors.

> In our study of bias in cost and demand forecasting in capital-investment transport projects, my colleagues and I found strong evidence of heavy political pressures on executives to make rosy forecasts and minor penalties for having made such forecasts. Indeed, during the 70 years covered by our study, forecasters consistently made errors of the same size and frequency, resulting in repeated cost overruns and demand failures.

This introduces perhaps the most sobering aspect of this chapter: the evidence that senior and responsible managers and government officials regularly practice "deliberate deception." But perhaps we should not be so surprised. This chapter opened with the suggestion that the study of human behavior should lie at the heart of project management studies, if we are to understand complexity in projects. If we are to take that seriously, then we should pay attention to the words of a professor of cognitive science and evolutionary psychology who wrote, "Deceit is the Cinderella of human nature; essential to our humanity, but disowned by its perpetrators at every turn. It is normal, natural and pervasive. It is not, as popular opinion would have it, reducible to mental illness or moral failure. Human society is a 'network of lies and deceptions' that would collapse under the weight of too much honesty. From the fairy tales our parents told us to the propaganda our governments feed us, human beings spend their lives surrounded by pretense."

References

P101, line 3. Lechler, T. (1998). When it comes to project management, it's the people that matter: An empirical analysis of project management in Germany. In F. Hartman, G. Jergeas, & J. Thomas (Eds.), *Proceedings of IRNOP III. The Nature and Role of Projects in the Next 20 Years: Research Issues and Problems.* University of Calgary, Calgary. and Strang, K. D. (2005). Examining effective and ineffective transformational project leadership. *Team Performance Management, 11*(3/4), 68–103.

P101, lines 4, 11. Slevin, D. P., & Pinto, J. K. (2004). An overview of behavioral issues in project management. In P. W. G. Morris & J. K. Pinto (Eds.), *The Wiley guide to managing projects* (pp. 67–85). Hoboken, NJ: John Wiley and Sons.

P101, line 14; P102, lines 20, 24. Cicmil, S., Cooke-Davies, T., Crawford, L., & Richardson, K. (2009). *On the complexity of projects: Exploring the implications of complexity theory for project management theory and practice.* Newtown Square, PA: Project Management Institute.

P101, line 19. Zack, J. G. Jr. (2007). *The greatest project risk of all. Cost Engineering, 49*(5), 3–4.

P102, line 15. Might the proper study of management be the man? (2004, April 15). *The Economist.* Retrieved from http://www.economist.com/node/2592934?Story_ID=2592934

P102, line 31. Turner, J. R., & Müller, R. (2004). Communication and co-operation on projects between the project owner as principal and the project manager as agent. *European Management Journal, 22*(3), 327–336.

P102, line 44; P103, line 3. Flyvbjerg, B., Garbuio, M., & Lovallo, D. (2009). Delusion and deception in large infrastrucure projects: Two models for explaining and preventing executive disaster. *California Management Review, 51*(2), 177.

P103, lines 14, 16. Sutherland, N. S. (1992). *Irrationality.* London, England: Printer & Martin Ltd.

P103, line 19. Janis, I. L. (1982). *Groupthink: Psychological studies of policy decisions and fiascoes* (2nd ed.). Boston, MA: Houghton Mifflin.

P103, line 21. Kramer, R. M. (1998). Revisiting the Bay of Pigs and Vietnam decisions 25 years later: How well has the groupthink hypothesis stood the test of time? *Organizational Behavior & Human Decision Processes, 73*(2-3), 236–271.

P104, line 15. The Sveriges Riksbank Prize in Economic Sciences in Memory of Alfred Nobel 2002. Nobelprize.org. Retrieved from http://nobelprize.org/nobel_prizes/economics/laureates/2002/

P104, line 18. Kahneman, D., & Tversky, A. (2000a). Prospect theory. An analysis of decision under risk. In D. Kahneman & A. Tversky (Eds.), *Choices, values and frames* (pp. 17–43). Cambridge, UK: Cambridge University Press.

P104, line 39. De Martino, B., Kumanran, D., Seymour, B., & Dolan, R. J. (2006). Frames, biases and rational decision-making in the human brain. *Science, 5787*(313), 687.

P105, line 39. Ariely, D., & Loewenstein, G. (2006). The heat of the moment: The effect of sexual arousal on sexual decision making. *Journal of Behavioural Decision Making, 19*(2), 87–98.

P106, lines 8, 10. Ariely, 2008, p. 96.

P106, line 16; P108, line 39. Wason, P. C. (1960). On the failure to eliminate hypotheses in a conceptual task. *Quarterly Journal of Experimental Psychology, 12,* 129–140. and Wason, P. C. (1966). Reasoning. In B. Foss, (Ed.), *New horizons in psychology.* Harmondsworth, UK: Penguin.

P106, line 20. Damasio, A. (1994). *Descartes' error. Emotion, reason and the human brain.* New York, NY: G. P. Putnam's Sons. (Electronic Edition by Vintage, London, England, 2006). and Bechara, A. (2004). The role of emotion in decision-making: Evidence from neurological patients with orbitofrontal damage. *Brain and Cognition, 55*(1), 30–40.

P106, line 37; P108, line 32. Gilovich, T. (1991). *How we know what isn't so: The fallibility of human reason in everyday life.* New York, NY: The Free Press.

P107, line 5. Kahneman, D., & Tversky, A. (1972). Subjective probability: A judgement of representativeness. *Cognitive Psychology, 3*(3), 430–454.

P109, line 10. Lorenz, K. (1978). *Behind the mirror.* London, England: Mariner Books.

P109, lines 21, 29. Lovallo, D., & Kahnemann, D. (2003, July). Delusions of success: How optimism undermines executives' decisions. *Harvard Business Review,* 57–63.

P109, line 37; P110, line 1. Argyris, C. (1991). Teaching smart people how to learn. *Harvard Business Review, 69*(3), 99–109.

P111, line 4. Roth, G. (2008, April). *The complex brain and its impact on project management.* Paper presented at the Second Knowledge Sharing Forum of the College of Complex Project Managers, Frankfurt, Germany.

P111, line 17. Lovallo, D., & Kahnemann, D. (2003, July). Delusions of success: How optimism undermines executives' decisions. *Harvard Business Review,* 57–63.

P111, line 42. Flyvbjerg, B. (2003, December). Delusions of success: Comment on Dan Lovallo and Daniel Kahneman. *Harvard Business Review,* 121–122.

P112, line 8. Alexander, 1975, p. 96

P112, line 10. Livingston Smith, D. (2004). *Why we lie. The evolutionary roots of deception and the unconscious mind.* New York, NY: St. Martin's Griffin.

HM Treasury. (2002). *Supplementary green book guidance: Optimism bias.* Retrieved from http://www.hm-treasury.gov.uk/d/5(3).pdf

Kahneman, D., & Tversky, A. (1979). Intuitive prediction: Biases and corrective procedures. *TIMS Studies in Management Science, 12,* 313–327.

Kahneman, D., & Tversky, A. (2000b). *Conflict resolution: A cognitive perspective.* In D. Kahneman & A. Tversky (Eds.), *Choices, values and frames* (pp. 473–487). Cambridge, UK: Cambridge University Press.

Orwell, G. (1949). *1984.* New York, NY: Penguin Books.

Turner, J. R., & Keegan, A. (1999). The versatile project-based organization: Governance and operational control. *European Management Journal, 17*(3), 296–309.

Zack, J. G. Jr. (2007). *The greatest project risk of all. Cost Engineering, 49*(5), 3–4.

Chapter 9

Controlling Chaos?
The Value and the Challenges of
Applying Complexity Theory to
Project Management

Kaye Remington and Roxanne Zolin

A Problematic Application of Theory?

The literature abounds with descriptions of failures in high-profile projects and a range of initiatives has been generated to enhance project management practice. Estimating from our own research, there are scores of other project failures that are unrecorded. Many of these failures can be explained using existing project management theory; poor risk management, inaccurate estimating, cultures of optimism dominating decision making, stakeholder mismanagement, inadequate timeframes, and so on. Nevertheless, in spite of extensive discussion and analysis of failures and attention to the presumed causes of failure, projects continue to fail in unexpected ways. In the 1990s, three U.S. state departments of motor vehicles (DMV) cancelled major projects due to time and cost overruns and inability to meet project goals. The California DMV failed to revitalize their drivers' license and registration application process after spending $45 million. The Oregon DMV cancelled their five-year, $50 million project to automate their manual, paper-based operation after three years when the estimates grew to $123 million; its duration stretched to eight years or more and the prototype was a complete failure. In 1997, the Washington state DMV cancelled their license application mitigation project because it would have been too big and obsolete by the time it was estimated to be finished. There are countless similar examples of projects that have been abandoned or that have not delivered the requirements.

A question plaguing researchers and practitioners alike is what can be discovered about the nature of these projects that defies the application of "best practice." Complexity theory is one discipline that seems to be yielding plausible explanations and to be helping researchers to shed light on phenomena that contribute to the downfall of some projects. The terms complexity, complexity theory, and complex adaptive systems are appearing with increasing frequency in project management literature. Project management as a discipline has a history of appropriating ideas from other fields, such as economics, the social sciences, and management science, to find answers for phenomena that cannot be explained by existing theoretical constructs. While this practice is healthy, it can be problematic.

This chapter is presented in two sections. Part One defines and describes some concepts associated with complexity theory and explores how the idea of complex adaptive systems has been adopted, adapted, and applied by project management theorists and practitioners to explain particular project phenomena. Part Two discusses conceptual and methodological questions associated with appropriating ideas from other, quite disparate disciplines, such as complexity theory, in order to explain project phenomena. Finally, we raise questions for research about how complexity theory and its various derivatives might be used to help project managers work more effectively in difficult projects exhibiting various forms of complexity. In so doing we draw upon our current research with defense acquisition projects[1] and previous research in the public sector and construction industries.

Part One: Complexity Theory and Projects
Defining Complexity

Complexity theory is an amalgam of ideas that seeks to explain phenomena not explainable by traditional (mechanistic) theories. It has been developed in several disparate fields, including the natural sciences, mathematics, and economics, integrating ideas from chaos theory, cognitive psychology, computer science, evolutionary biology, general systems theory, fuzzy logic, information theory, and other related fields. Rather than breaking them down into their constituent parts, (decomposition) complexity theory seeks to deal with natural and artificial systems as they are, holistically. Complexity theory has received a mixed reception in the general management literature, with opinions polarized between strong advocates and adversaries.

One of the aspects of complexity theory that management practitioners and theorists find most difficult to accept is the implication that organizations can become "chaotic" and therefore unmanageable, making outcomes impossible to predict. This is not an attractive prospect, especially in an outcome-oriented profession like project management. Therefore, it is puzzling that complexity theory seems to be attracting even stronger interest in project management literature than it has in the field of general management. Qualitative differences in types of projects have been recognized for some time. Probably following this realization, project management theorists seem to have absorbed and understood a very important aspect of complexity theory.

Complexity theory describes states varying from comparative order to complete disorder, or chaos, where the system defies prediction or control. However, even in a "chaotic" system, some structure is evident. In a chaotic system, at any point in time, parts of the system can be quite stable, even predictable. Over time, patterns can even be observed. Anyone who has managed a project that involves significant organizational change will recognize that some segments of the project behave pre-

---

[1]Research is currently being funded by the Defence Materiel Organization of the Australian Department of Defence.

dictably while other parts appear to be out of control. It is the recognition that some projects, or parts of projects, do not behave predictably, even when under the guidance of experienced project teams, whereas some parts will be very stable and behave in a predictable manner that has sustained continued interest in complexity theory. An IS integration project might have very predictable components like the data transfer from the old to the new system; it might have complicated, but manageable, segments, involving integration of new programming components. There might be other aspects that behave quite unpredictably, such as the adaptation of the system for use by a range of operators across the world. Also, in aircraft construction, there will be some routine processes, some complicated and very challenging operations, and some truly unpredictable events.

A Question for Project Management

Some authors have questioned whether the projects that are described as complex are just very complicated, suggesting that complexity might be yet another management fad. Are we really just observing the product of lack of experience? Cilliers famously argued that building a jumbo jet is complicated whereas making mayonnaise is complex. In so doing, he touched on an important aspect that distinguishes the two terms. As flippant as this metaphor first appears, and with apologies to those involved in the aircraft industry, a jet aircraft can be constructed using logical project management tools and methods based on decomposition. Furthermore, once it is constructed it can, theoretically, be deconstructed into its component parts. In praise of cooks worldwide, on the other hand, the delicate operation of slowly trickling olive oil into egg yolk produces a product that has no relation, physically or gastronomically to the original ingredients. Mayonnaise is the result of emergence. The original ingredients have been totally transformed in the act of combination and, try as you might, they cannot be separated and returned to their original states. Additionally simple visual inspection of mayonnaise would not allow you to observe the original ingredients, thereby disassociating cause from effect.

Complex Adaptive Systems

Systems thinking, the holistic idea that components can best be understood through their relationship to other parts of the system, has interested project management theorists for some time. The particular branch of complexity theory that draws upon systems thinking, and which has attracted the most recent attention by project management theorists, is complex adaptive systems. Also known as dynamic systems, complex adaptive systems are characterized by nonlinearity, emergence, path dependency, irreversibility, and disconnection between cause and effect.

Emergent Phenomena

However, not all systems or subsystems within a complex adaptive system exemplify all of these characteristics. Cillier's jumbo jet/mayonnaise metaphor really describes different aspects of complex adaptive systems. Mayonnaise production exhibits emergence and irreversibility, but with knowledge and experience success is relatively easy to predict. The aircraft also illustrates emergent properties. It started as a collection of separate materials and components: aluminum, plastics, engine components, and cables. When properly combined, the separate components emerge to become a machine that transports people in the air over long distances. Like making mayonnaise, with knowledge and experience, the outcomes in aircraft production can be predicted with reasonable confidence.

Therefore, it is helpful to think of different degrees of complexity in a complex adaptive system. As they become more complex, dynamic systems, like the weather and the human body, have high levels of connectivity and inter-dependence between events, resulting in nonlinear behavior, from which it is very difficult to link cause and effect. Nonlinear behavior has been observed and described in large projects. Nonlinear effects relate not only to the number and interdependencies in the schedule or network but also to the organizational layers that might be imposed on the project. We have found evidence of high levels of interdependence and nonlinear behavior due to the imposition of multiple organizational layers in the defense projects currently under investigation. Particularly, in international procurement projects, an action can be delayed or blocked anywhere in any one of several organizational networks, for reasons of which the project manager is not aware and therefore did not anticipate and, in some cases, cannot pinpoint. A study of complexity in ACAT1 (Acquisition Category 1) projects for the Australian Defence Materiel Organization discovered that reported complexity increased when projects were interdependent with other projects and required configuration of components from several different countries. This could result in bottlenecks delaying the project through cycles of rework. Figure 9-1 illustrates a cycle of rework caused by a delay in decision making on a public sector change project that affected almost all subsequent activities in the network. The project illustrated was eventually shut down before completion.

Feedback Loops

Stability in a system is maintained by negative feedback often manifested as negative feedback loops. For example, the human body, which is a dynamic system, has negative feedback loops that maintain life; when blood oxygen levels drop (negative feedback), the urge to breathe results in blood oxygen levels being reestablished within an acceptable range. However, another interesting characteristic of dynamic or complex adaptive systems is the propensity for events to reinforce each other in cycles, forming what are known as positive reinforcing cycles or positive feedback loops (Figure 9-1). Positive feedback loops can create, vicious (undesirable) or sometimes virtuous (desirable) cycles. "Vicious" cycles are often associated with disease states, such as type 2 diabetes. The inability of cells to uptake insulin, leads to poor metabolism of glucose, leads to exhaustion and weight gain, leads to increased insulin resistance at the cellular level, and so on. The nonlinear behavior, results in adaptation and emergent phenomena, which cause the system to change and to assume a different state. The system will tend to move further and further away from anticipated behavior until it is interrupted; either the person dies or intervention stops the vicious cycle. A number of project management studies have been conducted that clearly demonstrate the role of nonlinear processes, including positive reinforcing loops, or vicious cycles, in the emergence of uncontrollable risk patterns in projects. Figure 9-2 illustrates this phenomenon in a construction project for a city building.

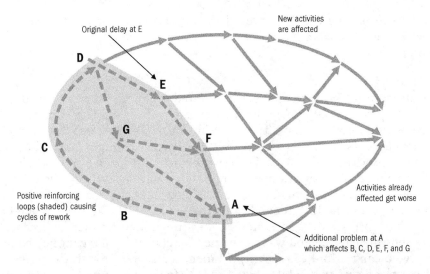

Figure 9-1: Part of a network of activities showing cycles of rework caused by a delay in decision making affecting almost all subsequent activities in the network

The construction project illustrated clearly exhibits nonlinear behavior, particularly the positive reinforcing loops, or vicious cycles (shaded). The smaller cycle, on the right hand side of the diagram illustrates the effect of very wet weather, which caused damage on the site and an accident, both contributing to delays, exacerbated by continued wet weather and more subsequent damage. This cycle continued and contributed to the large cycle, which eventually ended the project.

Dependence on Initial Conditions, and the Butterfly Effect

Another aspect, also illustrated in Figure 9-2, is something that complexity theorists refer to as *sensitive dependence on initial conditions*. Also known as the *butterfly effect*, it was first reported by the meteorologist, Lorenz, who found that minute variations in the initial values of variables in a weather model, even with a small number of initial variables, resulted in very divergent weather patterns. Any project manager working in the construction or engineering industries will be fully aware of the need to check initial site conditions, for example, before embarking on the project.

In the example illustrated in Figure 9-2, a number of initial conditions contributed to the nonlinear behavior. These can be seen at the bottom of the map and include unusually adverse weather conditions, which continued beyond expected timeframes; a sudden decrease in interest rates, stimulating a temporary building boom; a change in legislation, restricting availability of guest work visas; and unusual site conditions. Most of these, with the exception of the change in legislation and the unseasonal and prolonged bad weather, had been identified as risks early in the project. However, their affect had not been considered in aggregate. When triggered in a temporally related manner, small risks contributed in aggregate to the emergence of risk patterns that were unable to be controlled and continued until the works were shut down. It is possible to speculate on other contributing reasons why these patterns emerged. However, the point of this example is to illustrate that nonlinear patterns, causing positive reinforcing cycles, can occur even in relatively simple projects.

Phase Transition

At a certain point in time, the project illustrated in Figure 9-2 went through, what is described by complexity theorists as, a *phase transition*. The complexity term 'phase transition does not have the same meaning as the term "project phase," which refers to parts of a project life cycle. Both involve changes, but a phase transition is usually unexpected and can be very spectacular, like an avalanche. The 2009 global financial crisis is an example of a phase transition. Prior to the crisis, lending institutions had huge debts but were stable because they had the confidence of investors. These are the initial conditions that ended in the global financial crisis: extremely high private debt in America; an unregulated finance industry, which allowed subprime lending and was a scheme that claims to make money by lending to people who can't afford to repay it; payment for debts through the purchases of bonds from financiers in the false belief that they were genuinely safe, AAA-rated assets; banks and financial institutions that kept many of these toxic bonds on their books, and used them to raise more money; on-selling of bonds between banks, and so on. This lead to rapidly decreasing confidence in financial institutions and panic.

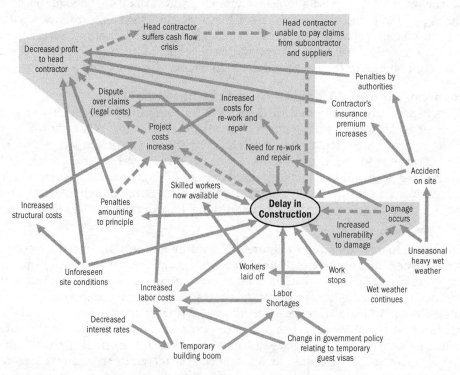

Figure 9-2: Construction example illustrating positive feedback loops of activities that continued to reinforce each other until the project was shut down

Under certain conditions, a system or its parts can operate at the boundary between stability and instability. In complexity theory, this has been referred to as the "edge of chaos" or "onset of chaos." At such a boundary, a very small disturbance can have a dramatic effect. During a phase transition, the system components are the same; the system itself just exhibits different properties. This is usually an internal response to an external change. In the example illustrated in Figure 9-2, the emergent properties caused by aggregated initial conditions and nonlinear, or positive feedback, cycles caused a cash flow crisis and, what seemed to the parties concerned to happen overnight, the head contractor filed for bankruptcy. The result of the phase transition was immediate cessation of work. The nature of relations between parties associated with the project changed dramatically from this point on. As the work stopped and litigation ensued the parties ceased to co-operate and became openly hostile to each other. Postimplementation analyses of much larger projects, carried out to assist with litigation proceedings, have uncovered similar effects of nonlinearity.

Classifying Complexity

In an attempt to assist practitioners and researchers and to make sense out of what appears to be a confused array of ideas and theories in the literature, a number of classification systems have been developed for complex projects. Several of these have attempted to define different characteristics of complexity as it affects projects. Models include those by Santana, Williams, D'Herbemont and César, Commonwealth of Australia, Hass, Remington & Pollack, Vidal and Marle, Bosch-Rekveldt and Mooi; Maylor, Vidgen, and Carver. These authors have variously classified projects according to either characteristics or sources of complexity. Recurring categories include physical structural or organizational complexity of the network; experience of complexity caused by uncertainty, technical, relational, or semantic; and complexity associated with temporal conditions, or environmental impacts over time from outside the project, such as impacts of political, regulatory or key stakeholder changes. Structural and organizational complexity has already been discussed in terms of the effects of nonlinearity and emergence. The following sections will provide an overview of thinking about uncertainty, technical challenges, the effects of time on project complexity, and leadership and management challenges.

Uncertainty

Uncertainty is discussed by many project management complexity writers as a characteristic of project complexity. We argue that uncertainty can be both a source of project complexity and a consequence of nonlinearity and emergence. Difficulty in linking cause and effect has an important effect on the project team and key stakeholders because of the uncertainty that arises. Factors that contribute to perceptions of uncertainty could include technical complicacy, unclear or untimely decision making, unexpected environmental changes, and many others. Resultant uncertainty, or ambiguity, can manifest as loss of faith or trust in the technology management of the project and in other parties involved in the project. In this case, uncertainty and associated reactions, such as loss of faith and trust are contingent factors. They are consequences of nonlinearity and emergence. Uncertainty can arise due to confusion and lack of clear causal relationships at any time in the project. However, uncertainty can also be a primary cause of nonlinearity. At project initiation, a lack of a shared understanding about goals and goal paths, or goals that are understood differently by different stakeholders, can increase feelings of uncertainty. If not dealt with decision making is affected and, if not recognized and addressed early, uncertainty may increase as the project progresses. Uncertainty as a causal factor has been explored by a number of authors.

Technical Challenges

Understandably, one aspect of interest to project management is technical difficulty. Technological novelty, task uncertainty, and the ability of the organization to cope with technological novelty have been cited specifically. Technical and design challenges are commonplace in projects, however, if they appear to be insurmountable, or at least insoluble in the required time frame, feelings of uncertainty and ambiguity can lead to lack of trust between key stakeholders, which might increase the perception of complexity In addition, design and creative activity is by definition nonlinear. Inherent in the design process are positive reinforcing loops, hopefully virtuous rather than vicious circles, leading to new ideas and knowledge. However, there can be many frustrating dead ends in the process of exploration. Jones and Deckro added another aspect to technical complexity, that of instability of the assumptions upon which the tasks are based. This has resonance with Williams who also defined aleotoric uncertainty, uncertainty inherent in the reliability of calculations, which can be alleviated by contingency planning, and epistemic uncertainty, stemming from either poor mental models or lack of knowledge.

Time and Project Complexity

There are many temporal sources of nonlinearity, particularly as many projects last for extended periods over several years. These projects are subject to a large range of environmental impacts, including political upheavals, local and worldwide economic crises, major regulation changes, and replacement of key personnel. At the other end of the time scale, Clift and Vandenbosch and Williams argued that an increasing desire to reduce time to market is another source of complexity. For those exploring computational complexity, time is to do with the number of steps involved in a solution. Traditionally that is how time has been measured and managed in projects but it is not the only way to manage projects. Some relevant research in the product development area investigates overlapping or entrainment of time sequences and more recently this research has been extended to large scale transformation projects. Gärling, Gillhom, and Montgomery investigated the role of anticipated time pressure in activity scheduling and studies of concurrent engineering have shown that overlapping project activities can save time up to a point. At some stage, excessive overlap of activities can lead to increased project duration, probably due to the increased propensity for nonlinearity and uncertainty. We know that personal perceptions of time change throughout a normal project, with time available perceived as greater at the start of a project, contracting as the project progresses. Nevertheless, there is little understanding of how pressure due to time affects decision making in teams and among other key stakeholders when complexity is a factor. Some of the change management literature and the psychology literature dealing with decision making under stress might provide useful insights for project management.

Leadership and Management Challenges

Research focusing on how people perform in projects described as complex has been informed by some of the leadership and change management literature and the sociology of communication. Laufer, Gordon, and Shenhar differentiated between management styles associated with simple and complex projects, and Müller and Turner have begun to explore leadership styles appropriate to different types of projects. They found that on medium complexity projects, emotional resilience and communication are important. On high complexity projects, they found that competencies required are more likely to be associated with transformational leadership than transactional leadership. Keegan and den Hartog argued that the complex reality of projects suggests that reciprocal and dynamic relationships and shared leadership are increasingly important. This is due to the temporary nature of projects and multiple and overlapping leader-follower relationships. Consequently, project managers must be both technically and socially competent to develop teams that can work dynamically and creatively toward objectives in changing environments across organizational functional lines.

Management challenges relating to sources of project complexity have also been examined. Remington and Pollack argued that certain manifestations of complexity require particular skills. Projects with high levels of structural or organizational complexity require strong formal project management capabilities; high levels of uncertainty require advanced relationship management skills and high levels of complexity due to extreme variations over time require developed political acumen. However, many complex projects exhibit all of these characteristics, suggesting that project leadership is best accomplished by carefully selected leadership teams representing this range of skills. Hällgren and Maaninen-Olssen also argued that in conditions of uncertainty deviations are successfully managed using both formal and informal communication and interaction. For Thomas and Mengel, these needs should be reflected in specialized education for complex project management. They agree with Chia who argued that it is important for managers of complex projects to be able to stay with the "ambivalence and ambiguity of the not-yet-known; recognizing that how a situation emerges crucially shapes its meaning, interpretation and social significance."

Nevertheless, if complexity theory is to be a useful tool for practitioners and researchers a number of seemingly insurmountable challenges present themselves for researchers.

Part Two: Conceptual Hurdles

Defining Complexity

While the previous sections summarize some of the research around the topics of complexity and project management, there are conceptual hurdles associated with applying complexity theory to project management. The first hurdle to overcome is the problem of what is considered complex. Semantic issues associated with the use of the term complexity abound. For example, the word complex is interchangeable in common parlance with complicated, difficult, multifaceted, convoluted, knotty, 'wicked', and multifarious.

As we suggested in the introduction, opinions about what is entitled to be labeled complex vary. Even within the natural sciences, debates suggest there is a qualitative difference in meaning between complexity and difficulty. Simply put these are the main sides to the argument. Some argue that only systems, networks and programs that are neither deterministically nor stochastically predictable, (based upon randomness), are entitled to be labeled complex. Others argue that an object may be perceived as complex based on how much information we have, on our ability to make distinctions or detect differences and, therefore, our ability to extract relevant information. Still others argue that something is complex if those who are associated with it believe it to be so.

Assessing Levels of Complexity

From a purely mathematical perspective, assessing complexity presents a significant conceptual problem because measuring complexity requires computational capacity far beyond current means. Things might be predictable in the short term but not in the long term. What is complicated or difficult is deterministically or stochastically predictable whereas what is complex is not predictable using known mathematical models. In the project management field, some argued that complexity can be measured "objectively." For example, in project management, there might be real characteristics that can be observed and measured: interdependencies among activities, limited information about activity durations, and unfamiliarity and variety in project work. Even so, reliance on computational methods alone might actually result in failure to appreciate important manifestations of complexity. There are aspects of complexity that are ambiguous, not understood, or not known, which cannot be modeled, regardless of the efficacy of the model. Moldoveanu questioned the validity in attempting to assess complexity, questioning whether we would "know a complex phenomenon if we saw it" or even whether "complexity of different phenomena be compared?"

We argue, with others that it is the "subjective" assessment of complexity that matters, and therefore, complexity is most usefully conceptualized cognitively in subjective terms. "Objective" measures of complexity, like the degree of nonlinearity, might be more convenient to measure but they don't give the whole story. Associated with this is the idea that the information we have, and our ability to make distinctions or detect differences and extract relevant information, will determine whether or not we perceive something to be complex. In relation to everyday practice, how people assess the level of project complexity is dependent upon how they construe the structure and behavior of the system, or the part of the system that they can observe. Moreover, our research to date supports observations by others who also observed that, at any point in time, even if one person were able to recognize complexity in a system, other players might have very different understandings of what that complexity looks like, or might not perceive that complexity is present at all. Best practice sets an industry standard. If the project cannot be managed using best practice, then lack of ability to control and predict outcomes is not just down to a lack of skill or experience.

Assessment is further complicated because the ability to define or measure the complexity of a system is itself defined by the model chosen, the ability of the assessor to apply the model, the presence of the assessor, and the information known or unknown, or indeed unknowable, about the system. Although some computational measures might be applicable, ultimately a cognitive approach to understanding complexity will prevail as it takes into account the fact that different people associated with the project will have different experience, knowledge, and capability, all of which will influence their assessment of the complexity. Perceptions also vary between individual observers and over time. For example, a novice does not necessarily see aspects of complexity that the experienced person sees or a novice might perceive something to be complex that an experienced person might see as challenging but manageable. Finally, individual personality characteristics are also likely to influence how the aspects of complexity, particularly uncertainty aspects, are conceptualized. In reality, we are not going to be able to fully define or measure complexity because we are dealing with the unknown. It is likely that the best that we can do will be to provide forewarning within the bounds of the project context and the capabilities of the people concerned.

Appropriating Concepts from Other Disciplines

More fundamentally, there are epistemological objections to appropriation by management disciplines of ideas from complexity science. One of the major critics, Rosenhead, argued that there is no evidentiary basis for claims made by various management authors for the application of complexity theory to management. The main arguments center on whether it is feasible, or indeed rational, to make a direct transfer of observations based on mathematical modeling in the natural sciences, such as those performed by Kaufmann and Lorenz, to human systems which have not been proven to be analogous.

In the sense that management theorists have employed qualitative descriptions from complexity science, they have done so metaphorically. As Brodbeck argued, causal relationships between groups of concepts in one domain are not implicitly preserved between their equivalents in another domain. Using complexity theory in a metaphorical sense does not give its use validity. A metaphor is a figure of speech, a term, or phrase that is applied to something to which it is not literally applicable in order to represent something else. To make things worse, many of the arguments put forward by management writers about the value of complexity thinking as a management tool are supported by anecdotal rather than empirical evidence and subject to obvious distortions, validity, and reliability issues.

Even within the natural sciences and economics, conclusions are based on mathematical modeling rather than direct observation. Kauffman's modeling of the adaptation of organisms and Krugman's modeling of the economics of land use are examples. Both authors are circumspect about the extension of their work for application to other areas of study. Rosenhead noted that not all nonlinear dynamic systems exhibit chaotic behavior but they can also become stable quite quickly. In such cases, small differences in initial conditions have only a minimal effect. Either way, the field is lacking empirical research that supports or refutes whether this and other claimed effects do occur in social systems.

Also problematic is the fact that some of the mathematical work cited by management complexity writers relates to deterministic chaos. Deterministic chaos is a branch of complexity theory that is based on the premise that the unpredictability arises without any random elements as input to the system or random processes within the system. However, it would be very hard to deny that apparently random behavior is very much in evidence in social systems, and it is surprising that randomness is not seen as further complicating the system. It can be argued that human systems are affected by several sources of complexity but it does not also follow that no prediction at all can be done or that the only criterion for decision making is randomness.

Nevertheless, empirical evidence is being accumulated. Even in small systems, we know that tiny errors in estimating initial conditions or small approximations in step-by-step calculations can result in large differences in outcomes. A dynamic system can become unpredictable quite rapidly, many different trajectories may be followed and many unanticipated patterns may emerge. That kind of behavior occurs in a complex system without even considering the additional possibilities created by human action or inaction. Increasing the number of elements and the number of interactions can create unexpected, emergent phenomena.

Challenges for Research

Complex projects are difficult to study because of extreme differences in industries, organization type, location, and cultures (national, industrial, and organizational). There are unresolved questions about what differentiates a large organization or project from a medium or small one and whether complexity is related to budget, time frame, or risk. Most studies to date have used organizational assessments of project complexity or assessments of key stakeholders, which are invariably subjective. Access to all management levels, particularly senior executive levels may be restricted, as is access to organizational data. Research is often limited to case studies because longitudinal studies and studies with multiple stakeholders are difficult logistically.

Mathematical, and other types of modeling, have focused on postevaluation. Subjectivity is also an issue, as is intersubjectivity, through the affect of the observer on the subject studied. Managers also perceive and interpret the external and internal organizational world in different ways. These issues affect social research in general and are not specific to project management research.

Encouragingly, a number of studies have been conducted that clearly demonstrate the role of nonlinear processes, including positive reinforcing loops, or vicious cycles, in the emergence of often uncontrollable risk patterns. Some of these behavior patterns closely resemble the "edge of chaos" in scientific models. Other large projects have also been studied that demonstrate characteristics that can be linked to complexity. Even relatively small studies, such as the example shown in Figure 9-2, illustrate the emergence of positive reinforcing cycles that caused the project to escalate into a critical state.

Challenges for Practice

Given that it is theoretically impossible to predict outcomes in a complex system with any kind of accuracy, we must ask the question whether it is possible to provide some kind of forewarning to practitioners and key stakeholders. Ideally, a forewarning system could alert key stakeholders to the fact that they are not dealing with a run-of-the-mill project but something that requires extraordinary management. Furthermore, if we picture a project made up of component parts on some kind of continuum from stability to chaos, the question arises whether it is possible to anticipate in advance which aspects of the project are likely to behave more indeterminately than others. As there will be aspects of the project or program that behave relatively deterministically, it would be useful if we could separate in advance those parts that can be managed with ordinary project management processes and those parts that require extraordinary management.

Stacey defined extraordinary management as a management practice, which goes beyond competent ordinary rationalistic forms of decision making. It requires extensive use of tacit knowledge and creativity to work with unstable situations in which normally accepted "givens" no longer exist. Fluid spontaneous groups need to be self-organizing, capable of redefining or extending their remit rather than being bound by fixed terms of reference. For projects, there are practical limits to this idea. Project teams are staffed from available qualified people and in large projects, they are often co-located and dedicated to the project.

Ultimately, the goal is to manage the range of complex events in projects, more successfully. There will always be aspects that are impossible to predict, the "unknown unknowns," however, there is much to be understood and anticipated. Williams argued that while foreseen uncertainty can be managed by contingency plans, unforeseen uncertainty cannot be planned for, and systemicity can help move events from unforeseen to foreseen uncertainty.

Conclusion

There is increasing agreement in the academic literature that complexity theory can provide a useful lens through which to study extremely challenging projects. Viewing a project as a complex adaptive system assists researchers and practitioners to understand previously unexplainable project phenomena. Arguments that there is no support for theoretical claims have been repudiated by evidence from detailed analyses of projects. Through postimplementation studies of projects, it has now been demonstrated that nonlinear patterns of events can lead to emergence and other characteristics that are also associated with complex adaptive systems. Of particular interest to project management researchers are emergent risk patterns, which might threaten the viability of a project.

The reality is that project managers are expected to deliver the projects, at least within a semblance of agreed outcomes. Nevertheless, some management complexity writers argue that control is impossible in a complex adaptive system. This is an oversimplification. Complex adaptive systems include subsystems that may range widely in levels of predictability, from control through to chaos. Those parts of a project that are behaving chaotically therefore require different management approaches, and possibly extraordinary management capabilities. Like any other management field, project management is not over-endowed with extraordinary managers. It is also unreasonable to expect managers, no matter how extraordinary, to operate constantly at the edge of chaos. If we acknowledge that some projects, or parts of projects, behave in ways that defy determination, the challenge for researchers is how to provide early warning systems so that managers can be better prepared and so that scarce resources can be utilized effectively.

In many ways, project management exists at the intersection between the technical and social worldviews. Therefore, project management researchers are exploring complexity from both computational and cognitive perspectives. Computational modeling and postproject analysis, revealing the existence of nonlinear and emergent characteristics, can demonstrate that the project is behaving as a complex adaptive system. Cognitive approaches are likely to become the preferred basis for development of practical assessment and early warning tools. This is because cognitive methods accommodate the subjective perceptions and capabilities of the people associated, which are likely to differ for each project.

The real test of a theory is its impact on practice, and then time will tell whether complexity theory produces a suite of tools and approaches for complex projects, which will assist project managers to tackle the seemingly impossible.

References

P115, line 3. Morris, P. W. G. (2006). How do we learn to manage projects better? In H. Smyth & S. Pryke, *Managing complex projects: A relationship approach* (pp. 58–77). London, England: Blackwell.

P115, line 12. IT-Cortex. (2010). Project failures. Retrieved from www.it-cortex.com/Examples_f.htm

P116, line 13; P122, line 4. Remington, K., Zolin, R., & Turner, R. (2009, October). *A model of project complexity: Distinguishing dimensions of complexity from severity.* Paper presented at IRNOP IX Conference, Berlin, Germany.

P116, line 13. Turner, J. R., Zolin, R., & Remington, K. (2009, October). *Modelling success on complex projects: Multiple perspectives over multiple time frames.* Paper presented at the *IRNOP IX Conference,* Berlin, Germany.

P116, line 14; P117, line 35. Remington, K., & Pollack, J. (2007). *Tools for complex projects.* Aldershot, UK: Gower Publishing Company.

P116, line 24; P116, line 38. Kauffmann, S. A. (1993). *The origins of order: Self-organization and selection in evolution.* New York, NY: Oxford University Press.

P116, line 24. Kauffmann, S. A. (1995). Escaping the red queen effect. *The McKinsey Quarterly, 1,* 119–129. and Stewart, I. (1989). *Does God play dice? The mathematics of chaos.* Oxford, UK: Blackwell.

P116, line 25; P123, line 3. Stacey, R. D. (1991). *The chaos frontier.* Oxford, UK: Butterworth-Heinemann. and Stacey, R. D. (1992). *Managing the unknowable.* San Francisco, CA: Jossey-Bass. and Stacey, R. D. (1996). Management and the science of complexity: If organizational life is nonlinear, can business strategies prevail? *Research Technology Management, 39*(3), 8–10. and Snowden, D. F., & Boone, M. E. (2007). A leader's framework for decision making. *Harvard Business Review,* 69-76.

P116, line 26; P125, line 18. Rosenhead, J. (1998). Complexity theory and management practice. *Science as Culture.* Retrieved from http://human-nature.com/science-as-culture/rosenhead.html

P116, line 34; P122, line 27. Clift, T. B., & Vandenbosch, M. B. (1999). Project complexity and efforts to reduce product development cycle time. *Journal of Business Research, 45*(2), 187–198.

P116, line 34. Payne, J. H., & Turner, J. R. (1999). Company-wide project management: The planning and control of programmes of projects of different type. *International Journal of Project Management, 17*(1), 55–59.

P116, line 34; P122, line 8. Turner, J. R., & Cochrane, R. A. (1993). Goals-and-methods matrix: Coping with projects with ill defined goals and/or methods of achieving them. *International Journal of Project Management, 11*(2), 93–102. and Shenhar, A. J. (2001). One size does not fit all projects: Exploring classical contingency domains. *Management Science, 47*(3), 394–414.

P116, line 41. Stewart, I. (1989). *Does God play dice? The mathematics of chaos.* Oxford, UK: Blackwell.

P117, line 15. Whitty, S. J., & Maylor, H. M. (2009). And then came complex project management (revised). *International Journal of Project Management, 27*(3), 304–310.

P117, lines 16, 40. Cilliers, P. (1998). *Complexity and postmodernism: Understanding complex systems.* London, England: Routledge.

P117, line 32. Checkland, P. (1981). *Systems thinking, systems practice.* Chichester, UK: John Wiley & Sons.

P117, line 33. Kerzner, H. (2005). *Project management: A systems approach to planning, scheduling and controlling,* New York, NY: John Wiley and Sons.

P117, line 35; P126, line 37. Alderman, N., & Ivory, C. (2007). Partnering in major contracts: Paradox and metaphor. *International Journal of Project Management, 25*(4):386–393.

P117, line 35. Aritua, B., Smith, N. J., & Bower, D. A. (2009). Construction client multi-projects: A complex adaptive systems perspective. *International Journal of Project Management, 27*(1), 72–79. and Baccarini, D. (1996). The concept of project complexity: A review. *International Journal of Project Management, 14*(4), 201–204. and Cooke-Davies, T., Cicmil, S., Crawford, L., & Richardson, K. (2007). We're not in Kansas anymore, Toto: Mapping the strange landscape of complexity theory, and its relationship to project management. *Project Management Journal, 38*(2), 50–61. and Danilovic, M., & Browning, T. (2007). Managing complex product development projects with design structure matrices and domain mapping matrices. *International Journal of Project Management, 25*(3), 300–314.

P117, line 35; P122, line 9. Pundir, A. K., Ganapathy, L., & Sambandam, N. (2007). Towards a complexity framework for managing projects. *E: CO, 9*(4), 17–25.

P117, line 37. Kauffmann, S. A. (1993). *The origins of order: Self-organization and selection in evolution.* New York, NY: Oxford University Press.

P118, line 8. Simon, H. A. (1962). *The architecture of complexity.* (Reprinted from *The sciences of the artificial,* 1982). Cambridge, MA: MIT Press.

P118, line 9; P121, line 15; P126, line 34. Ackermann, F., & Eden, C. (2001, August). Using causal mapping with computer based group support system technology for eliciting an understanding of failure in complex projects: Some implications for organizational research. *American Academy of Management Conference,* Washington, DC, USA.

P118, line 9; P121, line 21. Williams, T. M. (1999). The need for new paradigms for complex projects. *International Journal of Project Management, 17*(5), 269–273.

P118, line 9; P121, line 15; P122, lines 5, 8, 27; P126, line 34. Williams, T. M. (2002). *Modelling complex projects.* London, England: John Wiley & Sons, Ltd.

P118, line 44; P121, line 15; P126, line 34. Ackermann, F., Eden, C., & Williams, T. (1997). Modelling for litigation: Mixing qualitative and quantitative approaches. *Interfaces, 27*(2), 48–65. and Ivory, C., & Alderman, N. (2005). Can project management learn anything from studies of failure in complex systems? *Project Management Journal, 36*(3), 5–16. and Maytorena, E., Winch, G., Freeman, J., & Kiely, T. (2007). The influence of experience and information search styles on project risk identification performance. *IEEE Transactions on Engineering Management, 1*(2), 315–325.

P119, Figure 9-1. Remington, K. (2011). *Leadership for complex projects.* Aldershot, UK: Gower Publishing (in press).

P119, line 12. Palmer, T. (2008). Edward Norton Lorenz. *Physics Today, 61*(9), 81–82.

P120, Figure 9-2; P121, line 22; P123, line 18. Remington, K., & Pollack, J. (2007). *Tools for complex projects.* Aldershot, UK: Gower Publishing Company.

P121, line 3. Langton, C. G. (1990). Computation at the edge of chaos. *Physica D, 42.* and Crutchfield, J. P., & Young, K. (1990). Computation at the onset of chaos. In W. Zurek (Ed.), *Complexity, entropy, and the physics of information* (Vol. VIII) (pp. 223–269). Reading, MA: Addison-Wesley.

P121, line 4. Schroeder, M. R. (1991). *Fractals, chaos, power laws: Minutes from an infinite paradise.* New York, NY: W.H. Freeman.

P121, line 15; P122, line 5; P126, line 34. Williams, T. M. (2005). Assessing and moving on from the dominant project management discourse in the light of project overruns. *IEEE Transactions on Engineering Management, 52*(4), 497–508.

P121, line 19; P121, line 23. Bosch-Rekveldt, M. G. C., & Mooi, H. G. (2008, October). *Research into project complexity classification methods.* Paper presented at IPMA Research conference, Rome, Italy.

P121, line 21. Santana, G. (1990). Classification of construction projects by scales of complexity. *International Journal of Project Management, 8*(2), 102–104. and D' Herbemont, O., & César, B. (1998). *Managing sensitive projects: A lateral approach.* London, England: Macmillan Press Ltd.

P121, line 22. Commonwealth of Australia (Department of Defence), College of Complex Project Managers and Defence Materiel Organisation. (2006). *Competency standard for complex project managers,* Public release version 2.0. Available from http://www.defence.gov.au/dmo/proj_man/Complex_PM_v2.0.pdf. and Hass, K. (2007). Introducing the project complexity model: A new approach to diagnosing and managing projects—part 1 of 2. *PM World Today, IX*(VII), 1–8. and Vidal, L-A., & Marle, F. (2008). Understanding project complexity: Implications on project management. *Kybernetes, 37*(8), 1094–2001.

P121, line 23. Maylor, H., Vidgen, R., & Carver, S. (2008). Managerial complexity in project based operations: A grounded model and its implications for practice. *Project Management Journal, 39*(S1), S15–S26.

P121, line 43. Geraldi, J., & Adlbrecht, G. (2007). On faith, fact, and interaction in projects. *Project Management Journal, 38*(1), 32–43. and Geraldi, J. (2008). Patterns of complexity: The thermometer of complexity. *Project Perspectives 2008, The Annual Publication of IPMA,* 4–9.

P121, line 43; P122, line 13. Müller, R., & Geraldi, J. G. (2007). *Linking complexity and leadership competences of project managers.* Paper presented at the IRNOP VIII Conference, Brighton, UK.

P122, line 5. De Meyer, A., Loch, C. H., & Pich, M. T. (2002). Managing project uncertainty: From variation to chaos. *MIT Sloan Management Review, 43*(2), 60-67. and Loch, C. H., De Meyer, A., & Pich, M. T. (2006). *Managing the unknown: A new approach to managing high uncertainty and risk in projects.* Hoboken, NJ: John Wiley & Sons.

P122, line 8. Payne, J. (1995). Management of multiple simultaneous projects: A state-of-the-art review. *International Journal of Project Management, 13*(3), 163–168.

P122, line 9. Taikonda, M. V., & Rosenthal, S. R. (2000). Technological novelty, project complexity, and product development project execution success: A deeper look at task uncertainty in product innovation. *IEEE Transactions on Engineering Management, 47*(1), 74–87.

P122, line 15. Kokotivich, V., & Remington, K. (2008, October). *Enhancing innovative capabilities: Developing creative thinking approaches with tomorrow's project managers.* Paper presented at IRNOP Conference, Brighton, UK.

P122, line 17. Jones, R., & Deckro, R. (1993). The social psychology of project management conflict. *European Journal of Operational Research, 64*(2), 216–228.

P122, line 19. Williams, T. M. (1994). Managing risk in development and initial production. *International Journal of Production Research, 32*(7), 1591–1597.

P122, line 27. Clift, T. B., & Vandenbosch, M. B. (1999). Project complexity and efforts to reduce product development cycle time. *Journal of Business Research, 45*(2), 187–198.

P122, line 31. Lundin, R., Söderholm, A., & Wilson, T. (2001). *On conceptualization of time in projects.* Paper presented at the Nordic Conference on Project Management, Uppsala University, Uppsala, Sweden.

P122, line 33. Brown, S., & Eisenhardt, K. (1997). The art of continuous change: Linking complexity theory and time-paced evolution in relentlessly shifting organizations. *Administrative Science Quarterly, 42*(1), 1–34. and Eisenhardt, K. M. (1999). Making fast strategic decisions in high-velocity environments. *Academy of Management Journal, 32*(3), 543–576. and Söderlund, J. (2002). Managing complex development projects: Arenas, knowledge processes and time. *R&D Management, 32*(5), 419–430.

P122, line 34. Söderlund, J. (2010). Knowledge entrainment and project management: The case of large-scale transformation projects. *International Journal of Project Management, 28*(2), 130–141. and Gärling, T., Gillholm, R., & Montgomery, W. (1999). The role of anticipated time pressure in activity scheduling. *Transportation, 26*(2), 173–191.

P122, line 38. Salazar-Kish, J. M. (2001). Modeling concurrency tradeoffs and their effects on project duration and rework [Doctoral dissertation, Stanford University].

P122, line 41. Gersick, C. J. G. (1988). Time and transition in work teams: Toward a new model of group development. *Academy of Management Journal, 31*(1), 9–41.

P122, line 43. Carr, A. (2006). *Space and time and organization change,* Bradford, UK: Emerald Group Publishing Limited.

P122, line 45. Cohen, I. (2008). Improving time-critical decision making in life-threatening situations: Observations and insights. *Decision Analysis, 5*(2),

100–110. and Maule, A. J., & Svenson, O. (Eds.). (1993). Time pressure and stress in human judgment and decision making. New York, NY: Plenum.

P123, line 3. Kahane, A. (2004). *Solving tough problems: An open way of talking, listening, and creating new realities.* San Francisco, CA: Berrett-Koehler Publishers.

P123, line 4. Luhmann, N. (1995). *Social systems.* Stanford, CA: Stanford University Press. and Laufer, A., Gordon, R. D., & Shenhar, A. J. (1996). Simultaneous management: The key to excellence in capital projects. *International Journal of Project Management, 14*(4), 189–199.

P123, line 5. Müller, R., & Turner, J. R. (2007). Matching the project manager's leadership style to project type. *International Journal of Project Management, 25*(1), 21–32.

P123, line 10. Keegan, A. E., & Hartog, den D.N. (2004). Transformational leadership in a project-based environment: A comparative study of the leadership styles of project managers and line managers. *International Journal of Project Management, 22*(8), 609–618.

P123, line 25. Hällgren, M., & Maaninen-Olssen, E. (2005). Deviation, ambiguity, and uncertainty in a project-intensive organization. *Project Management Journal, 36*(3), 17–26.

P123, line 27. Thomas, J., & Mengel, T. (2008). Preparing project managers to deal with complexity: Advanced project management education. *International Journal of Project Management, 26*(3), 304–315.

P123, lines 29, 32. Chia, R. (1997). Process philosophy and management learning: Cultivating 'foresight' in management education. In J. Burgoyne & M. Reynolds (Eds.), *Management learning* (pp. 71-88). London, England: Sage Publications.

P124, lines 6, 16. Biggiero, L. (2001). Sources of complexity in human systems. *Nonlinear Dynamics, Psychology and Life Sciences, 5*(1), 3–19.

P124, lines 9, 34. Bateson, G. (1980). *Mind and nature.* New York, NY: Bantam Books.

P124, line 9. Foerster, von H. (1984). Principles of self-organization in a socio-managerial context. In H. Ulrich & G. J. B. Probst (Eds.), *Self-organization and management of social systems (pp. 2–24).* Berlin, Germany: Springer.

P124, lines 10, 28. Fioretti, G., & Visser, B. (2004). A cognitive interpretation of organizational complexity. *E: CO Special Double Issue, 6*(1-2), 11–23. and Rescher, R. (1998). *Complexity: A philosophical overview.* New Brunswick, NJ: Freeman & Co. and Simon, H. A. (1962). *The architecture of complexity.* (Reprinted from *The sciences of the artificial,* 1982). Cambridge, MA: MIT Press.

P124, line 17. Arrecchi, F. T. (2003). Complexity and emergence of meaning. In V. Benci, P. Cerrai, P. Fregugulia, , G. Israel, & C. Pellegrini (Eds.), *Determinism, Holism and Complexity* (pp. 3–26). New York, NY: Kluwer Academic/Plenum Publishers.

P124, line 17; P125, line 2. McLain, D. (2009). Quantifying project characteristics related to uncertainty. *Project Management Journal, 40*(4), 60–73.

P124, line 25. Moldoveanu, M. (2004). An intersubjective measure of organisational complexity: A new approach to the study of complexity in organizations. *Emergence: Complexity and Organization, 6*(3), 9–16.

P124, line 41; P125, line 11. Grenier, S., Barrette, A.-M., & Ladouceur, R. (2005). Intolerance of uncertainty and intolerance of ambiguity: Similarities and differences. *Personality and Individual Differences, 39*(3), 593–600.

P124, line 41. Remington, K., Zolin, R., & Turner, R. (2009, October). *A model of project complexity: Distinguishing dimensions of complexity from severity.* Paper presented at IRNOP IX Conference, Berlin, Germany.

P125, line 19. Rosenhead, J., & Mingers, J. (Eds.). (2001). *Rational analysis for a problematic world revisited: Problem structuring methods for complexity, uncertainty and conflict.* Chichester, UK. John Wiley and Son.

P125, line 25. Brodbeck, M. (1968). Models, meaning, and theories. In M. Brodbeck (Ed.), *Readings in the philosophy of the social sciences* (pp. 579–600). New York, NY: Macmillan.

P125, line 35. Kauffmann, S. A. (1993). *The origins of order: Self-organization and selection in evolution.* New York, NY: Oxford University Press.

P125, line 36. Krugman, P. (1996). *The self-organizing economy.* Cambridge, MA: Blackwell.

P125, lines 38, 44. Rosenhead, J. (1998). Complexity theory and management practice. *Science as Culture.* Retrieved from http://human-nature.com/science-as-culture/rosenhead.html

P126, line 10. Ruelle, D. (1991). *Chance and chaos.* Princeton, NJ: Princeton University Press.

P126, line 15. Hall, N. (1991). *The new scientist guide to chaos.* London, England: Penguin.

P126, line 29. Foerster, von H. (1984). Principles of self-organization in a socio-managerial context. In H. Ulrich & G. J. B. Probst (Eds.), *Self-organization and management of social systems (pp. 2–24).* Berlin, Germany: Springer.

P126, line 30. Alvesson, M., & Berg, P. O. (1992). *Corporate culture and organizational symbolism.* Berlin, Germany: de Gruyter. and Weick, K. E. (1995). *Sensemaking in organizations.* Beverly Hills, CA: Sage.

P127, line 9. Stacey, R. D. (1993). *Strategic management and organizational dynamics.* London, England: Pitman.

P127, line 14. Stacey, R. D. (1996). Management and the science of complexity: If organizational life is nonlinear, can business strategies prevail? *Research Technology Management, 39*(3), 8–10.

P127, line 20. Williams, T. M. (2005). Assessing and moving on from the dominant project management discourse in the light of project overruns. *IEEE Transactions on Engineering Management, 52*(4), 497–508.

Casti, J. L. (1994). *Complexification.* New York, NY: HarperCollins.

Williams, T. M. (2004). Why Monte Carlo simulations of project networks can mislead. *Project Management Journal, 25*(3), 53–61.

Chapter 10

Systems Thinking and the Systems Movement

Peter Checkland and Terry Williams

Overview

The word "system" is usually understood to refer to a set of elements joined together to make a complex whole. The word may be used to refer to an abstract whole (the principles constituting a system of justice, say,) or a physical whole (a railway engine); but, in both cases, the justification for using the word is the same: The whole is seen as having properties that make it "more than the sum of its parts." This is the everyday language expression of the idea of "emergent properties"—that is to say properties, which have no meaning in terms of the parts, that make up the whole. Thus, a heap consisting of the individual parts of a bicycle does not have vehicular potential. However, when the parts are linked together in a particular structure to make the bicycle as a whole, which does have the potential to get someone with the ability to ride from A to B, that is an emergent property of the bicycle as a whole.

The idea of emergent properties is the single most fundamental systems idea and to use this (and other) systems ideas in a conscious organized way is to do some "systems thinking." To use systems thinking to tackle some perceived problem is to take "a systems approach" to it. Since the field of management deals with complex matters, and systems thinking has been developed to cope with complexity, it is not surprising to find systems thinking closely associated with the field. Indeed, many systems ideas and several versions of both systems thinking and a systems approach have all been developed in work on management problems.

This chapter will review the origin and nature of systems thinking and describe a number of varieties of it as they have been developed to tackle problems in the management field.

The Origins of Systems Thinking

Around the turn of the century, when biologists were considering the fundamental nature of their science, a school of thought arose, which argued that biology's object of concern was the living organism as a whole. It was suggested by these "organismic" biologists that the science should develop by creating descriptions of the basic processes, which characterize a living organism, processes of growth and decay and so on. They developed the concept of an organism as an "open" entity, which exchanges materials, energy, and information with an environment to which it can adapt (a metaphor that has been much taken up in organization theory). Beginning in the 1940s, Ludwig von Bertalanffy argued that the ideas about organisms that he and his colleagues had developed could in fact be applied to wholes of any kind: to "systems" in general. This initiated systems thinking in a formal sense and in 1954, the first institution in this new field was set up. This was the Society for General Systems Research (SGSR), committed to the development of a general system(s) theory (GST), which could be applied within any field where phenomena concerned with organized complexity were studied. The pioneers hoped that communications between different scientific fields would be helped by such theory.

These aspirations of the pioneers have not been fulfilled; rather, systems thinking has been developed within particular fields, although the outcomes continue to provide, in systems ideas, a language applicable within many different disciplines. This means that as a field, systems has the same status as mathematics: it is a meta-discipline, a language, which can be used to talk about the subject matter of other areas. Thus, for example, there are systems thinking geographers, sociologists and management scientists, and other geographers, sociologists and management scientists who do not use the systems language.

The Nature of Systems Thinking

Throughout the systems' literature, the core image or concept upon which systems thinking is based is that of the adaptive whole. The concept is of some whole entity (which may be seen as a whole because it has emergent properties) existing in an environment that may change and so deliver shocks to it. The adaptive whole may then survive in the changing environment if it can adapt to the changes.

Ordinary everyday experience offers many examples of this process, which is what makes systems thinking intuitively attractive. For example, when the temperature of our environment rises, our bodies open pores and produce sweat, which evaporates and helps to cool us down. The Boy Scouts movement has survived for more than one hundred years, but it is not the same organization created by its founder. It has adapted to a changing society. Furthermore, manufacturing companies using oil as a raw material had to change their policies and operations very rapidly when the price of oil increased fourfold between 1973 and 1974 and then doubled again in 1979, if they were to survive in their changed economic environment. All these happenings can be expressed in systems language. They represent the behavior of entities that may be treated as if they were adaptive wholes.

In order to describe something as an adaptive whole, four fundamental ideas are needed. First, the whole will be seen as a system (rather than simply as an aggregate) if an observer can identify some emergent properties of it as an entity. Second, the whole system may contain parts which are themselves smaller wholes (or "sub-systems"). Thus, the human body can be regarded as a system but also, within it, subsystems such as the respiratory system or the blood-circulation system can be identified. This means that systems thinking postulates a layered or hierarchical structure in which systems, part of wider systems, may themselves contain sub-systems, which may contain sub-subsystems, and so on. Finally, if a system is to survive in a changing environment, it must have the processes of communication and control. It must be able to sense the change in the environment and adopt a suitable response in the form of some "control action." In our bodies, many such actions are automatic, as when our core temperature is maintained within quite narrow limits. In designed systems, engineers have to create mechanisms, which keep performance within chosen limits, Watt's governor controlling the speed of a steam engine being the paradigm example.

With the four concepts of emergent properties, a layered structure and processes of communication and control a very wide range of wholes may be described as systems capable (within limits) of surviving in a changing environment. Systems thinking applies these ideas to a wide range of observed features of the world, the purpose being, in general, either to understand the world better or to intervene to improve some part of it.

Three broad categories of work can be seen in which the idea of an adaptive whole has been developed and exploited. Biologists and, especially, ecologists study the wholes that nature creates, which are often referred to as "natural systems," for example, frogs, forests, and the biosphere of the planet. Engineers, on the other hand, create "designed systems"—systems planned to exhibit some desirable emergent properties and to survive under a range of environmental conditions. Note also that designed systems may be abstract rather than concrete, as in systems of philosophy or a set of connected principles (as in, say, a "design philosophy").

It is the third broad area of systems thinking, however, which is of greatest interest to those studying the problems of management. For example, it was realized in the 1970s in action research which tackled messy real world problem situations, that a connected set of human activities, joined together to make a purposeful whole could, with the addition of a monitoring and control sub-system, be treated as a new kind of system. Models of such systems can be built and used to explore real world purposeful action. This yields a wide-ranging approach to the problems within and between organizations, since the taking of purposeful action is a ubiquitous characteristic of human affairs at many different levels, from the short-term tactical to the long-term strategic and over many time scales.

These three broad categories of work are all similar in that they exhibit the key characteristic of systems thinking, namely the conscious use of systems concepts, especially that of the adaptive whole, to understand some phenomena in the world or to guide intervention aimed at improvement. In more technical language, systems ideas provide an epistemology within which what counts as knowledge for the systems thinker will be defined.

The Evolution of the Systems Movement in the Field of Management

The systems movement has evolved steadily since the late 1940s when GST emerged. In the 1950s, much of the work done was of a practical kind and represented the application to civilian situations of the lessons learned from the development of operations research (OR) during the World War II.

The application of the lessons learned in wartime or to postwar activity in industrial and other organizations led to a number of organized forms of inquiry and problem solving. Bell Telephone Laboratories, for example, formalized their approach to new technology projects in "systems engineering"; and the RAND Corporation developed "systems analysis." When the first mainframe computers became available, the analysis needed to design and establish a computer system drew on the same set of ideas.

This was the dominant systems thinking in management in the 1950s and 1960s. Its essence was to define very carefully a desirable objective or need, to examine possible alternative systems that might achieve the objective or meet the need, and to select among the alternatives, paying great attention to formulating the criteria upon which selection is based. This is what is now known as "hard" systems thinking, a systematic approach to achieving defined objectives.

It was in the 1970s and 1980s that a more systemic use of systems ideas was developed in a program of action research aimed at finding better ways of tackling the kind of ill-structured problem situations in the real world in which objectives are multiple, ambiguous, and conflicting. This produced what is now known as "soft systems methodology" (SSM), a much-used complementary approach to that of systems engineering/systems analysis. Many practitioners around the world have contributed to this development of so-called "soft" systems thinking.

SSM is a learning system, a system of inquiry. It makes use of models of purposeful human activity, each based on a particular, declared, worldview (since purposeful activity seen as "freedom fighting" by one observer may be interpreted as "terrorism" by another). These models are used as intellectual devices to explore problematical situations. Comparing models with the perceived real world structures a debate about change, a debate that seeks accommodations between conflicting interests and enables "action to improve" to be taken.

The difference between "hard" and "soft" systems thinking lies in how systems thinking is used. In the hard mode, the world is assumed to contain systems; and they can be "engineered" to work effectively. In the "soft" mode, the world is taken to be problematical, but it is assumed that the process of inquiry into it can be organized as a system. It is this shift of systemicity, from the world to the process of inquiry into the world, which marks the hard/soft distinction. In practical terms, the "hard" approaches are appropriate where objectives or needs are well-defined, and the "soft" approaches in "messier" situations.

More recently, Ulrich's development of the work of Churchman has drawn attention to the need, where practical social planning is concerned, to open up the proposals of experts to examination by lay persons who will be affected by what the planners design. Ulrich's "critical heuristics" stresses that every definition of a problem and every choice of a system to design and implement will contain normative assumptions, which need to be teased out and subjected to critical scrutiny. The aim is to enable practical uses of systems thinking to be emancipatory for both those who are involved and those who are affected.

Varieties of Systems Thinking

It is not possible to cover all the many varieties of systems thinking in one chapter. However, it is possible to define a set of categories that at least enables us to make sense of any version of systems thinking which we may come across, whether in the literature of the past, in present practice, or in potential future developments. The categories that make this possible are shown in Figure 10-1.

It is important to see Figure 10-1 not as a map of systems work but as a way of making sense of the wide range of examples of such work. Any actual use of systems ideas may draw on several categories; but it will be describable using these categories. It will be useful to give some examples.

Thus, area 1 in Figure 10-1 would include the development of cybernetics, which its pioneer Wiener called the entire field of control and communication theory whether in the machine or in the animal. Many people have used cybernetics within area 2.1, and users of organizational cybernetics could do so in several ways, consciously using the cybernetic model either as an account of the real world (area 2.11) or as a device to explore complex reality (area 2.12) or, indeed, both.

Similarly, a study in an organization, using SSM, part of area 2.12, might well reach the conclusion that, say, a system to control product quality to meet certain criteria ought to be set up. Designing and implementing such a system might then be done using the approach of hard systems engineering, area 2.11. As a final example, a RAND-style study using, say, cost-benefit analysis to help managers facing a major policy decision (area 2.13) would be enriched by placing the decision in question in a systems context such as could be provided by soft systems thinking.

The systems literature contains more than enough accounts of systems approaches in the management field. This chapter concentrates on methodologies that have been used extensively, that have generated secondary literature, and that have been shown to be transferable from the pioneers to other groups of users. Several have been described earlier: systems engineering, RAND systems analysis, SSM,

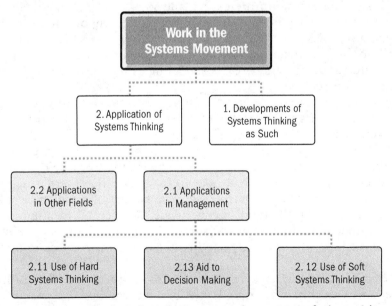

Figure 10-1: Categories that can make sense of the wide range of work within the systems movement

and critical heuristics. This section will end with brief indications of eight other approaches that have had a significant impact on management practice.

1. Studying inventory problems in manufacturing companies, Forrester developed a simple way of modeling material storage and flows governed by policy criteria. This "industrial dynamics," as it was first called, was later generalized to "system dynamics" (SD) and extended well outside the field of inventory problems. SD modeling was the basis of the world models, which were in vogue in the 1970s. The SD community flourishes and has its own journal and conferences. (Later material in this chapter will expand this basic account of an important version of systems thinking in action.)

2. When the technology of the U.K. coal mining industry changed radically in the 1950s, the change affected not only the technical aspects of winning coal from a harsh environment but the whole social structure of the industry. Studying this, the researchers from the Tavistock Institute proposed a "sociotechnical system" as an explanatory device. Based upon viewing an organization as an open system in interaction with its environment, the sociotechnical model makes technology, social system, and environment interdependent: you cannot change one without changing all. This has been a very influential concept, a mainstream of thinking in organization theory of a functionalist kind, concerned to explain how the parts of an organization contribute to a coherent whole.

3. After 40 years of experience in the world of affairs, Sir Geoffrey Vickers sought in retirement to make sense of what he had experienced. He found systems thinking helpful and developed his theory of "appreciative systems" as an epistemology of the social process. In an "appreciative system," we notice certain features of our world as significant, as a result of our previous experience. We discriminate and judge such features using standards of good/bad, interesting/uninteresting, and so on, and we take action in terms of managing networks of relationships that are important to us. However, in doing so, the *source* of the standards is the previous history of the system itself, so that our social world continuously reconstructs itself out of its own past. Interest in Vickers' work is spreading as its relevance to modern management is perceived.

4. In his "interactive planning," Ackoff argues for a systems approach to societal problems. His influential work is based on the idea that the real world is characterized not by "problems" but by "systems of problems" or "messes" and requires a highly participative approach based on planning. He describes five interacting phases, planning for ends, means to those ends, resourcing achievement of ends, organizational arrangements necessary to achieve them and implementation and control, the latter being important since all outputs call for revision in the light of experience. The central idea is to start from an imagined ideal future for a system being planned for, one which ignores all constraints. The effort is then directed to getting as close to that ideal as possible.

5. Though Wiener's original cybernetics focused on the nature of control systems, whether in machines or animals, the best-known work on organizational or management cybernetics was that of Beer, which extends that concept. He developed a sophisticated model, the viable systems model (VSM), which has five

interacting subsystems. He argued that these subsystems are necessary and sufficient for the survival of an autonomous whole in its environment. In terms of an organization, system one is a set of operational elements, which make up an organizational entity; system two is an anti-oscillatory mechanism; system three is the management unit responsible for system one, internally, now; system four is responsible for the external and future; and system five is for monitoring the three-four interaction. The sophistication of the model lies in its never-ending, recursive nature: systems two, three, four, and five constitute the system one of another level. Many managers have made use of the VSM in understanding and ordering their organizations.

6. There is ongoing interest in the implications of a systems model created by Maturana and Varela to make sense of living systems. Their autopoietic (self-producing) model has elements whose action creates the system itself as a stable pattern of relations. They had reservations about applying the model to a social whole, such as an organization, but it is proving to be at least a rich metaphor for thinking about organizational phenomena.

7. Not surprisingly, the field of information systems has seen much use of systems thinking. This approach has been helpful in distinguishing information systems (IS) from information technology (IT): IS being the "what" and IT is the "how." Checkland and Holwell provide a systems-thinking-based account of the field as a whole in which IS are human systems which attribute meaning to data which computers can efficiently manipulate and process in systems based on IT.

8. Finally, there has recently been something of a rediscovery of systems ideas by some academics under the banner of "Complexity Theory." Many a *problematique* in the real world can be viewed as a "complex adaptive system," and some of the resulting insights from this approach are reviewed in Chapter 9.

The Future of Systems Thinking

In everyday language, we casually speak of "the legal system," "the education system," and "healthcare systems" as if these were systems unequivocally existing in the world. In fact, these features of our world reveal imperfect versions of systemic properties as these have been defined in the field of systems. Everyday language uses system to mean simply some complex whole. Systems thinking has supplied a variety of accounts of that complexity and has created an epistemology and a language that can be used to discuss many different phenomena: natural or designed, concrete or abstract. "System" properly used is the name of a concept that may or may not map the world as we experience it.

In the past, most work in the systems movement followed everyday language in assuming the world to consist of interacting systems. More recently, emphasis has been on using the systems language to try to make sense of the world as we experience it, in particular modeling processes rather than entities.

Helped by the ease and density of instant communication, old boundaries dissolve and former taken-as-given hierarchies become irrelevant. Managers increasingly need to "read" their world as if it were a text that can be interpreted in multiple ways. The crucial management skill remains that of making sense of the complexity faced. Process modeling based on systems thinking offers a powerful tool for managers in the future.

System Dynamics

The first half of this chapter described systems thinking generally and the benefits of systems thinking. This has covered a wide variety of accounts of the complexities of the world.

The remainder of this chapter takes one particular account, which takes a relatively well-defined view of a complex project and attempts to structure then quantify that structure. This method is known as system dynamics (SD), and it is well known as a means of understanding the complexities of projects (a good review of literature up to 1996 is given by Rodrigues & Bowers, 1996).

These models originated from the operational research world, but with two differences. First, there are aspects that are of increasing importance in understanding the behavior of projects, with which conventional models do not deal—the "softer" variables that are more difficult to quantify. Forrester, the inventor of system dynamics, spoke against "...the omission of admittedly highly significant factors (most of the 'intangible' influences on decisions) because these are unmeasured or unmeasurable. To omit such variables is equivalent to saying they have zero effect...probably the only value that is known to be wrong." Postmortem research on projects has often shown that these soft variables are often the very variables that determine the project behavior, and it is the omission that causes the project models to become less acceptable. Williams devoted a whole chapter to case studies of these effects, which include the following:

- The effects caused by the project client, including scope changes and multiplicities of scope changes, delays, requirement to do extra supporting work, interference, the effect of client-contractor trust and so on.
- The effects of management decisions during the project.
- Subjective effects within the workforce, such as morale, schedule pressure, the effects of overtime and overcrowding and so on.

Second, management, of course, does not sit idly by during a project but takes actions to try to bring late running or overspending actions under control, and it is these that require a new way of modeling.

Our understanding of how complex projects behave has developed in recent years, particularly through the work of two teams. The first is based at Strathclyde University, Glasgow, Scotland. Eden, Williams, Ackermann, and Howick have been involved in postmortem analysis of a range of projects. Eden and Ackermann had already developed cognitive/causal mapping techniques, which were immediately appropriate to study structures of causality in a project, which could be combined with system dynamics to produce quantitative results. The techniques used on the first claim, the Channel Tunnel "shuttle" train-wagons, are described by Ackermann, Eden, and Williams, and all successive claims have been characterized by the use of these techniques. Explanations for project behavior derive from systemic inter-related sets of causal effects; and in particular, where overruns turn into catastrophic overspends can frequently be traced to dynamics set up by these effects turning into positive feedback loops, or vicious circles.

Perhaps the most important way such loops are set up and exacerbated is through management response to project perturbations, hence, the sometimes counterintuitive effect of such actions. Eden, Williams, Ackermann, and Howick described some of these effects, as does Williams, Eden, Ackermann, and Tait for the shuttle project (drawing some simple feedback-loop diagrams). These describe how feedback structures can be set up and how they can highly magnify small effects in a project. A key lesson here is that a major cause of feedback, and thus badly failed projects, is management action taken to accelerate a time-constrained project after a delay. Here, mathematical models have made a considerable contribution in being able to demonstrate and quantify effects that are intuitively unexpected but which correspond well both to empirical evidence and experience.

The other team (the first to begin chronologically) is Cooper and others at PA Consulting, who also used SD. The lessons learned have been similar and in parallel. This work began more than 20 years ago, and has analyzed project behavior in various domains. Cooper, Lyneis, and Bryant pointed to a number of factors that inhibit successful project analysis, including "the difficulty in determining the true causes of project performance." They also discussed feedback structures as the root of the complexity, but point to three particular structures that they say generally underlie project dynamics: the re-work cycle (including discovery of unexpected rework), feedback effects on productivity and work quality, and knock-on effects from upstream phases to downstream phases.

Thus, simply mapping out the causality involved in the effects of a project can reveal many of the reasons for complexity. Ramified chains of effects, which ripple out to cover many of the aspects of the project, can show the systemicity involved that it is difficult to see intuitively. Then as soon as the ramified chains meet up with their starting points to produce feedback loops (whether balancing "negative" feedback loops or positive "reinforcing" vicious circles or if they are unwanted or virtuous circles if they are good), complex behavior is displayed which would be difficult to understand without the explanations of the mapping. This can be useful in preproject risk analysis (to understand what might happen and what the "big" risks would be that would set off feedback or runaway behavior), in operational control of projects (which is less prevalent), or in our understanding of how projects have behaved and our ability to learn from them.

While powerful, these are qualitative arguments, and the validation necessary to convince the modeler that these are effective representations of the "real" project as experienced requires quantification. Causal modeling of the type described earlier does, however, lend itself naturally to quantification by system dynamics, which allows the flows and feedback loops within the causal models, including the soft effects, and the flow of information upon which actors within the project make their decisions, all to be modeled and calibrated. Howick, Eden, Ackermann, and Williams described a good process, based upon the causal modeling and then quantification of the behavior of projects. In this, qualitative cognitive maps or project cause maps, gained through interviews and workshops, aim to capture the key events that occurred on the project. Facilitated group workshops where participants can contribute directly (sometimes anonymously and simultaneously), to the construction of a cause map enable "piggy backing" off one another, triggering new memories and challenging views, and eventually developing together a comprehensive view of the whole project in the form of an integrated causal map. Technical analysis of this map enables the core/endogenous variables and trigger/exogenous variables to be identified and the map to be turned into a formal—and reduced—influence diagram and allows quantification into a system dynamics simulation model.

Analyzing the behavior of projects postmortem with the aid of system dynamics models reveals some interesting behavior that does not fit easily into conventional project management. Current project management practice and discourse is dominated by the "bodies of knowledge" or BoKs, which professional project management bodies consider to be the core knowledge of managing projects, presenting sets of normative procedures that appear to be self-evidently correct. However, there are three underlying assumptions to this discourse

- Project management is self-evidently correct: it is rationalist and normative.
- The ontological stance is effectively positivist.
- Project management is particularly concerned with managing scope in individual parts.

These three assumptions lead to three particular emphases in current project management discourse and thus in the BoKs:

- A heavy emphasis on planning.
- An implication of a very conventional control model.
- Project management is generally decoupled from the environment.

The SD modeling work provided explanations for why some projects severely overrun, which clash with these assumptions of the current dominant project management discourse.

- Unlike the third assumption, the SD models show behavior arising from the complex interactions of the various parts of the project, which would not be predicted from an analysis of the individual parts of the project.
- Against the first assumption, the SD models show project behavior that is complex and nonintuitive, with feedback exacerbated through management response to project perturbations, conventional methods provide unhelpful or even not beneficial advice and are not necessarily self-evidently correct.
- The second assumption is also challenged. First, the models differ from the BoKs in their emphasis on, or inclusion of, soft factors, often-important links in the chains of causality. Second, they show that the models need to incorporate not only "real" data but also management perceptions of data and capture the socially constructed nature of "reality" in a project.

The SD models tell us why failures occur in projects that exhibit complexity—that is, when they combine structural complexity—many parts in complex combinations and uncertainty in project goals and in the means to achieve those goals. Goal uncertainty in particular is lacking in the conventional project management discourse, and it is when uncertainty affects a traditionally managed project that is structurally complex that the systemic effects discussed above start to occur. But there is a third factor identified in the SD modeling. Frequently, events that compromise the plan occur at a faster rate than that at which it is practical to re-plan. When the project is heavily time constrained, the project manager feels forced to take acceleration actions. A structurally complex project, when perturbed by external uncertainties, can become unstable and difficult to manage. Often, time constraints accelerate actions and then management must make very fast and sometimes very many decisions, and the catastrophic over-runs described can occur.

Conventional techniques are designed for projects with large numbers of elements, but the assumed structures are subject to very limited types of interdependence, and conventional methods are even more unsuited to projects under high uncertainty. It is when uncertainty affects a traditionally managed, time-constrained project that is structurally complex that the systemic effects discussed start to occur. However, the systemic models demonstrated an important aspect: It is management actions to accelerate perturbed projects that particularly exacerbate the feedback. When the project is heavily time-constrained, the project manager feels forced to take acceleration actions, and this produces the problems from feedback. Thus, we have identified the three compounding factors that come together in complex structures of positive feedback to cause extreme overruns when projects are managed conventionally: structural complexity, uncertainty, and a tight time-constraint.

Work from different directions seeking to establish characteristics that cause complexity projects come up with similar characteristics. But the SD modeling explains how the tightness of the time-constraints strengthen the power of the feedback loops, which means that small problems or uncertainties cause unexpectedly large effects. It also shows how the type of underspecification identified by Flyvberg, Bruzelius, and Rothengatter brings what is sometimes called "double jeopardy"—underestimation (when the estimate is elevated to the status of a project control budget) causing feedback that causes much greater overspend than the degree of underestimation.

References

P136, line 4. Bertalanffy, L. V. (1968). *General system theory.* New York, NY: Braziller.

P137, line 27; P138, line 15. Checkland, P. (1981). *Systems thinking, systems practice.* Chichester: Wiley.

P138, line 2. Hall, A. D. (1962). *A methodology of systems engineering.* Princeton, NJ: Van Nostrand.

P138, line 3; P139, line 17. Optner, S. L. (Ed.). (1973). *Systems analysis.* Harmondsworth, UK: Penguin.

P138, line 33. Checkland, P., & Poulter, J. (2006). *Learning for action.* Chichester, UK: Wiley.

P138, line 34. Ulrich, W. (1983). *Critical heuristics of social planning.* Bern, Switzerland: Haupt. and Churchman, C. W. (1971). *The design of inquiring systems.* New York, NY: Basic Books.

P139, line 8; P140, line 45. Wiener, N. (1948). *Cybernetics [enlarged edition 1961].* Cambridge, MA: MIT Press, and New York, NY: J. Wiley.

P139, line 10; P140, line 47. Beer, S. (1979). *The heart of enterprise*. Chichester, UK: Wiley.

P140, line 3; P142, lines 15, 19. Forrester, J. W. (1961). *Industrial dynamics*. Cambridge, MA: MIT Press.

P140, line 8. Meadows, D. H., Meadows, D. L., Randers, R., & Behrens, W. (1972). *The limits to growth*. New York, NY: Universe Books.

P140, line 14. Trist, E. L., Higgin, G. W., Murray, H., & Pollock, A. B. (1963). *Organizational choice*. London, England: Tavistock Publications.

P140, line 25. Vickers, G. (1965). *The art of judgement*. London, England: Chapman and Hall.

P140, line 34. Ackoff, R. L. (1974). *Redesigning the future*. New York, NY: Wiley.

P141, line 12. Maturana, H., & Varela, F. (1980). *Autopoiesis and cognition: The realisation of the living*. Dordrecht, The Netherlands: Reidel.

P141, line 20. Checkland, P. & Holwell, S. (1998). *Information, systems, and information systems*. Chichester, UK: Wiley.

P141, line 25. Stacey, R. D., Griffin, D., & Shaw, P. (2000). *Complexity and management: Fad or radical challenge to systems thinking?* London, England: Routledge.

P142, line 9. Sterman, J. D. (2000). *Business dynamics: Systems thinking and modeling for a complex world*. Chicago, IL: Irwin/McGraw-Hill.

P142, line 11. Rodrigues, A., & Bowers, J. A. (1996). System dynamics in project management: A comparative analysis with the traditional methods. *Systems Dynamics Review, 12*(2), 121–139.

P142, line 22; P143, line 5. Williams, T. M. (2002). *Modelling complex projects*. London, England: Wiley.

P142, line 37. Eden, C., & Ackermann, F., (1998). *The journey of strategic change*. Chichester, UK: Sage.

P142, line 41. Ackermann, F., Eden, C., & Williams, T. (1997). Modeling for litigation: Mixing qualitative and quantitative approaches. *Interfaces, 27*(2), 48–65.

P143, line 5. Eden, C., Williams, T., Ackermann, F., & Howick, S. (2000). On the nature of disruption and delay (D&D) in major projects. *Journal of the Operational Research Society, 51*, 291–300.

P143, line 6. Williams, T., Eden, C., Ackermann, F., & Tait, A. (1995). The effects of design changes and delays on project costs. *Journal of the Operational Research Society, 46*(7), 809–818.

P143, line 16. Graham, A. K. (2000). Beyond PM 101: Lessons for managing large development programs. *Project Management Journal, 31*(1), 7–18. and Cooper, K. G. (1980). Naval ship production: A claim settled and a framework built. *Interfaces, 10*(6), 20–36.

P143, lines 17, 19. Cooper, K. G., Lyneis, J. M., & Bryant, B. J. (2002). Learning to learn, from past to future. *International Journal of Project Management, 20*(3), 213–219.

P143, line 23. Cooper, K. (1993). The rework cycle: Benchmarks for the project manager. *Project Management Journal, 24*(1), 17–21. and Lyneis, J. M., Cooper, K. G., & Els, S. A. (2001). Strategic management of complex projects: A case study using system dynamics. *Systems Dynamics Review, 17*(3), 237–260.

P143, lines 35, 44. Howick, S., Ackermann, F., Eden, C., & Williams, T. (2009). Understanding the causes and consequences of disruption and delay in complex projects: How system dynamics can help. In R. A. Meyers (Ed.), *Encyclopedia of complexity and system science* (Vol. 2, pp. 1845–1864). New York, NY: Springer Verlag.

P143, line 43. Howick, S., Eden, C., Ackermann, F., & Williams, T. (2008). Building confidence in models for multiple audiences: The modelling cascade. *European Journal of Operational Research, 186*(3), 1068–1083.

P144, line 13. Project Management Institute. (2008). *A guide to the project management body of knowledge (PMBOK® Guide)* (4th ed.). Newtown Square, PA: Project Management Institute.

P144, lines 15, 21. Williams, T. M. (2005). Assessing and building on project management theory in the light of badly over-run projects. *IEEE Transactions in Engineering Management, 52*(4), 497–508.

P144, line 16. Lundin, R. A. (1995). Editorial: Temporary organizations and project management. *Scandinavian Journal of Management, 11*(4), 315–317. and Packendorff, J. (1995). Inquiring into the temporary organization: New directions for project management research. *Scandinavian Journal of Management, 11*(4), 319–333.

P144, line 17; P145, line 1. Linehan, C., & Kavanagh, D. (2004, December). *From project ontologies to communities of virtue.* Paper presented at the Second International Workshop, "Making Projects Critical." University of Western England, Bristol, UK.

P144, line 19. Koskela, L., & Howell, G. (2002, August). The theory of project management: Explanation to novel methods. *Proceedings of the 10th Annual Conference on Lean Construction (IGLC-10)*, Gramado, Brazil.

P144, line 22. Packendorff, J. (1995). Inquiring into the temporary organization: New directions for project management research. *Scandinavian Journal of Management, 11*(4), 319–333.

P144, line 23. Hodgson, D. E. (2004). Project work: The legacy of bureaucratic control in the postbureaucratic organization. *Organization, 11*(1), 81–100.

P144, line 24. Malgrati, A., & Damiani, M. (2002). Rethinking the new project management framework: New epistemology, new insights. *Proceedings of the Project Management Institute Research Conference* (pp. 371–380), Seattle, WA.

P144, line 30. Lindkvist, L., Söderlund, J., & Tell, F. (1998). Managing product development projects: On the significance of fountains and deadlines. *Organization Studies, 19*(6), 931–951.

P144, line 40. Williams, T. M. (1999). The need for new paradigms for complex projects. International Journal of Project Management, 17(5), 269–273.

P144, line 41. Baccarini, D. (1996). The concept of project complexity: A review. *International Journal of Project Management, 14*(4), 201–204.

P144, line 42. Turner J. R., & Cochrane R. A. (1993). Goals-and-methods matrix: Coping with projects with ill defined goals and/or methods of achieving them. *International Journal of Project Management, 11*(1), 93–102.

P145, line 1. Engwall, M. (2002). The futile dream of the perfect goal. In K. Sahil-Andersson & A. Soderholm (Eds.), *Beyond project management: New perspectives on the temporary-permanent dilemma* (pp. 261–277). Malmo, Sweden: Libe Ekonomi, Copenhagen Business School Press.

P145, line 23. Shenhar, A. J., & Dvir, D. (2004). How projects differ and what to do about it. In J. Pinto & P. Morris (Eds.), *Handbook of managing projects* (pp. 1265–1286). New York, NY: Wiley.

P145, line 27. Flyvberg, B., Bruzelius, N., & Rothengatter, W. (2003). *Megaprojects and risk: An anatomy of ambition.* Cambridge, UK: Cambridge University Press.

Checkland, P., & Scholes, J. (1990). *Soft systems methodology in action.* Chichester, UK: Wiley.
Churchman, C. W. (1968). *The systems approach.* New York, NY: Dell Publishing.

Chapter 11

Systems Engineering and Project Management

Andrew Daw

This chapter considers the relationship between the complementary disciplines of project management and systems engineering in the context of project, program, and portfolio management. The quality of this relationship in terms of style and culture as well as in the assignment and ownership of technical and functional activities is crucial to the success of any project.

The combination of the natural human ambition to develop and progress and the perceived benefits of ever-increasing use and application of technology in achieving that advancement has generated a powerful dynamic in the way that projects and programs of development are defined. In a world that is closer together, particularly fueled by digital technology, the expectations among all areas of society are rising in all areas of technical activity. Projects and programs are increasingly defined not by the product or artifact that is the final tangible element but by the effects or influences that that artifact (or more likely) a set of artifacts can produce. Thus, there is a growing need to understand integration between the artifacts of a project or several projects, to understand, predict, and measure (preferably a priori) the interactions and interdependencies between disparate projects and to be able to demonstrate the value of the artifacts as an integrated whole to the numerous direct and indirect stakeholders of the project.

Value

In this environment of seeking benefits and effects within a constrained and constraining environment, the issue of value must be increasingly addressed. Value is present in whatever we do. It represents cultural norms; it represents those concepts, things, and activities against which we balance and prioritize our time, investment, and decision making. As always, value must also be related to context and perspective. In some circumstances the "value" of an item will be seen by the requirer/user and supplier in the same way while others will be opposed; hence, a trade will occur to normalize the relationship. Value is often mapped into financial terms. This is a straightforward mapping when the value statement between the parties can be quantified in this way: cost, amortized assets, (tangible values), etc. But what is the value of reputation, presence, societal benefit, and other more human perspectives (the intangible values)? In the arena of complex projects and programs and the associated decision making, it is these types of values and benefits that are the key outputs required. The project manager and systems engineer must now recognize that the drivers of the activity are significantly intangible and subjective and recognize that the traditional processes need to be addressed with a different emphasis, which may in turn require new personal skills and competencies to achieve success. Naturally, there may also be new processes and techniques required to address the problem in the first place.

Project Characterization

Consider "project style" as characterized by Figure 11-1, which presents a view of projects as a relationship between intricacy and uncertainty. It is presented in a traditional four-box model whereby the top right represents the unknown, difficult, wicked area and the bottom left the tamer more predictable/solvable problem space.

This model views the environment in an intricacy–uncertainty domain, where maximums of each represent problems of acquisition, whereby the requirements and scope are uncertain and the solution components and their interactions and interfaces have considerable intricacy. This is the domain of "strategic creativity" or the "edge of chaos."

The mapping through these perspectives enables the issues of connectivity to be identified and addressed. What links the chaotic edge with the volatile and complicated projects to enable the management of the move/transition to more straightforward projects? This model suggests the importance of coordination and communication, to which the construct of context should be added.

The ability to communicate and place in context the issues of the strategic domain is critical to the development of coherent solutions and programs, the understanding of the impact and implications of decisions, and the feedback from the implementation domains. These feedbacks will be both positive and negative. In

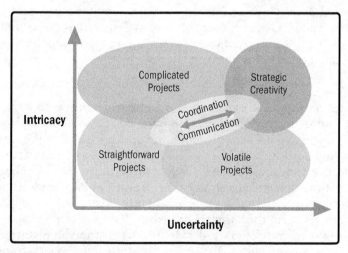

Figure 11-1: Considering a complexity perspective for project style/type

some circumstances, the positive feedback will allow for increased capability, cost effectiveness, etc., and a rebalancing of the solution space in favor of things that are going well to balance those that are falling short. In other circumstances, that feedback will be negative, reflecting an inherent inability to achieve within the constraints and parameters of the problem. Therefore, the feedback will highlight changes and adjustments to the national capability desired either by recognizing and understanding the constraint and then relaxing the issue or by appreciating that a solution is not yet viable. Then issues of research and development (or whatever is possible) to improve the underpinning technology, social or resource base from which solutions may be developed can be addressed.

As a comparative example, consider the U.S. space program from the late 1950s to early 1970s and that of providing military capability through defense acquisition in the current decade. Notwithstanding, the underlying political and military motives of the space program, the "civil" objective of the endeavor was articulated by President John F. Kennedy in 1961. He said, "This nation should commit itself to achieving the goal, before this decade is out, of landing a man on the moon and returning him safely to the earth." At the time, manned space flight was extremely limited, time in space was measured in hours, rather than days, resource and financial requirements were unknown. Many would have said that this was "impossible," beyond human ability, extremely complex, and then they would provide a range of reasons why it could not (and indeed should not be done). In many ways, those naysayers made valid points, but the ambition noted earlier and an inherent confidence and belief drove the United States to develop the necessary skills, resources, techniques, architectures, and program management skills to deliver the required outcome. The journey of Apollo 11 in 1969 is testament to that courage and activity. In the context of the start point, was this a complex problem to be managed or simply complicated? At the point of national commitment, the required functionality was known. Previous design activity had developed the fundamental architecture of the solution space, the product development program was in hand, many of the physical constraints were known, and an initial flight program (the Mercury flights) had begun the "setting to work" elements of the system. Much was still unknown and much still had to be resolved, but the basic tenets and constructs of reducing the problem to manageable chunks, developing systems, subsystems, equipment, and components were in place and operational. Project and program management was about the hard delivery disciplines associated with tangible items to time (the flight launch window) and performance. The systems engineering of the program was about the design development and production of products within a broader enterprise recognizing the human component, the simulation aspects, the technology pull through, etc. The space program was a (very) complicated activity, not necessarily a complex one (and in the context of discussion later in this chapter, not an activity we can currently replicate today).

Consider then the delivery over time of military capability in the United Kingdom. Military capability is not tangible, it is an effect or outcome relative to the context and circumstance of use, it is different every time it is generated, even if it is the same affect that is required. It is achieved through the total integration of multiple components—some of which are not even present at the point of use and delivery—and the effectiveness of the effect or outcome of the capability delivered is dependent on the actions and reactions of the enemy. Within the U.K. Ministry of Defence (MOD) today, the initiative of Through Life Capability Management and a number of associated and supportive initiatives (such as the system of systems approach) are seeking to address this issue to provide balanced, appropriate, effective, and affordable military and industrial forces that support the aspirations of the United Kingdom within the global environment. To accomplish this, MOD, through the Defense Equipment and Support Organization, (DE&S), has established a large number of individual project teams to manage the acquisition of equipment and elements of the necessary associated training. The equipment and elements are coordinated by a number of program boards that seek to achieve a degree of acquisition coherence.

Front line commands have roles and responsibilities in the final integration of the components that generate the required capability/military effect using whatever assets are available to them at the time. In these circumstances, project and program management can still be regarded as being about the hard delivery disciplines of tangible items procured to time, cost, and performance while systems engineering still needs to drive the design development and production of products within a broader enterprise recognizing the human component, the simulation aspects, the technology pull through, etc. However, a key difference is that the time of delivery of the artifact is fixed solely by the contract. The need for the capability and its contributing components occurs at unknown times in the future (or more hopefully is never used, e.g., the nuclear deterrent). In addition, the performance element is dependent upon factors outside the contractual boundary and the financial criteria are not open ended (as was the case with the space program). Furthermore, while the means of generating and delivering the required effect and military output are known today for today's circumstance, those same means (artifacts, products services, etc.) may be neither appropriate nor good enough for a future delivery event. The presence of these uncertainties, new variables (which are themselves always changing), the dynamic nature of the environment, etc., means that defense acquisition is an activity that borders the complex-chaotic boundary, where simple reductionist techniques are inappropriate until a "higher" level of program and system work has been completed and the implications of that work understood and accepted.

Thus, one result of this combination of human ambition, technological development, greater fluidity and uncertainty in the environment and the need for greater integration across numerous disparate entities and organizations, is that the span of project types undertaken embraces the complete spectrum of project style and tends to move relentlessly from the straightforward through the complicated to the complex. Then it leads to a chaotic environment whereby the interactions and dependencies and the conflicting stakeholder demands and values, etc., cannot be reconciled in any meaningful fashion. Projects operating in this latter arena of the complex-chaotic boundary are often seeking to address "wicked problems."

Wicked Problems

In a seminal article, Rittel and Webber noted, "As we seek to improve the effectiveness of actions in pursuit of valued outcomes, as system boundaries get stretched, and as we become more sophisticated about the complex workings of open societal systems, it becomes ever more difficult to make the planning idea operational," and this is true when defining such issues as "capability" and other abstract notions of effect, and articulating and bounding the multidimensional space of interfaces and interactions that are present within the defense domain. Rittel and Webber suggested that wicked problems have 10 characteristics:

- They have no definitive formulation.
- They have no stopping rule (i.e., they do not have unambiguous criteria for deciding if the problem is resolved, and getting all stakeholders to agree that a resolution is "good enough" can be a challenge).
- They have solutions that are not true or false, but rather good or bad, (or better or worse [current author addition]).
- They have no immediate and no ultimate test of a solution.
- There is no opportunity to learn by trial and error, every attempt (at solution) counts significantly and every solution is a "one-shot operation."
- They don't have an enumerable (or exhaustively describable) set of potential solutions, nor is there a well-described set of permissible operations that may incorporated into the plan
- Each wicked problem is essentially unique.
- Each wicked problem can be considered to be a symptom of another problem.
- They can be explained in numerous ways, through many stakeholders who have various and changing ideas about what might be a problem, what might be causing it and how it might be resolved.
- The planner/designer has no right to be wrong.

In some sense, these characteristics can be considered as expressing an ill-posed question with an open-ended set of interrelationships and dependencies requiring a formulation of constraint mathematics that might preclude a solution space in the first place.

Thus, the classical systems approach, based upon the four distinct phases:

- Understanding the problem
- Gathering information
- Analyzing and refining information
- Developing solutions

can be seen as being inappropriate at best and inoperable at worst. In drawing from the literature, John noted:

- "One cannot understand the problem without knowing about its context, one cannot meaningfully search for information without knowing what to look for in the solution space; one cannot first understand, then solve."
- "With an ill-defined problem, from the beginning, it is not clear what the problem is and thus, what a solution is. Solving and specifying the problem develop in parallel and drive each other."
- "Attempting to baseline requirements and then use an analytical approach to deal with wicked projects is a recipe for disaster."

In these circumstances, the "traditional" mechanisms of both project management and systems engineering, concentrating upon the delivery of a product that meets a requirement, is built to a known and established specification, etc., find themselves wanting. Unfortunately, society has no interest in the type of question it is posing or the style of project that is required to achieve the outputs; it just requires/demands the outputs. Thus, for these project types in the complex-chaotic area (the wicked ones), the issue for the project team becomes one of management, the wicked problem cannot be solved but the output artifacts are required and hence management of the wickedness is required in such a way that allows acceptable outcomes to be developed and derived.

The key to achieving the successful management of the wicked problem—once it has been accepted that the problem cannot be solved in the first place—is to establish an organization that enables the execution of a variety of project and program types. Each should be completed within a framework of processes, competencies, and commercial skills that allows the enterprise to make informed, evidence-based decisions with known and understood impacts and implications. These decisions and the implied risks and opportunities associated with those decisions then permit tangible outputs and components to be developed that might be expected (within a set of circumstances and assumptions) to have value and usefulness in the environment and to the user. These individual components can then be addressed as complex-complicated projects in their own right and a more traditional sequence of project and systems engineering activities can be pursued. However, it should not be thought that by establishing a set, n, of these complex-complicated projects that the full extent of the complex-chaotic problem has been resolved.

Consider the organizational structure illustrated in Figure 11-2. This generic organizational model is derived from the published U.K. MoD Acquisition Value Chain and is equally applicable to any hierarchical decision-making organization within government, industry, etc. The figure expresses a series of relationships and interfaces that provide the context for the decision making and trading that should occur across all components of the environment and community in establishing what (product and or service) should be procured. Each area provides a context for the subsequent area and the feedback loops represent a formal set of communication mechanisms that enable challenges and corrections from one area to another in a series of informed decision-making activities. Reading from left to right, therefore, develops the national (political) aspiration into a capability contribution to the specific solution concepts and then to the implementation and delivery mechanisms of the individual project teams. The embracing context of this "left to right" view of the "wicked-problem management" space is the underpinning budget and aspiration. Reading in the reverse direction come the mitigating issues and boundaries (expressed as reality and costs), and these act as the constraints on the system context, defining what is and is not achievable. Thus, the system can be closed loop and stable, with informed decision making and a full understanding of the impact and implications of decisions.

So, if a wicked problem cannot be expressed in solvable terms (but Figure 11-2 represents a framework for its expression), then the transition from the wicked capability expression of the problem (the left-hand area) can be managed to enable the development and acquisition of pertinent products and services within the constraints of the problem (as required at the right-hand area). This may be considered as a tame(r) problem. Functionally, the activities of each of the four areas of this model are congruent—that of management and decision making in context. As the decision-making process transitions from left to right, the underpinning aspects of trading between options, constraints, and value continue to expose awkward questions, incorrect assumptions, incompleteness of data and information, and un-

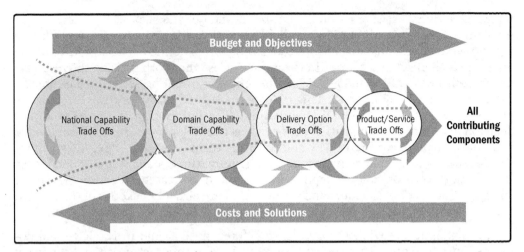

Figure 11-2: Capability value chain

certainty in concept development all within a potentially rapidly changing context and internal competitive rivalries. The interactions within and between these functional areas therefore all contributes to the presence and style of "wickedness" in the domain.

However, wickedness within the problem domain is not restricted to the left-hand side of this model, and the "type" and example of wickedness changes within the process. At the left-hand side, the wickedness is manifest primarily as diversity and uncertainty; in the second area, wickedness is more characterized by choice, technology options, and trading while at the right-hand side, it remains within the system through the issues of competition, changing context, and system solution maturity. The concept of potential residual wickedness is introduced to recognize that the issues of acquisition of the identified artifacts are complicated and complex and that even straightforward projects (at the right-hand end of the acquisition model) may have problems that reflect in some degree or scale the attributes of wickedness. It should be noted that the problem at the right hand end, the implementation and delivery end, is not necessarily tame, in that it is well bounded and understood, but that it is potentially tamer.

Wickedness may also be considered as being "internal" and "external," which impacts throughout the overall process to varying degrees. At the left-hand end, wickedness is essentially external, driven by the external environment and its relation to the highest-level objective (the national aspiration). At the right-hand end, it is internal (or residual) driven through the issues and relationships of solution development, delivery, and integration into a changing environment. Vested interest is one particular common example of internal and external wickedness, and this can be manifest at all levels and in many ways.

It may also be useful to introduce an eleventh attribute of wickedness—time, which appears in two forms: tempo and duration. Each of the decision-making areas and their associated activities has an associated time constant, an associated tempo of activity. At the national—left-hand—end of the acquisition process, the problem definition is a "sample and hold" function and provides a sampling rate against which decisions are considered and objectives defined. The activities of the other areas then act as a set of filters on the process that both provide the response to the decision stimulus and negate any benefit that might be derived from increasing the national sampling rate. This reflects the second aspect of time through the process, the duration of overall (acquisition). The duration of the process makes decision making on solution attributes, such as technology, for example, impossible to achieve in any meaningful way and so limits the potential for flexibility and responsiveness and to change in the face of changing threats and issues. Such issues limit both the customer and supplier options and in the case of technology, almost ensure the delivery of products and services that are either at best out of touch with the changed problem space or at worst obsolete or wholly inappropriate.

In managing the wicked problem, therefore, those at and in the left-hand domains must recognize that the environment is high in uncertainty and intricacy and not attempt to apply reductionist theories to simplify the problem. There must be an embracing of the issues not a shirking from them; an identification of all contributing environments to the solution; and a communication and coordination of activities across the framework to ensure consistency and coherence of the endeavors within the defined context.

Influence and Control

The transition from left to right in this decision-making program space can be thought of as translating the abstract concepts, such as capability, national aspiration, etc., to the definition and delivery of hard products and services available for the benefit of society, specific users, etc., items such as phones, tanks, cars, and buildings. Throughout, the human element is considered part of the solution, and hence, technical-socio systems develop. However, the process of understanding the abstract and getting a grip on the issues and constraints—particularly those drivers defined by sociological, technical, economic, environmental, political, and values (STEEPV)—and the definition of the opportunity is an area of the domain in which the project manager and systems engineer have very little "control" over the ultimate direction and structure of the later activities. They are able to exert and have exerted upon them considerable "influence" through their technical and social experience.

Conversely, at the right-hand side of the diagram where the project activities are concerned with the hard delivery of the identified products and services, the project manager and systems engineer have significant control; these are the key cooperating and directing elements of the project team and its activities. At this point, the opportunities for influence in the design and development space are much reduced and are potentially limited to minor variations to current activities and adjustments of future incremental planning activities.

Over the course of the translation, therefore, from the abstract to the tangible, the balance of influence and control within the problem and solution space are constantly changing. However, in order to make progress, there must be clear informed decision making, each of which marks a step away from the abstract (intangible, influence) space towards the product/service delivery and achievement space (tangible, controlled).

Associated with this influence and control perspective is the complementary one of skills and associated activity. While project/program management always contains an element of the hard delivery perspectives—a project manager's priority is after all to get the project/activity out on time and within budget—even at the abstract end of the project space, there will be a need to drive functional activity to support decision making. The relationship with the systems engineer is extremely close with significant overlap in activity and responsibility. In this domain, the systems engineer, whose priority is to design and assure a system that will meet the agreed operational requirements over the future life cycle, is key to articulating and bringing together the issues of the stakeholders and beginning the journey of putting flesh upon the decision making, which will ultimately lead to tangible deliveries and the value generation. It should not be forgotten that throughout this translation process, the systems engineer also stands as proxy for the silent majority of the future users and stakeholders whose views must be reflected as best as possible within the decision-making process.

The significant overlap in this area of the project space includes the following: those activities associated with stakeholder identification, engagement, and management; the definition of strategic aims objectives and project functions; and the initial identification of interfaces and interdependencies within the program space and their impact and implication upon future opportunities. Most importantly, however, there must be a complete union of the disciplines with respect to risk and opportunity identification and management. Agreement and understanding of the issues associated with risk ownership, the impact, and implications of those risks is vital to establishing coherent plans and an appropriate understanding of the context for all parties and for maintaining the necessary inclusivity of all pertinent parties to the problem.

At the delivery end of the project, the roles of project manager and systems engineer are more "traditional." They still have the responsibilities noted earlier, but now decision making is more bounded, the wickedness level lower (or non-existent), and the drivers of time, cost, and performance are paramount for the project manager and assurance of compliance in the design development and delivery activities key for the systems engineer. Naturally, there remain common areas of responsibility and ownership—again the risk arena is paramount here—but the separation of the disciplines is clearer and the competencies required more traditional.

Throughout this transition, it is essential that the values of the project manager and systems engineer are complementary, that neither is dominant, and that they merge into an integrated system understand-decide-develop-deliver-operate team for the long term, whose underpinning understanding recognizes that the system is the means for delivering future operational value.

Project Engineering Perspectives

Consider now how these individual styles of project might be supported in engineering/process terms. What sort of project activity set would have to be conducted, and how, in order to pass through a decision or capability need that was articulated and refined from left to right in the model, particularly if the primary theme and underpinning requirement was to provide evidenced information for informed decision making?

Figure 11-3 presents an overlay of possible systems engineering styles and process life cycles that might enable such a journey. Again, drawn from Conway and Mawby, these models are considered as:

- Emergence model,
- Option model,
- 'V' model, and
- Waterfall model.

These various models do not have necessarily completely independent definitions and can, in general, be grouped into two pairs: the higher level option and emergence Models and the V and waterfall models.

The traditional industry process for systems engineering and the development of a comprehensive product portfolio, within its definition of capability, is the 'V' model as illustrated in Figure 11-4 and the associated waterfall model whereby each activity is a natural sequential progression from the last. This has served well in various implementations for some time, particularly through the formal processes of requirements engineering, system analysis, and systems design. The right hand side of the 'V' offers Test Acceptance and Integration - each of which enables validation and verification of the design and product.

However, it is product based and neither the waterfall nor 'V' model inherently includes and reflects the issues associated with a nonlinear problem-solving requirement, or with the recursive nature of iterations, incremental integration across numerous stakeholders, or multiple contributing components to the required capability. How do the complex intersystem reactions take place and get valued within this structure? It is postulated that this type of "sequential" process is inadequate and ill posed for the much broader canvas that is required when considering capability or the underlying issues associated with the emergence or options models.

A detailed comparison of the traditional 'V' model with a new "reaction chamber" systems engineering process life cycle is presented by Price and John, which

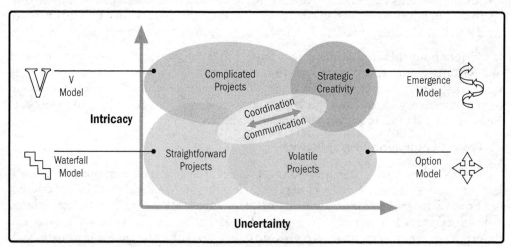

Figure 11-3: A (systems) engineering overlay of process styles

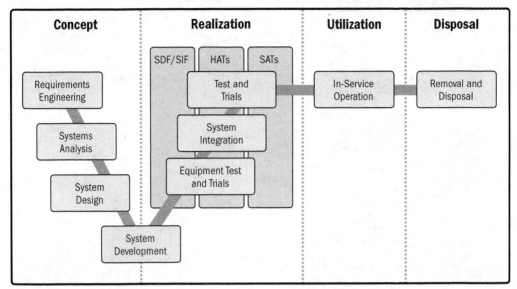

Figure 11-4: Traditional 'V' diagram systems engineering process life cycle

also described a number of extensions to that original model that offer the required articulation of capability development than the 'V' model suggests/permits. Figure 11-5 presents this new perspective.

Together with a formal recognition that certain aspects of those activities must occur in parallel, the new model places systems analysis processes in a much more dominant and important role—the continuous, through life tail of the process life cycle. This tail now enables a more defined and coherent through life management policy to be adopted as each of the systems analysis activities offers the opportunity for a measurable system delivery. The use of techniques in this area enables the derivation and management of information and the identification of emergent opportunities and option analysis necessary for the two higher-level models identified previously.

This model also offers a direct linkage with the concepts of experimentation. If, in the context of a wicked problem, experimentation is considered in the broadest definition, opportunities for trial and experiment with concepts, ideas, system balances, etc., occur at every stage of the process life cycle. In the very early stages of the problem, solution development and experimentation can be applied across the first four boxes of Figure 11-5 embracing the top-level documentation development and ideas, the analysis of the requirements, the scope of the real world solution opportunity, and then the traditional measurement of systems analysis. This construct of representation and iteration can and should be applied throughout the program life cycle and act as a key part of the overall through life management issues.

Information Management
To support such a project life cycle, the management of information through the generic organizational model is essential and becomes an issue of scale. Building

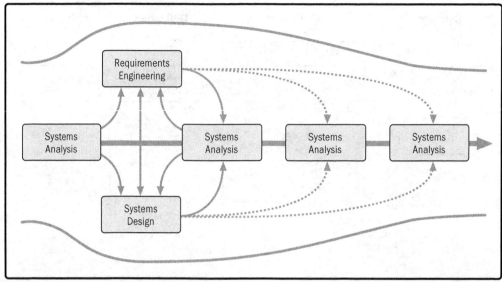

Figure 11-5: Reaction Chamber Systems Engineering Process Life Cycle Model

on the multiple system representations of the analysis, the flow of information in terms of context, decision-making details, and the underpinning evidence is crucial to ensuring the consistency and coherency of the environment. Similarly, issues of configuration management become of great importance as this forms the basis of the management of change processes. In ensuring the maintenance of pertinent acquisition, particularly in capability terms, continued understanding of the external environment and the impact and implications of change in that environment must be built upon sound information and knowledge management techniques.

In the steady state situation, much of this becomes an issue of the management of change. These changes occur in each of the decision environments encapsulated by the model and a detailed understanding of the component contributors to the required capabilities, the product and service life cycles, the balances achieved and the reasons behind decisions must be managed.

There are many information sources within this model. The information model must be initiated through an understanding of value in order that the context for the acquisition is well understood and that the decision making has sufficient context to be able to rank and prioritize alternatives at the highest level. This value statement, which becomes increasingly well defined in terms of measures of capability, effectiveness, and performance as progress through the process is made, is expressed in as many terms as is necessary; it is not necessarily a purely financial statement and in some circumstances may not even contain a financial statement.

It is important to recognize that the objective of the information views at this stage of trade space identification and analysis is to determine the solution space in which a viable/feasible solution may sit. It is not about determining the exact solution. The trade space is defined in terms of the solution attributes and characteristics that any solution must exhibit in order to be compliant. This trade space will be bounded by a range of factors including policy, industrial constraints, performance issues, financial constraints, the scenarios of operation, the tactics doctrine, and policy of use, among others. Thus, the combination of information types and sources may be considered as providing a set of "system characteristics" against which the final acquisition is achieved/contracted, rather than formal restricted and rigid requirements—specifications based process where language and vested interest all too often color the solution environment. The system characteristics are defined by the constraints applied to the acquisition, and they define the solution volume across all pertinent views, stakeholders, and disciplines in which it is reasonable to seek solutions. They also provide confidence that a solution from that space will have value to the community of users and stakeholders, and can be utilized within the operational construct required. Such a set of characteristics also feed into the relevant contractual model as a necessary part of the acceptance and assurance criteria.

Throughout this information model, the content and context of the interfaces is driven by the decision making of the area to the left of the current position. Thus, as information flows through the model, this information set is available to and used by all stakeholders in the domain; there cannot be a "them and us" and "information is power" situation.

In support of recent initiatives, particularly in the defense environment, significant developments in the application of information management, modeling, and visualization in support of decision making have occurred. One of the primary developed visualizations is based upon revisiting and reinterpreting the ideas of incremental acquisition (and the inherent insights afforded to the management of risk in delivery and performance contribution terms) and the conventional program Gantt chart.

Daw noted that one of the primary outputs from the reaction chamber model is the development of integrated, through life management planning artifacts. At the left-hand side of the capability value chain, these represent a view of the required capability over time, while on the right-hand side (implementation and delivery), they represent the through life management plans for the individual products and services that contribute to the capability, considered across all the contributing factors and components. The plans constitute, therefore, a coherent and consistent set of representations and visualizations of the problem and solution space. The development of these plans and their perspectives is a joint project manager and systems engineer activity recognizing that it is necessary to provide appropriate detail for planning purposes in capability terms when considering the timescales and time frames of all the component parts (e.g., recruitment, training).

Consider a simple construct for the definition of the plan; the customer has an important system measure of interest, which traditionally is required to improve over time to cope with increasing threats, improved performance, etc. Consider also the opportunity to deliver 80 percent to 85 percent of the required capability quickly, supported by a series of increments to the solution over time. The resulting staircase could look as shown in Figure 11-6.

The tread of the staircase is time, the pitch the expected capability increase with respect to the measure of interest. To achieve this, a program must be established that can be cost/is costable. Hence, the Cost–Time–Performance trio of the procurement can be determined. The increase in capability is achieved across all of the contributing components to the solution, through the standards tenets of incremental acquisition and technology insertion, for example, through pull through of research, development, and focused investment, etc.

There are many additional elements that can be derived from such a representation, but a key benefit is one of flexibility, particularly of industry to respond to radical changes in the measure of interest. The development of a "staircase" requires a different set of risk methodologies and perspectives. Each element of a step—the tread and the pitch—is subject to uncertainty; there is uncertainty in the time of the delivery and again in the actual of capability increment against the measure of interest. The issue for the new management processes should, therefore, be to ensure that the uncertainty at all times is bounded and recognize that the "opportunity" side to risk is one offering nimbleness of response to changing measures of interest, of flexibility in delivery, and direction and focus in investment.

A properly managed and contracted staircase offers considerable openness and visibility to the ministry for planning purposes (both long term and short term), and to industry who, in some cases, could be competed and judged not just upon the initial product but also on the quality and confidence of the supporting through life planning.

Schematically, the overall capability derived from these contributing components can be represented as a typical Gantt chart (Figure 11-7). At the highest level, the rows of the Gantt chart represent not program activities but the life cycles of all the necessary contributing components of the solution system.

Reading from left to right, therefore, provides a clear view of the schedule and interactions/dependencies between the component life cycles—offering views of

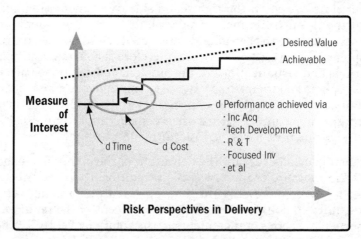

Figure 11-6: Staircase Model of Through Life Acquisition and Risk Perspectives in Delivery (t) and Performance Increment (p)

proposed in service, out of service dates, spend peaks in demonstration/manufacture, even start dates for future programs to support an enduring capability need. This view is simply an extension of standard the project management Gantt chart. Reading from top to bottom however affords the opportunity to 'sum'/aggregate the contributions to capability provided by the individual components at any one time and thence through life, and the simple graphic at the bottom of the chart represents some presentation method against a particular measure of interest from the customer. This can be established wrt scenarios, operational metrics (values), success criteria, etc.

This planning and information visualization is at the heart of an integrated "dashboard" that reflect the required components of the following:

- Required outcome and its predicted trends over time,
- The inclusive view of the risk to cost time and performance of the expected project artifacts, and
- The supply view of contract progress and structure.

The "Dynamic Gantt Chart" or integrated management plan contains all the necessary components that contribute to the required capability. It includes detail across all the customer components of the required outcome, across the industrial (supplier) capability/capacity, across the relevant research and technology program

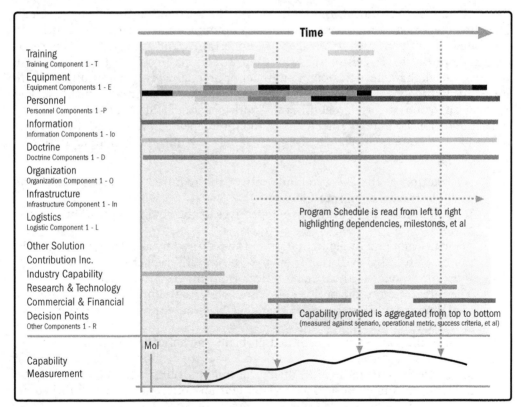

Figure 11-7: Combined Gantt and Capability Aggregation

and includes information about the decision points and timings necessary to enable commercial and financial developments. This plan also highlights the dependencies across the programs and highlights mismatches in expectation, planning, timing, etc. It is from this plan that all details of the current and expected acquisition activities and their products are taken and used in the associated analysis techniques.

The dynamic part of this plan and its associated analysis is that the schedules of the acquisition elements can be moved and adjusted and the results of those adjustments perceived in the direct changes associated with the other visualizations.

It should also be noted that this is not about forecasting the future; rather, it is about enabling a consolidated view of the management of the capability in and across all domains and contributing elements, not just the cost function of a particular piece of equipment or system, as is currently the case. Such a plan is predicated upon the ability to measure and evaluate the system and to understand the value or worth of an activity. Again, it is in this context that system analysis plays such a major role in supporting the management opportunities.

Skillset and Competencies

If these are the project/program environments and techniques in which people and organizations are going to have to work and interact, what sort of skills and competencies will they have to have and what sort of people are required in order to make these programs effective and the management of wicked/complex problems viable?

In the emergence model, the skills reflect the abstract nature of the problem. The characteristics of these practitioners are found primarily in their abilities to correlate abstract concepts, to engage with uncertainty and ambiguity, and perhaps have a more intuitive feel for the ways and directions in which to move. These are not typical characteristics of an engineer or an engineering community. There are no formal requirements or specifications; these are areas in which the wicked problem characteristic are predominant—multiple stakeholders, no right or wrong answer, multiple complexly interrelating and interdependent issues, confused value definition and statement. Figure 11-8 provides a view into these characteristics by highlighting the required abilities as:

- **Abstraction** of the key fundamentals of the required characteristics of the problem and solution space;
- **Representation** from multiple perspectives of the potential solution sets and options;
- Identification and implementation of the required **measurement techniques**, metrics, etc., that will represent the "how well" aspect of the solution options in response to the value required from the solution space;
- The **integration** of the option sets into a preferred solution set, including the initial metrics, interfaces, etc., that develop a route through the overall problem space;
- Communication of the combined problem and solution space in a way that engages, informs, provides confidence, and offers inclusive engagement of stakeholders. Given the multidiscipline and multidimensional nature of this problem, this is expressed as a **visualization** ability/skill that is linked di-

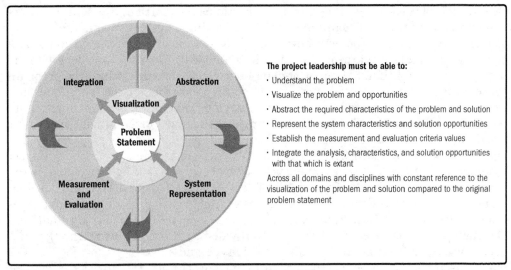

The project leadership must be able to:
- Understand the problem
- Visualize the problem and opportunities
- Abstract the required characteristics of the problem and solution
- Represent the system characteristics and solution opportunities
- Establish the measurement and evaluation criteria values
- Integrate the analysis, characteristics, and solution opportunities with that which is extant

Across all domains and disciplines with constant reference to the visualization of the problem and solution compared to the original problem statement

Figure 11-8: Emergence model techniques and skills

rectly to the original requirement/problem definition and then supports all the other skills as noted above.

Individual personal behaviors in this model are also likely to include:

- Refined interpersonal skills,
- Strong intuitive and intuition based aspects, and
- Supportive team working traits.

In this domain, the overlap between project management and systems engineering skills is likely to be significant. In the "V" and Waterfall models, however, the divergence of the project management and systems engineering skills will be greater as these models demand the harder edged issues of "completer/finisher" to ensure delivery of the required artifacts.

In managing the varying issues as they move through the transition from complex to straightforward, the five skills noted earlier are constantly utilized, but the degree to which one or other is the dominant skill varies with the level of decision making, problem management, and context. By the time the "V" and Waterfall models are realized on the right-hand side of the diagram, the delivery skills are of higher importance. The definitive actions and activities of the individual processes are well defined, and the issues of information configuration management and integration are the dominant needs, underpinned by visualization of the overall integration and development of the solution space.

There is a significant time dimension that must also be considered in relation to the skills and competencies noted and, which if left unattended, "disables" the future. Individual understanding, competencies, and application skills are perishable attributes and if left unattended dissipate and become obsolete, overtaken by progress and lack of practice. There is and has been for some time growing evidence that in complex systems, the careers of participants (particularly senior players and expertise within the team) may only span a single system such is the acquisition life cycle, the development cost, etc. Thus, the experiential dimension of any competencies and the learning gained by individuals diminishes considerably. This now places an additional element of complexity and wickedness into the problem; those engaged in the endeavor have not done the job before, or the techniques and experience necessary were last used in the previous generation without appropriate recording and learning. Consider the example of the new Queen Elizabeth Aircraft Carriers—the previous U.K. design was cancelled in 1965 and was prepared by specialist teams in the main within the U.K. Ministry of Defence. Even the youngest member of that team at that time would have been approaching retirement at the time of the recent U.K. Queen Elizabeth Class Aircraft Carrier design and development decisions and the number of resources available with direct operational experience of fast jet operations from carriers and the associated issues is very small and decreasing. Further, the new designs are provided by a U.K. industry that has not been engaged in such detail for ships of this type and size since the 1950s. These platforms are (very) complicated in their own right, the additional risks associated with the additional elements of lack of direct referential experience, and differing responsibilities and ownership must be factored into the project planning and activities of the community associated with the development.

Conclusion

The ambition in human endeavor and societal need expressed in the context of today's circumstance of constraint combine to form a environment of increasing complexity in which to design develop and operate system solutions. It has been suggested that in these circumstances, the environment represents a wicked problem that cannot be solved (analytically) but must be managed to provide an acceptable solution and set of appropriate artifacts. In this domain, the project manager and the systems engineer must establish a partnership of equals that enables the appropriate emphasis and focus to be placed upon the necessary techniques and activities but with explicit concentration upon the support to decision making in the face of uncertainty, ambiguity, and incomplete knowledge and information.

The topics discussed have highlighted the need to establish an organizational decision-making framework within which a series of transitions are made that enable the design definition and subsequent delivery of system solutions of value. These topics have been combined and expressed within the framework (Figure 11-9).

It must be emphasized that the complete transition from left to right in any of these perspectives does not constitute a solution, merely a management of the wickedness and complexity to achieve a solution that provides some extent of the original required value, outcome, and effect. However, a potential residual wickedness remains at the point of implementation/delivery, which reflects the complexity and high levels of complication required in today's solution set for capability, whether that be driven by the number and type of interface, interaction, and interdependency between systems or simply by the nature of human action, understanding, and perception. The key issue is that it exists because the environment is uncertain. These management issues are not established to remove that uncertainty and

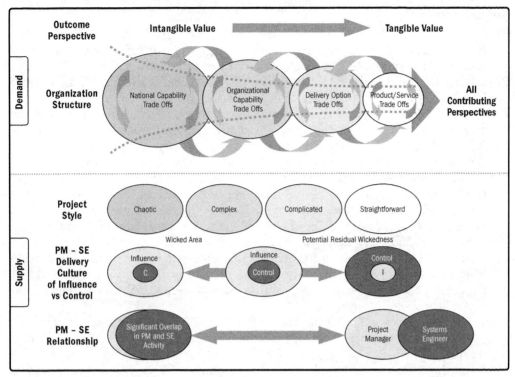

Figure 11-9: Composite framework highlighting perspectives of transition for the project manager and systems engineer

the project manager and systems engineer together act to minimize its effect and enable informed decisions to be made regarding its impact and implications.

If successfully applied, the execution of these transitions and the understanding of the relationships developed will enable

- coherent and consistent (evidence) information for informed decision making;
- inclusivity of stakeholder, system perspective, and development opportunities;
- integration, capability acceptance/assurance;
- support to flexibility and the management of change; and
- a focused investment and identified opportunities for research pull through.

In wicked problem terms, while the planner/designer may still have no right to be right, he or she will at least be able to break even, so that customers know what they are getting when and to what level of quality and confidence. In addition, the supplier will know that his or her delivery is managed and has confidence in its applicability and acceptance. Both have a strategy to manage the inevitable set of changes that will occur through life.

References

P150, line 11, Figure 11-1; P158, line 3, Figure 11-3. Conway, B., & Mawby, D. (2006, October). *Early lessons for establishing through life capability programs.* Paper presented at the RUSI Defence Project Management Conference.

P152, lines 42, 46; P153, line 34. Rittel, H. W. J., & Webber, M. M. (1973). Dilemmas in a general theory of planning. *Policy Sciences, 4*(2), 155–169.

P153, line 31. John, P. (2007, February). *Contracting against requirements documents or shared models.* Paper presented at BAE Systems R&T Conference.

P153, line 39. Aaby, A. (2002). *Computational complexity and problem hierarchy.* Retrieved from http://cs.wwc.edu/~aabyan/Theory/complexity.html

P154, line 10. Daw, A. J. (2007, August). *On the wicked problem of defence acquisition.* Paper presented at the AIAA Conference Challenges in Systems Engineering for Advanced Technology Programs. Reprinted November 2009. In C. E. Dickerson & D. N. Mavris (Eds.), Architecture and Principles of Systems Engineering (pp. 353–387). Boca Raton, FL: Auerbach Publications.

P154, line 21. HMG MOD Apr 2007 'Acquisition Operating Framework, sub-section 'What is the Scope of Capability Management?'" http://www.ams.mod.uk/aof content/operational/business/capabilitymanagement/capabilitymanagement_scope.htm

P156, line 30. Loverage, D. (2002). *The STEEPV Acronym and Process: A clarification.* Paper presented at Ideas in Progress, University of Manchester, Manchester, UK.

P158, line 28; P160, Figure 11-5. Price, S. N., & John, P. (2002). *The status of models in systems engineering.* Paper presented at IFORS 2002, Shrivenham, UK: Royal Military College of Science.

P161, line 22. Symes, G., & Daw, A. J. (2009, December). On the use of information management in the context of through life capability management (TLCM). *Journal of Naval Engineering.*

P161, line 26. Daw, A. J. (2004, September). *New process and structure thinking for capability development.* Paper presented at the Ninth International CCRP Symposium, Copenhagen, Denmark.

Summary

Chapter 12

Toward a Coherent Research Agenda

Terry Williams

Introduction

Complexity has been important in the project management community for many years. Chapter 1 discussed workshops conducted by Project Management Institute (PMI), and it gave a high-level overview of the complexity topics and issues raised at these meetings. Chapters 2–11 explored these topics and issues further. Specifically, Chapters 2–7 covered the implications for practitioners of what is currently known, and Chapters 8–11 dealt with complexity as it relates to project management.

However, this is just the start of a journey. Chapters 8–11 laid the groundwork and have been effective determining the problems, but these chapters do not highlight solutions well, and even Chapters 2–7 identified a wide range of areas where further research is needed.

This chapter reviews the previous 11 chapters and tries to identify where further research is needed and where the project management community could work to push forward the understanding of complex projects, and therefore our effective management of these projects.

Conceptual

Chapter 1 raised the fundamental question, what does "complexity" actually mean when applied to projects? It also asked these questions: What causes complexity, and why is it a problem?

There are a number of levels at which this can be answered. Herbert Simon's definition is often quoted: A complex system is "one made up of a large number of parts that interact in a non-simple way. In such systems the whole is more than the sum of the parts, not in an ultimate, metaphysical sense but in the important pragmatic sense that, given the properties of the parts and the laws of interaction, it is not a trivial matter to infer the properties of the whole." This definition gives us a starting point, but the previous chapters built on that considerably. In Chapter 10, Checkland's theory gave the four concepts of emergent properties, a layered structure, and processes of communication and control—the first particularly being a continual theme throughout the book. Chapter 1 highlighted additional issues that identify "complexity," including behavior, systemicity (sometimes referred to as being "complicated"), "diversity of models," "incomplete or inappropriate" project management, and the overall "system of systems" effect of strategic management. Chapter 4 covered "external" complexity, which is increasingly seen as a key driver of complexity; 'the most important point is that the environment in which one is delivering the project is complex and dynamic' said an interviewee in Klakegg, Williams, Walker, Anderson, & Magnussen.

In addition, complexity theory yields other concepts that might contribute to our understanding. Chapter 9 mentioned some of these concepts, in particular the tipping point and the butterfly effect —the former having been identified a number of times about projects, and the latter giving useful advice on the difficulty in forecasting project out-turns. Cicmil, Cooke-Davies, Crawford, and Richardson discussed these issues further, in particular focusing on the concepts of Stacey's "complex responsive processes of relating in organizations."

Before we look at the combinations of some or all of these ideas, more research is needed. More research will provide an understanding of each concept's meaning in the context of projects and their implications for the practice of project management—from the basic ideas of epistemic and aleatoric uncertainty, technical difficulty, and through the systemic and behavioral concepts. Each concept and its implications could form the basis of a research study.

As Chapter 1 implies, a key need is to bring structure to this discussion and try to categorize or classify the various meanings of complexity when it is applied to projects. Conway and Mawby, as quoted in Chapter 11, referred to this discussion, and Chapter 9 gave a wider view. Chapter 4 provided a different definition, while Chapter 5 took the argument further (and shows a 2x2 matrix when just two dimensions are considered). Another good definition is found in Chapter 3. Much of this work points in a similar direction, and indeed much of the literature points in similar directions. Geraldi, Maylor, and Williams (in press) summarized the literature and classified complexity into structural, uncertainty, dynamics, pace, and socio-political complexity (here can be seen echoes of other project classification systems, such as Shenhar's), which is likely to cover most ideas.

Clearly, more research is needed on classification schemes, to try to bring more acceptance and uniformity to the discussion. As stated in Chapter 5, "The first stage in helping to solve some of the challenges of delivery, is to provide a conceptualization for practitioners that assists in gaining a common language and understanding." In addition, as Chapter 9 mentioned, our work needs to be able to apply to the great diversity in different project types.

However, it is just as urgent to have empirical evidence. First, there is the difficulty in assessing levels of complexity in any of these dimensions (as identified in Chapter 9). Then, even if we can agree on how they should be measured, a large research effort is needed to look into the actual occurrence of such complexity in practice, the distribution of different amounts of the different complexity dimensions in practice, how difficult complexities affect projects, whether the measures might be useful, and so forth.

The People-Basis of Projects

Research on project complexity has made a number of advances in some of these aspects. However, a particularly important part of the necessary additional research on the nature of project complexity, where work has perhaps made less progress, is in the last of five categories provided by Geraldi et al.—socio-political complexity.

There is a lot of work in this area outside of the project domain. In Chapter 11, there is a quote by Rittel and Webber on "wicked" problems, and this is advanced by Roth and Senge, who defined a matrix of "dynamic complexity" against the complexity of the human- and/or group-effect. They labelled problems with high behavioral complexity problems "wicked"; those high in dynamic complexity were called "wicked messes."

Clearly, projects consist of individuals making decisions, and both Chapters 1 and 8 have cited human behavior, judgment, and decision making as significant sources of complexity. However, the issues go beyond rational decision making. Apart from the more obvious biases that Chapter 8 cited from Kahneman and Tversky, there are the quirks on how people draw conclusions and make decisions (Chapter 8), and how humans exhibit nonrational or irrational behavior.

Projects are carried out by teams, and complexity comes not only from the individuals within the teams but also from the interrelationships between them. For example, Cicmil et al. emphasized complex responsive processes of relating in organizations. The work this team is trying to carry out may add complexity in particular. Chapter 8 stated, "Projects have always been delivered by people working together, and leading and motivating them to align their efforts behind the project goal has always been an important task for the project manager." If the "goal" is ill defined and the way toward it is complex, then there are extra layers of complexity.

Looking beyond the project team, there are interpersonal complexities within the organization. Chapter 8 referenced Turner and Müller on seller/buyer relationships and the wider stakeholders in society.

Of course, there are many theoretical resources in the wider academic literature to approach these problems. When looking at the individual and his or her position within the organization, Bourdieu provided useful theoretical constructs to understand the relationship between what people actually do in practice/why they make decisions, and the objective social structures within the organization and their discourses, relationship networks, and "taken for granted." Power relationships between the actors have long been recognized as important elements, and the work of Foucault has been taken up occasionally. The ideas of Habermas' "sincere communicative speech acts" (discourse unfettered by the coercive use of power) might also be valuable. Where we add the complexities in establishing the goals and the work to be done, Weick's sensemaking is a concept sometimes consdiered by researchers.

These concepts appear to have the potential to advance our models of how projects and project teams work; however, they have been seldom used in project management. (O'Leary is a notable exception, especially as it is based on an empirical case). Clearly, there is much more research to do here by researchers who are willing to comprehend these theoretical constructs and are able to apply them to the real world of complex projects. In doing so, hopefully project management will move on to a firmer theoretical basis.

Managing Projects

While research into the conceptual basis of project complexity has moved forward somewhat, little progress has been made on its implications for how to manage projects. Simple "dominant discourse" models such as A *Guide to the Project Management Body of Knowledge (PMBOK® Guide)*—Fourth Edition and PRINCE2 for defining output and execution are inadequate for complex projects; we need models that are more sophisticated. As stated in Chapter 4, "If complexity, and especially its roots stemming from the portfolio level, are not recognized and incorporated in project execution tools, then project and portfolio managers are sent into minefields studded with traps that they have not been warned about."

Examples of different ways of thinking include Daw's time-dependent models in Chapter 11 (which, in his words, do "not constitute a solution—merely a management of the wickedness and complexity to achieve a solution that provides some extent of the original required value, outcome and effect."); "overlapping or entrainment of time sequences" in Chapter 9; and lean/agile methods. Chapter 4 cited some actions to reduce or deal with complexity (reduce complexity: decouple and modularize, freeze components, control/fast response, and small steps/controlling variability)—although sometimes complexity is desirable (as explained in Chapter 4), or even necessary.

However, this picture needs more structuring. Chapter 3, or rather Remington and Pollack, gave some structure to the different methods that might be required. As mentioned in Chapter 3, "Managing a complex project successfully requires unconstrained thinking; thinking that embraces more than the standard textbook approaches to project management or the standard tools and methods." Multiple methods (or "systemic pluralism" [Chapter 3]) are needed, with different methods at different points in the life cycle. New words and terms (such as "anatomy" or "semi-structures") are brought in, which might move us forward but have not yet stood the test of empirical time. The categorizations mentioned previously, such as Geraldi et al. and Chapter 4, also describe a diagnosis system for complexity, which will tell us the tool to use and when to use it. Remington and Pollack and Geraldi et al. advised on the complexity types that suggest the type of tools to use.

However, the step to providing firm, research-based, practitioner-friendly advice on how to manage projects depending on the mix of complexity involved has not been taken or empirically tested. Such new knowledge must be co-created by researchers and reflective practitioners working together to understand how real projects behave. Methods that both comprehend the complexity of projects and that are useful operationally are likely to be hybrid models (as indeed has long been the case for applying systemic models in an operational project environment). We need not only need an apriori system for understanding complexity at the start of a project—although that would be extremely valuable—but also models to understand and to diagnose the development of complexity as a project proceeds. Therefore, we will be able to adapt our methodologies accordingly.

Projects are not isolated but set within complex programs and complex organizations. Therefore, the Introduction discusses the need to understand how projects contribute to the goals of a program and the interaction among projects and programs. As a result, our research agenda needs to go wider than the individual project and move toward looking at these complex interactions. As discussed in Chapter 4, research needs to examine the strategies that can be pursued by the corporation (e.g., de-complexing the choice of projects, reducing number of projects, etc.) and show how to understand these strategies and their impact on the complexity of the organizational activity; traditional project selection criteria-based methods are likely to be quite inadequate. Further, as discussed in Chapter 2, we need to look into the organizational capacity for managing complexity, which needs to consider the issues of organizational culture as discussed in the previous section, as well as competences. (Chapter 2 also discusses the need to change institutionalized procurement practices, which are likely to be more aligned to noncomplex projects and environments.)

Other Issues

The need to understand the complexity of projects and their environment raises many other issues apart from the individual question of how to manage those projects.

The first clear issue, introduced in Chapter 5, is the need for new estimating tools that can comprehend the complexity of projects. The work of the colleges in Chapter 2 identified that future capability (i.e., future projects) is predicated on attaining rational estimates for those projects. Chapter 6 covered the basics of parametric estimating (along the lines of Pugh's work). But much more research is needed for the effect of different types of complexity, increasing complexity throughout the project, emergent issues, and the difficult of estimating a project, which is going to proceed toward an as-yet ill-defined goal as project team sensemaking. Furthermore, current tools and decision processes are unsuitable for analyzing uncertainty (Chapter 2 mentioned a lack of understanding or acknowledgment of nontechnical risk in analyzing such uncertainty), making our current risk analysis weak, and undoubtedly disregarding of complexity. The concept of complexity and the models of complex projects that we build in our research agenda have to be sufficient to be able to estimate those projects, and empirical testing of those methods must be sufficient for us to be confident in those estimates.

A second issue that has arisen is the need for training that comprehends project complexity. Chapter 7 noted that standard methods are "essentially geared toward threshold competence represented by minimum standards for project management knowledge and practice considered necessary for effective workplace performance." This is well recognized, and the PMI research project on complexity concluded and as stated in Chapter 8, "Project managers deal with project complexity by utilizing standard project management tools and techniques in combination with a set of alternative skills and competencies that are not codified or captured in the conventional recommendations of good practice." This clearly covers various relationship skills. Chapter 3 noted that project managers should be "like politicians in their ability to influence and manage a network of relationships," and have a good understanding of systemicity (Chapter 8) and emergence (Chapter 11). The need for different and more appropriate training is clearly important, but our training must be based on a clear understanding of what complexity is and how it affects projects.

Our research agenda needs to both develop that understanding and consider its implications for project manager training.

Project managers are not the only audience for our research agenda. There are various stakeholder audiences, including, *among others*, senior management who have the governance role, and project management offices (PMOs) that need to understand and predict the behavior of the project. Such audiences, especially those set in conventional project management thinking, can have difficulty in understanding models that comprehend complexity. An important education task here needs to be a firm conceptual basis informed by research. This is particularly so when hybrid combinations of complexity models and conventional models are used, which might need to be the case to actually operationalize this research as mentioned previously. Chapter 2 mentioned some of the issues caused by stakeholders who do not have a common understanding of project success or project activity. Our research agenda needs to consider these differing audiences.

Learning lessons from complex projects, where the root causes of problems is not clear particularly because of what Chapter 4 calls "causal ambiguity," is known to be a problem. As our research develops models that understand complexity and its effect within projects, this research needs to inform how projects can be understood mid-project and post-mortem, with methods that can comprehend the various dynamic and behavioral aspects of complexity. Again, any practical methods are likely to be co-created between researchers and practitioners.

Finally, the preceding chapters looked at leadership challenges relating to sources of project complexity (e.g., Chapter 9) and the need for "systems thinking and paradoxical leadership" (e.g., Chapter 2). Our discussion of complex projects illustrated how "sensemaking leaders makes sense," and there is a research agenda looking at how leaders shape complex projects and appropriate leadership styles.

The Future

This chapter has highlighted a number of directions for future research, from the conceptual to the practical. All are needed if we are to understand and manage complex projects. However, this is not an agenda for researchers alone. Chapter 7 discussed the need for reflective practitioners and industry/university alliances in this applied area.

Much of what we have discussed is understood intuitively by experts, which is why Part 1 concentrated on the experiential learning of experts and was discussed by Whitty in the Introduction. Conceptual knowledge, empirical application, and testing need to be cocreated between researchers and reflective practitioners in the actuality of projects. Chapter 13 will consider advice for management and senior practitioners on how their practice needs to change in the face of increasing complexity, but that chapter and this chapter need to be seen as moving hand-in-hand as we develop this field.

References

P171, lines 21, 26. Simon, H. A. (1982). Sciences of the artificial (2nd ed.). Cambridge, MA: MIT Press.

P172, line 8. Klakegg, O. J., Williams, T. M., Walker, D., Andersen, B., & Magnussen, O. M. (2010). *Early warning signs in complex projects*. Newtown Square, PA:

Project Management Institute. and Kreiner, K. (1995). In search of relevance: Project management in drifting environments. *Scandinavian Journal of Management*, 11(4), 335–346.

P172, line 13; P173, line 20; P175, line 38. Cicmil, S., Cooke-Davies, T., Crawford, L., & Richardson, K. (2009). *On the complexity of projects: Exploring the implications of complexity theory for project management theory and practice.* Newtown Square, PA: Project Management Institute.

P172, line 24. Conway, B., & Mawby, D. (2006, October). *Early lessons for establishing through life capability programs.* Paper presented at the RUSI Defence Project Management Conference.

P172, line 29; P174, lines 32, 34. Geraldi, J. G., Maylor, H., & Williams, T. M. (in press). Now, let's make it really complex (complicated): A systematic review of the complexities of projects. *International Journal in Operations and Production Management.*

P173, line 7. Rittel, H. W. J., & Webber, M. M. (1973). Dilemmas in a general theory of planning. *Policy Sciences*, 4(2), 155–169.

P173, line 8. Roth, G., & Senge, P. (1996). From theory to practice: Research territory, processes, and structure at an organizational learning centre. *Journal of Organizational Change Management*, 9(1), 92–106.

P173, line 16. Kahneman, D., & Tversky, A. (1972). Subjective probability: A judgment of representativeness. *Cognitive Psychology*, 3(3), 430–454. and Kahneman, D., & Tversky, A. (1979). Intuitive prediction: Biases and corrective procedures. *TIMS Studies in Management Science*, 12, 313–327. and Kahneman, D., & Tversky, A. (2000a). Prospect theory: An analysis of decision under risk. In D. Kahneman & A. Tversky (Eds.), *Choices, values and frames* (pp. 17–43). Cambridge, UK: Cambridge University Press. and Kahneman, D., & Tversky, A. (2000b). *Conflict resolution: A cognitive perspective.* In D. Kahneman & A. Tversky (Eds.), *Choices, values and frames* (pp. 473–487). Cambridge, UK: Cambridge University Press.

P173, line 27. Turner, J. R., & Müller, R. (2004). Communication and co-operation on projects between the project owner as principal and the project manager as agent. *European Management Journal*, 22(3), 327–336.

P173, line 39. Weick, K. E. (1995). *Sensemaking in organizations.* Beverly Hills, CA: Sage Publications.

P173, line 43. O'Leary, T. (2010). *Managing business change projects: A social practice perspective* (Unpublished doctoral dissertation). University of Southampton, Southhampton, UK.

P174, line 8. Project Management Institute [PMI], 2008

P174, lines 24, 33. Remington, K., & Pollack, J. (2007). *Tools for complex projects.* Aldershot, UK: Gower Publishing.

P174, line 40. Rodrigues, A., & Williams, T. M. (1997). Systems dynamics in software project management: Towards the development of a formal integrated framework. *European Journal of Information Systems*, 6(1), 51–66.

P176, line 18. Williams, T. M. (2008). How do organizations learn lessons from projects—And do they? *IEEE Transactions in Engineering Management*, 55(2), 248–266.

P176, line 38. Cicmil, S., Williams, T. M., Thomas, J., & Hodgson, D. (2006). Rethinking project management: Researching the actuality of projects. *International Journal of Project Management*, 24(8), 675–686.

Chapter 13

Toward Project Management 2.0

Terry Cooke-Davies

Introduction

There are no reliable data on the percentage of all projects and programs that can be regarded as "complex," because not all projects contain sufficient complexity to warrant such a label. However, regardless of how small that percentage is, there are two good reasons why they need to be given special treatment.

First, complex projects are frequently highly visible and central to national or corporate strategy, therefore, their failure leads to banner headlines and media frenzy. Second, it is reasonable to assume that such projects are disproportionately important. It could be that some kind of Pareto distribution applies to them, so that although they represent only (say) the top 20 percent of all projects undertaken, they account for (say) 80 percent or so of the significant strategic value and management attention of those responsible for delivering projects and programs.

The first 12 chapters of this book presented a rich variety of insights and suggestions for the way that project management practice can or should evolve to master these ambitious and challenging enterprises. This chapter assembles these suggestions and arranges them into a framework that could possibly be considered as a direction for the development of the next generation of practices suitable for the management of complex projects. You could think about it, if you wished, as "project management 2.0."

Two things need to be said at the outset. First, the term "project management" is not meant to suggest that it related purely to the practice of someone with the job title of "project manager." On the contrary, as it has been clearly seen already and it will be emphasized once again in the remainder of this chapter. Managing projects is a "whole organization" activity, involving many people in different functions and at different hierarchical levels. Second, branding it as "PM 2.0" is not to imply that current practices and standards for project, program, and portfolio management (perhaps referred to collectively as PM 1.x) are no longer relevant or appropriate. Once again, the opposite is true. PM 2.0 builds on and incorporates PM 1.x; it is still relevant to 80 percent or more of all projects and programs that do not warrant the label "complex."

A Framework for Making Sense of Practice

Having argued for why the practices described in this chapter are vitally important and having suggested that they augment rather than replace existing project management practice, the rest of the chapter reviews the practices as they relate to three hierarchical bands in an organization. These are the three hierarchical bands: the organizational level, where executives establish policies, structures, and process frameworks that apply to the whole organization; the governance level, where those charged with the governance of a complex project or program have their own decisions to make; and at the project delivery level, where the project leader and/or manager and project team are tasked with delivering the complex project successfully.

At these three levels, some of the practices are about policies, some are about structures, some are about people, and some are about processes. Therefore, this chapter will summarize the 50 or 60 recommendations that appear earlier in the text in the form of a grid, grouping the practices into one of four areas (policy, structure, people, and process) as they are established and implemented at one of three hierarchical levels (organization, governance, and project) as shown in Table 13-1.

Organization Level
Policy

As Chapter 1 emphasized, the starting point for any organization wishing to seriously implement organization-wide management of complex programs and projects is appropriate organizational attention to program and project management. Paradoxically, it is only when an organization's senior management recognizes just how important it is to manage its total set of "change" activities *strategically*. Then it can start to create a framework for managing these activities in a way that reflects both their value to the organization, and the implications of how complex individual programs and projects will need to be if they are to support the organization's strategic objectives.

It is all too easy to repeat a mantra of "keep it simple," but sometimes an organization's strategy calls for it to create competitive advantage through deliberately seeking to develop highly complex solutions. Chapter 11 argued that the basis to such decisions should always be the "value" that the organization derives from such strategies, just as decisions about which programs and projects to include in the strategic portfolio should be taken based on optimized value to the customer and to the business. So what is an organization to do, if value is best provided through complex solutions?

The suggestion made in Chapter 4 is to embrace the necessary complexity and, while striving to avoid making any activities more complex than necessary, create an organization-wide framework that allows complex programs and projects to be undertaken with confidence. Such an approach carries with it a number of very practical implications. Chapter 6, for example, points out the folly of insisting on the provision of detailed budgets and plans early in the life of such complex programs and projects, when there is still only the haziest of notions as to what the actual design for the solution will be. This has led others to develop frameworks to allow organizations to identify the sources of dysfunctional complexity, while Chapter 5 recommends the development of simple frameworks that allow practitioners throughout the organization to talk to each other using a common vocabulary to describe complexity.

Adding a word of caution to this discussion, Chapter 2 suggested that organizations should ask themselves serious questions about whether or not they have the capacity to create appropriate project and program management systems that are capable of controlling projects that have the degree of complexity required to meet their strategic objectives.

Structure

Policies such as those suggested previously are likely to be embodied in organizations through structures and processes. The problems can start at the outset as the author of this chapter mentioned elsewhere, if tasks that are most usefully classified as programs or projects are assigned as operations to "business as usual" sections of the organization. Chapter 5 offered useful advice about classifying tasks according to their complexity into one of four types, and then managing them through an appropriate organizational structure. As Chapter 1 pointed out, this can be supported through the intelligent use of project management offices (PMOs) advocating governance structures, groups of projects and/or programs, or individual projects and/or programs. When dealing with complex projects and programs, it is also particularly helpful to adopt structures that encourage the disciplines of systems engineering (or business analysis) and project management to work together easily during the early, definitional stages of programs and projects.

All structures, however, are only as good as the people who are working within them, and the strong suggestion to emerge from Chapter 7 is that organizations undertaking complex projects should create or develop structural units, such as project academies, tasked with the development and maintenance of a project capable workforce. These can be supported, as Chapter 2 mentioned, by the creation and support of discipline-based communities of practice that allow practitioners to maintain their professional knowledge at the highest possible level.

People

An emphasis on the people who lead, manage, and deliver programs and projects has been a characteristic of many of the chapters in this book. Chapter 2 revealed that many complex projects fail because of divergent interests of different stakeholders, some of which are the result of their differing relationships to the project, which is highlighted in Chapter 8. This revelation suggests that any organization that is serious about improving its ability to deliver complex projects needs to ensure at the very least that all its internal stakeholders—business unit managers, functional line managers, portfolio managers and the rest—are all aligned behind the policies described earlier and are committed to making the structures work.

The need for a structure that provides for workforce development has been mentioned previously, but the aim of the unit needs to be as much on developing sufficient people with the skills to lead and manage complex projects as it is on developing the entire project-capable workforce. Chapter 2 and Chapter 4, for example, emphasized the important of developing high-grade leaders for the most complex programs undertaken by an organization. Chapter 8 emphasized the need for development programs to include a focus on developing emotional intelligence, and Chapter 7 argued that this development would need to be carried out as much through experiential learning in the workplace as through more formal methods of development. Indeed, as Chapter 1 reported, the research workshops emphasized how important it is to tie a career ladder to both the development of skills in individual practitioners and to the capacity requirements of the organization.

One aspect of this, brought out clearly in Chapter 5, is the recognition that different kinds of jobs in the project and program space require different aptitudes, colorfully characterized as recognizing the different attributes of an "air traffic controller" from those of a "war room commander."

Process

The series of workshops that were summarized in Chapter 1 underscored how much attention had been focused on the development of processes for managing portfolios, programs, and projects. The general tenor of the observations were sympathetic to the point made strongly by Cooke-Davies, Crawford, and Lechler that there needs to be a "fit" between the project management processes and other elements of the project management system (such as policies, structures, and people) and the organizational context and strategic intent. If such a fit is patchy or absent, then as Chapter 2 stated, the business systems can become obstacles to program and project success. There also needs to be a fit between the different groups of processes that are called into play to manage portfolios, programs, and projects, as Chapter 1 described.

Processes themselves need to be adapted to their specific purpose, and "for instance, where the high levels of complexity are due to socio-political challenges, pace or fundamental uncertainties, the standards and generic models appear ineffectual," as is pointed out in Chapter 5.

For example, talk of fit between project and portfolio management processes can sound abstract, so it is helpful to think of specific instances. One such example where they touch each other closely and require especially good fit is in the application of selection criteria to projects at project decision points that provide information for portfolio decisions. Chapter 4 listed the nature of additional criteria that can be used to control complexity at the portfolio level, criteria such as the amount of complexity at portfolio level introduced by a specific project through technical, resource, market, or external interactions.

This statement implies that each organization has some means of categorizing projects in terms of their complexity; Chapter 9 illustrated this notion with a helpful table of alternative schemes. Regardless of which one of these (or any other) is adopted, there are several process implications that flow from it: for example, management information systems may need to be amended for different categories of complexity (Chapter 11); different methodologies may be more suitable to different categories (Chapter 11); project managers of differing skills and abilities may need to be appointed (Chapter 1); different tools might be more appropriate (Chapter 4);

and sophisticated methods of defining programs and projects might need to be adopted in order to contain complexity (Chapter 4).

Governance

Aside from the differences at organizational level that have been summarized, the first 11 chapters of this book also mentioned some additional practices at the level of the governance of individual programs and projects—practices for sponsors and steering committees to adopt.

Policy

Many of the more publicized failure of complex projects arise from the difference between their final costs and the expectations at the time of approval. Chapter 6 provided both suggestions and evidence for the need to adopt a much more intelligent and realistic approach to the use of parametric estimating techniques at the start of a project, taking into account not only historical trend analysis but also technological maturity. The point has already been made that organizational policy needs to account for this, but because the accuracy of the estimate is such an important factor in the business case for any project, that, particularly in the case of complex projects, it calls for special attention from those responsible for governance at the start.

Structure

Both Chapter 2 and Chapter 8 dwelled on the problems of "optimism" bias in forecasts and estimates, so Chapter 8 made a strong case for developing governance structures for individual complex projects that are specifically designed to inhibit it. In the case of public sector infrastructure projects, examples have been given elsewhere, but the number of embarrassing cases of complex projects massively exceeding both budget and schedule estimates suggests that there is still a need to turn this laudable ambition into common practice. Chapter 1 also noted the need to involve the right mix of business, line, and project/program management in the governance structures and to ensure that the governance structure is appropriately integrated with the project structure so that there is agreement among managers about which processes need to be "tightly controlled and rigorously followed, and those that are better applied flexibly."

People

The need for competent sponsorship and governance of programs and projects has been well attested elsewhere, but Chapter 5 stated that an additional requirement is for sponsors to understand not only the overall complexity in a project but also to have some way of representing it in a model. A further dimension of understanding is called for in Chapter 11, where it is pointed out "simply mapping out the causality involved in the effects of a project can reveal many of the reasons for complexity."

Process

Presentations given to the workshops reported in Chapter 1 cited evidence that smaller projects of shorter duration are considerably easier to control than larger projects of longer duration, which led to the suggestion that program or project design should make allowance for this when developing the project strategy in its early stages. This advice is reinforced in Chapter 5, which suggested that complexity could be reduced by a combination of decoupling elements from each other and by seeking ways of introducing modularity wherever possible.

Within the constraints set by the organizational process framework, there are a number of practices suggested for sponsors and steering groups: choosing the appropriate tools to be used for the specific program or project (Chapter 3); making sensitive use of earned value management to monitor value delivered (Chapter 3); ensuring that appropriate estimating processes are used at the appropriate project stage (Chapter 6); for understanding the implications of complexity and systemicity (Chapters 5 and 11); and for deciding when to freeze design (Chapter 4), which calls for both sensitive use of process and the exercise of judgment. Such judgment is likely to be refined if sponsors encourage the use of system dynamics modeling as a regular part of postimplementation reviews (Chapter 10).

Program or Project

At the project level, it is interesting to observe that relatively few new practices emerged from the earlier chapters in the areas of policy, structure, or process, but there was a substantial emphasis on people. Indeed, the centrality of people emerged not only from the workshops that are reported in Chapter 1 but also from the research directions identified in Chapter 12. It is perhaps not too speculative to suggest that if this book is dealing with the emergence of a portfolio, program, and project context that could be called Project Management 2.0, one of its most prominent characteristics will be an emphasis on the centrality of people.

Structure

Just three practices are suggested with respect to project structures, of which the most radical was to adopt an approach such as integration centric development (ICD) that allows a project team to adopt a "whole project approach" (Chapter 3). From the same paper, using the metaphor of "jazz," comes the suggestion of creating "time-linked semi-structures" as a means of structuring complex projects that are driven by set deadlines. The third suggestion (Chapter 2) is that the project leaders should "build each project team network by linking nodes in and between the communities of practice network." This has the benefit of moving toward the closer integration of the project management and systems engineering communities so strongly advocated in Chapter 11.

People

Practices advocated in respect of people, while many and various, fall into two basic categories: those that relate to the skills and behavior of project managers or leaders and those that relate to the holistic nature of project team activity.

By examining the first of these two categories, it would be fair to say that the suggested practices mainly arise out of the practices recommended at organizational level in terms of recruiting, developing, and retaining a project capable workforce with the right capacity and the right skills. The latter emphasized the need for leadership skills as well as management skills for the manager of a complex project

(Chapter 1). This recommends going to great lengths to identify extraordinary leadership skills for those being selected to manage the most complex projects (Chapter 8); for identifying the special skills required for dealing with "emergence" and the unexpected both by project managers and by systems engineers for projects that are intended to provide solutions to "wicked" problems (Chapter 11); to distinguish between the kinds of project managers that could be characterized as "civil pilots" from those that could be considered "fighter pilots" (Chapter 5); and that call for high levels of emotional intelligence (EQ) among the project leadership team.

In the second category, the practices most emphasized are those that relate to developing a broad and deep understanding by the project team as a whole of the "systemicity" inherent in the project (Chapters 1 and 8) so that this understanding is brought to bear on the tasks of project planning (Chapter 2) and on risk management (Chapter 3).

Process

It will come as no surprise that the first practice advocated for the processes of complex projects at the project level is to ensure that the most appropriate suite of conceptual and systems tools is adopted to suit the specific nature and context of each project (Chapter 3). A table of such tools is offered, and in an expanded form is available in Remington and Pollack.

Borrowing concepts from high-reliability organizations, such as a nuclear power plant or an aircraft carrier, two innovative processes are suggested in Chapter 4 for the management of complex projects: "control and fast response" and "small steps whilst controlling variability." Because the former was developed for what might be termed "steady state" operations, they need to be adapted for the project environment, but the authors of the chapter present a strong case for making the effort. They also referred to a paper, which provided many case examples of how the latter technique can be successfully applied.

Conclusion

A recent study of more than 1,500 CEOs concluded that, "Today's complexity is only expected to rise and more than half of CEOs doubt their ability to manage it. Seventy-nine percent of CEOs anticipate even greater complexity ahead. However, one set of organizations, we call them "standouts" has turned increased complexity into financial advantage over the past five years."

Inevitably, complexity will be experienced in the nature of programs and projects undertaken by organizations during the next decade or more.

This book has combined a host of insights from practitioners and researchers to provide help and advice for practitioners, for managers of practitioners, and for the project management research community. The contributors hope that the number of organizations that turn complexity into financial advantage will increase significantly.

Table 13-1: Practices recommended in this book, arranged by level and by area

	Organization	Governance	Project

Policy	1. Appropriate organizational attention to program and project management. (Chapter 1)
	2. View not only individual programs and projects but also the disciplines of project management and systems engineering from a value-creation perspective. (Chapter 11)
	3. Establish a framework that relates complexity to business strategy. (Chapter 4)
	  a. Allow the use of practices that are appropriate to complexity. (Chapter 6)
	  b. Establish a common language of complexity throughout the organization. (Chapter 5)
	  c. Assess organizational capacity to manage its complex programs and projects. (Chapter 2)
		1. Establish estimating policy after making due allowance for complexity and for technology maturity. (Chapter 6)	

Structure	4. Structure the organization to classify "tasks" in a way that is complementary to the structure of business operations and covers all portfolios, programs, and projects. (Chapter 5)
	5. Make smart use of PMOs. (Chapter 1)
	6. Ensure that the structures encourage the integration of systems engineering (or its cousin, business analysis) with project management. (Chapter 11)
	7. Institute structures to support the development of a project-capable work force. (Chapter 7)
	8. Create discipline-based communities of practice. (Chapter 6)
		2. Establish governance structures for programs, projects, and program and project management that minimize optimism bias in estimates and forecasts. (Chapter 8)
		  a. Ensure appropriate balance of authority between the line and project management. (Chapter 1)
		  b. Ensure that the project structure and the governance structure are integrated. (Chapter 1)
			1. Structure projects around integration for better understanding of system anatomy. (Chapter 3)
			2. Adopt flexible semi-structures linked to time constraints. (Chapter 3)
			3. Plug project team networks into organization-wide communities of practice. (Chapter 2)

People	9. Align the views of organizational program and project success among all organizational stakeholders. (Chapter 6)
	10. Recruit and develop program and project managers with strong leadership skills. (Chapter 6)
		3. Ensure that people in governance have a clear picture of the complexity of each program or project they are governing. (Chapter 5)
		4. Understand the dynamic linkages inherent in the project to assess the likely impact of both risks and corrective actions. (Chapter 10)
			4. Pay close attention to the appointment of all key positions in programs and projects, for example:
			  a. Emphasize leadership as well as management. (Chapter 1)
			  b. Look for exceptional leadership skills on complex projects. (Chapter 8)

c. Appoint both project managers and systems engineers (business analysts) based on skills to cope with "emergence." (Chapter 11)

d. Distinguish between "civil pilots" and "fighter pilots." (Chapter 5)

e. Ensure that leaders have high emotional intelligence (EQ). (Chapter 8)

5. Develop a shared understanding within the team of the "systemicity" inherent in the project. (Chapters 1 and 8)

a. Incorporate an understanding of "systemicity" into project planning. (Chapter 2)

b. Understand the systemic impact of combinations of risks. (Chapter 1)

6. Decide on the appropriate tools to manage complexity in the program or project. (Chapter 3)

7. On complex projects, use "control and fast response" approaches. (Chapter 4)

8. Take small steps and control variability. (Chapter 4)

5. Design the program or project to optimize delivery and to reduce unnecessary complexity. (Chapters 1 and 4)

6. Employ appropriate tools:

a. To map the complexity in a program or project. (Chapter 3)

b. To select the appropriate estimating process for the particular project and stage. (Chapter 6)

c. To apply earned value management appropriately. (Chapter 3)

d. Use judgment to know when to freeze design, and when to remain adaptable. (Chapter 4)

7. If appropriate, use system dynamics in post-implementation reviews. (Chapter 10)

11. Ensure that all people involved in managing programs and projects are involved in a strong work force development program. (Chapter 1)

a. Progress through a career ladder/personal development framework. (Chapter 1)

b. Experiential learning in the workplace integrated with developmental activities. (Chapter 7)

c. Personal aptitude for managing different kinds of programs and projects distinguished. (Chapter 5)

Process

12. Ensure that business systems do not become obstacles to program and project success. (Chapter 6)

a. Portfolio, program, and project systems are integrated among themselves and with other business systems. (Chapter 11)

b. Avoid numerous pitfalls implicit in the unthinking application of classical management "good practices." (Chapter 6)

c. Consider whether standards help or hinder for different types of tasks. (Chapter 5)

13. Widen project selection criteria to improve portfolio selection. (Chapter 4)

14. Categorize projects according to their degree of complexity. (Chapter 9)

a. Amend management information systems to reflect the nature of complex projects. (Chapter 11)

b. Develop sophisticated definition methods for containing complexity. (Chapter 4)

c. Use tools such as the design structure matrix. (Chapter 4)

d. Adapt different project methodologies for different types of projects. (Chapter 11)

e. Match the capabilities of individual project managers to the complexity of the programs or projects they are managing. (Chapter 1)

References

P180, line 44. Birkinshaw, J., & Heywood, S. (2010, May). Putting organizational complexity in its place. *McKinsey Quarterly*, Chicago, IL: McKinsey & Co.

P181, line 13. Cooke-Davies, T. (2009). Front-end alignment of projects: Doing the right project. In T. M. Williams, K. Samset, & K. J. Sunnevåg (Eds.), *Making essential choices with scant information: Front-end decision making in major projects* (pp. 106–124). Basingstoke, UK: Palgrave Macmillan.

P182, line 18. Cooke-Davies, T., Crawford, L. H., & Lechler, T. (2009). Project management systems: Moving project management from an operational to a strategic discipline. *Project Management Journal, 40*(1), 110–123.

P183, line 23. Flyvbjerg, B., Bruzilius, N., & Rothengatter, W. (2003) *Megaprojects and risk: An anatomy of ambition.* Cambridge, UK: Cambridge University Press.

P183, line 33. Crawford, L., Cooke-Davies, T., Hobbs, B., Labuschagne, L., Remington, K., & Chen, P. (2008). *Situational sponsorship of projects and programs: An empirical review.* Newtown Square, PA: Project Management Institute.

P185, line 19. Remington, K., & Pollack, J. (2007). *Tools for complex projects.* Aldershot, UK: Gower Publishing.

P185, line 26. Sommer, S. C., Loch, C. H., & Dong, J. (2009). Managing complexity and unforeseeable uncertainty in startup companies: An empirical study. *Organization Science, 20*(1), 118–133.

P185, line 33. International Business Machines (IBM) Corp. (n.d.). *Capitalizing on complexity. Insights from the 2010 IBM global CEO study.* Retrieved from http://www-935.ibm.com/services/us/ceo/ceostudy2010/index.html, p. 8.

Contributors

Editor-in-Chief

Terry Cooke-Davies is Chairman of Human Systems International Limited. He has a PhD in project management, a bachelor's degree in theology, and qualifications in electrical engineering, management accounting and counselling, Terry has worked alongside senior leaders and managers in both the public and the private sectors, to ensure the delivery of business critical change and enhance the quality of leadership. He is recognized as a 'thought leader', and has reviewed many national and international standards as a 'subject matter expert'. Terry is an OPM3® Assessor and Consultant and was awarded the APM Sir Monty Finniston Award in 2006. He has held a number of Adjunct and Visiting Faculty roles at universities in the UK, France and Australia and is a Visiting Fellow at Cranfield School of Management .

Contributing Editors

Lynn H. Crawford has a background as architect, project manager, regional planner and policy adviser, and with qualifications in human resource management and business administration, Lynn is a world authority on project management competence. She was a member of the Steering Committee for the development of Australian National Competency Standards in Project Management and is currently leading initiatives aimed at development of global standards for project management. She is Vice-Chair of the Global Accreditation Center of Project Management Institute. Lynn is a Professor of Project Management at ESC Lille School of Management, and Bond University in SE Queensland, Australia.

John R. Patton, PMP is President and CEO of Cadence Management Corporation. John founded Cadence in 1983, leading the planning, organization and startup activities for the company, with the vision of becoming a premier provider of project management training, consulting services, and support tools. John was the first chair of the OPM3® Certification Committee, 2006–2009. Elected to the Board of Directors of the PMI Educational Foundation for the term 2011–2013. He is a regular participant in PMI's Research Working sessions prior to Global Congresses. John has degrees from the University of Oregon, University of Barcelona (Diplomado), and Portland State University. The Cadence mission is connecting people worldwide and transforming businesses through project management. The company has established an international program of licensing Cadence training to consulting firms in Asia, Latin America and Europe, a program where courses taught by local seminar leaders in the local language of the country. John's consulting experience includes assignments on numerous multi-million dollar new product development projects around the world. He is bilingual in Spanish, and has additional abilities with French, Catalan and German.

Chris Stevens, PhD, has extensive senior management experience, nationally and globally, across many diverse industries where project-based delivery is a core commercial competency. His practical focus is conceiving and delivering innovation, transformation and change within large and international corporations. As a systemic problem solver, a thinker and doer, Chris mitigates risk and delivers better technology-enabled project and program outcomes, setting the vision and being pragmatic, producing improved governance, commercial efficiencies. Chris is an advisor to major international institutions as a *pro-bono* contributor to improving advanced knowledge of project, program and portfolio management including *Project Management Institute* and *International Astronautical Federation*.

Terry M. Williams is Professor of Management Science, Director of the Management School at the University of Southampton, UK. He previously worked in Operational Research (OR) at Engineering Consultants YARD developing project risk management and acting as Risk Manager for major projects, then at Strathclyde University, UK as Professor of OR and Head of Department. He continues research and consultancy modeling the behavior of major projects, both post-project review and pre-project risk, including work in major claims in Europe and North America. Terry is a member of a number of research networks worldwide and sits on PMI's Academic Members Advisory Group. Terry is a speaker on modeling complex projects and post-project reviews. Terry was appointed Dean of Hull University Business School, effective September 2011.

Contributors

Dan Bennett currently serves as Director of F-35 International Programs, responsible for ensuring successful delivery on all F-35 program commitments to international customers. His responsibilities include strategic integration, program planning, program performance and delivery, and ultimate customer satisfaction. Dan also holds allied responsibilities for management of international industrial participation, national disclosure policy engagements, and import/export control activities on behalf of the F-35 Program. Dan has performed as a skilled program manager, proposal leader, Integrated Product Team leader, and principle engineer in a variety of roles for Lockheed Martin Aeronautics Company. Dan also serves as a change agent and thought leader, applying formal learning from the EMCPM program within the Aeronautics Company and Lockheed Martin Corporation. He serves in formal roles as a member of the Corporate Global Diversity team, the F-35 Summit for Cultural Change, and as a leader/mentor for Program Management Mentoring Across Programs. Dan is currently engaged in formal one-to-one mentoring with three developing program managers. Dan completed the Executive Masters in Complex Project Management (EMCPM) program as a member of the inaugural cohort in 2008, and was awarded the QUT Faculty of Business Dean's Award for Excellence

Stephen Carver is rated as one of the top 3 lecturers at Europe's top MBA Business Schools—Cranfield. He has a reputation of taking complex management concepts and being able to distill them down, into highly informative, interactive and fun sessions—often using "storytelling" techniques. Unusual, for an academic, he has actually spent most of his working life in real business and still runs his own, highly successful, Consultancy Company (his client reads like the FTSE/Dow top 200!). He has managed projects from oil rigs to bank mergers, sailing ships to product launches and IT systems to advertising campaigns.

Peter Checkland joined the postgraduate Department of Systems Engineering at Lancaster University after 15 years as a manager in the synthetic fiber industry. There he led what became a thirty-year program of action research in organizations outside the university. Initially the research theme was to examine the possibility of using the well-developed methods of systems engineering in problem situations rather than in the technically-defined problem situations in which the methods had been refined. This attempt at transfer failed, and the action research moved in a different direction. The work finally established Soft Systems Methodology (SSM) as an approach to tackling the multi-faceted problems which managers face; in doing this, it also established the now well-recognized distinction between 'hard' and 'soft' systems thinking. SSM is now taught and used around the world. Its development through action research is described in many papers and in five books; *Systems Thinking, Systems Practice* (1981); *Soft Systems Methodology in Action* (with J. Scholes; 1990); *Systems Information and Information Systems* (with Sue Holwell, 1998); *SSM: A 30-Year Retrospective* (1999); *Learning for Action* (with John Poulter, 2006). Peter Checkland's work has been recognized in a number of awards: honorary doctorates from City University, the Open University, Erasmus University (The Netherlands), and Prague University of Economics, a Most Distinguished and Outstanding Contributor Award from the Bntish Computer Society, the Gold Medal of the UK Systems Society, The Beale Medal of the OR Society, the I+M Award (Information and Management) of Amsterdam University and the Pioneer Award of the International Council on Systems Engineering.

Andrew Daw. Having previously worked for a major Defence Industry prime and in defence IT consultancy, Andrew Daw is currently the Head of TLCM Services for Harmonic Ltd, an independent Professional Services company providing support to the Defence and Security Market for complex program definition and delivery. He has major project leadership experience as Chief Systems Engineer in programs such as the UK Future Aircraft Carrier, has undertaken oversight and review activities for a national research program and has been working jointly with the UK MoD in Defence Acquisition activities since 2000. He was instrumental in the design, development and deployment of an Information Management based Decision Support and visualization environment (TRAiDE™) assisting the UK Defence Acquisition initiative of Through Life Capability Management (TLCM). Andrew is a Chartered Mathematician, a past President of INCOSE UK (2006–08) and is a Visiting Professor of Systems Engineering at the University of Strathclyde in Glasgow.

Stephen Hayes is the Chief Executive Officer of the International Centre for Complex Project Management, an independent international not-for-profit company that aims to better enable the global community to deliver complex projects and manage complexity. Stephen is working extensively in the international community with other government agencies and corporations to deliver this new global resource. Stephen has a Masters of Management and is a graduate of Australian Command and Staff Course. He served in the Royal Australian Air Force for 29 years and has held a military command as well as posts in systems engineering and human resource management. Stephen has had six appointments within the Defence Materiel Organisation in addition to a project management exchange with the Royal Air Force. Stephen's project management work in the United Kingdom was recognized with the honor of being made a Member of the Order of the British Empire (MBE). He is also a Certified Practicing Project Director. As the Australian Department of Defence's Executive Director – Complex Project Management, Stephen was responsible for the development and delivery of the Department's Complex Project Management initiatives. These included the competency standard for complex project managers, the Executive Masters in Complex Project Management and formation of the International Centre for Complex Project Management.

Dr. Ed Hoffman is responsible for the development of NASA's program/project management and engineering workforce in his role as founding director of the NASA Academy of Program/Project and Engineering Leadership (APPEL). He received the NASA Outstanding Leadership Medal in 2010. He has co-authored *Shared Voyage: Learning and Unlearning from Remarkable Projects* (2005) and *Project Management Success Stories: Lessons of Project Leaders* (2000). He also serves as an adjunct faculty member at George Washington University. Dr. Hoffman holds a Doctorate and two Master degrees from Columbia University in social and organizational psychology. He received a Bachelor of Science in Psychology from Brooklyn College.

Christoph H. Loch is the Glaxo Smith Kline Chaired Professor of Corporate Innovation and Professor of Technology and Operations Management at INSEAD; he also serves as Director of the INSEAD Israel Research Center. He will assume the position of the director of the Judge Business School of the University of Cambridge in September 2011. His research revolves around the management of R&D and the product innovation process, particularly technology strategy, strategy cascading, project selection, concurrent engineering, project management under high complexity and high uncertainty, and performance measurement. He also examines the motivation of professional personnel in organizations (such as R&D organizations), in particular, the emotional aspects of motivation and performance

Dr. Harvey Maylor is Director of the International Centre for Programme Management (ICPM) at Cranfield School of Management (in partnership with HP), and lately founding Programme Director for Cranfield's MSc in Programme and Project Management. He is the author of seven books including Europe's best-selling Project Management text, (Maylor, H. (2010), *Project Management*, 4th edition, FT Prentice Hall) and 18 articles in peer-reviewed journals. He was involved in the EPSRC's Rethinking PM Network, and PMI's Value of Project Management study. He is a member of PMI's Academic Member Advisory Group and ESRC's peer review college. His research interests today focus on managing complexity, adoption (and non-adoption) of promising practices, and the development of organizational strategy for PPM.

Frederick C. Payne is Vice President and Global Program Management Director of Ricardo plc. He is a 30 year veteran of the defense, aerospace and automotive industries with an exceptional track record in program management and delivery. In his role with Ricardo, as Vice President and Global Program Management Director, Fred provides policy and guidance for the global Ricardo project management community, ensuring effective and appropriate application of the Ricardo's

Global Product Development Process across all projects and the development of project managers through training and certification programs. Currently, Fred represents Ricardo on the Project Management Institute (PMI) Global Executive Council. He has been the past chair of the Project Management PMI Global Corporate Council. In 2005 he was named by PMI as a 'Top 50 Power Program Management Leader'. Fred is also an officer of the International Centre for Complex Project Management. He holds BSEE and MBA degrees from Fairleigh Dickinson University as well as Graduate Certificate Degree in Project Management from Stevens Institute of Technology.

Dr Julien Pollack is a Senior Lecturer at the University of Technology, Sydney. His previous experience includes projects in the manufacturing, telecommunications, information technology and health care industries. He has worked in hard engineering and intangible organizational change projects. His early research focused on practical ways to combine project management techniques with soft systems approaches, to meet the needs of varying project contexts. More recently, he has been investigating the sources of project complexity and how complexity theory can be applied to project contexts.

Dr. Kaye Remington is Managing Director of ELEFSIS (www.elefsis.org), developing strategic and project leadership in complex organizational environments. She has also recently launched PLOPP (People Leading and Organising Projects for the Planet) a pro bono organization that works with voluntary groups to help them start-up and manage community projects more effectively. Formerly Program Director of Post-graduate Project Management at the University of Technology Sydney, she is now an Honorary Senior Research Fellow, dividing her time between research, writing and consulting. Kaye's 25-year career in project, program and senior management took her to the UK, Europe and the Middle East. She is co-author of the book, *Tools for Complex Projects* (2007), and has just completed another book, *Leadership for Complex Projects* (due November 2011) by Gower Publishing.

Dale Shermon is a Principal Consultant with with QinetiQ Limited. He has broad experience of Aerospace and Defence both from the customer and supplier perspectives. Dale has produced estimates using parametric, analogy and detailed estimating techniques for a number of projects managing a team or independently. Dale has presented and taught more than 50 courses on a diverse number of topics within the estimating and bidding domain both in the UK and abroad. He was the major contributor and editor of the "Systems Cost Engineering" book published by Gower in 2009 regarding the applications of parametric estimating. Dale was the creator of the TruePlanning for Concepts model and the PRICE Systems Life Cycle Enterprise Questionnaire. In 2009 he was presented with the prestigious International Society for Parametric Estimating (ISPA) Frank Freiman award for lifetime contributions to parametric estimating.

Dr. Roxanne Zolin is Associate Professor in the School of Management at Queensland University of Technology. She helped develop and teaches the Executive Masters in Complex Project Management in Canberra. Roxanne managed large and small projects in software development, new product development, enterprise development, advertising, marketing and promotions. Roxanne did her PhD in Construction Engineering Management at Stanford University, where she also obtained a Masters in Sociology. She researches the affects of complexity on project success and failure. Her software development company built organizational simulations and provided software development and technical writing services to organizations, such as Coles Myer Pty Ltd, Telecom and the Australian Navy. Her marketing company helped start over 500 new businesses with 80% self-supporting in their first year. Roxanne was National Marketing Manager for Myers, the world's 15th largest department store chain. Her sales promotions won three national awards from the Sales Promotion Association of Australia.

Index